YOUTH
AND
INEQUALITY

YOUTH
AND
INEQUALITY

edited by

Inge Bates and George Riseborough

Open University Press
BUCKINGHAM · PHILADELPHIA

Open University Press
Celtic Court
22 Ballmoor
Buckingham
MK18 1XW

and
1900 Frost Road, Suite 101
Bristol, PA 19007, USA

First Published 1993
Reprinted 1994

A catalogue record of this book is available from the British Library

ISBN 0 335 15695 9 (pb)

Library of Congress Cataloging-in-Publication Data
Bates, Inge.
Youth and inequality/Inge Bates and George Riseborough.
p. cm.
Includes bibliographical references and index.
ISBN 0–335–15695–9 (pb)
1. Youth – Great Britain – Social conditions. 2. Sex
discrimination – Great Britain. 3. Social classes – Great Britain.
4. Equality – Great Britain. I. Riseborough, George, 1943- .
II. Title.
HQ799.G7B37 1993
305.23′5′0941–dc20 92–43088 CIP

Typeset by Graphicraft Typesetters Ltd, Hong Kong
Printed in Great Britain by St Edmundsbury Press Ltd,
Bury St Edmunds, Suffolk

For Sven and Silverwood

Contents

Contributors

Patricia Allatt, Reader in Sociology, Teesside Business School, University of Teesside.

Inge Bates, Lecturer in Education, Division of Education, University of Sheffield.

Robert MacDonald, Research Fellow, School of Education, University of Durham.

John Quicke, Reader in Education, Division of Education, University of Sheffield.

George Riseborough, Senior Lecturer in Education, Manchester Metropolitan University.

Ken Roberts, Professor of Sociology, University of Liverpool.

Debra Roker, Research Fellow, Social and Applied Psychology Unit, University of Sheffield.

Preface

This book is about *unequal* opportunities and the ways in which these affect young people's lives and transitions into adulthood. The chapters explore the experience of transition in different class/gendered locations and reveal the influence of many hidden social advantages and disadvantages. The research on which the book is based comes from the ESRC's 16–19 Initiative. This was a programme of research on young people undertaken by research teams in ten universities and polytechnics. At the heart of the programme was a longitudinal study of 5000 young people growing up in different labour markets. This 'core' research was conducted by four teams at the Universities of Sheffield, Dundee, Edinburgh, Liverpool and Surrey and co-ordinated by John Bynner. The main report of this survey, *Careers and Identities* is published by Open University Press (1992). The 16–19 Initiative also included – both within the 'core' research and as part of a group of associated studies – more qualitative and ethnographic work intended to illuminate processes of socialization. The major proportion of ethnographic work was undertaken by the Sheffield University Division of Education team, co-ordinated by Inge Bates. This group, Inge Bates, George Riseborough and John Quicke, undertook five separate but interrelated studies. Other qualitative studies were undertaken by Lyn Jamieson and Helen Corr at Edinburgh University, Frank Coffield and Robert MacDonald at Durham University and Pat Allatt and Lyn Benson at the University of Teesside. In addition, Debra Roker, a 16–19 Initiative-linked ESRC student, based her doctoral study on girls in private education. These teams established an 'Ethnography' Working Group, which met in Sheffield in the course of the Initiative. *Youth and Inequality* collects together some of the work of this group.

The book was brought together in challenging circumstances. Our fieldwork with youth revealed deepening social divisions and inequalities. Some groups, for example the privately educated, were sailing forth towards higher education with the wind in their favour. Others, for example those involved in youth training, were often weighed down by family poverty and related social problems and struggling to last out until they could get a job. Moreover, we were conscious that our frame was limited for the purposes of exploring the full range of accumulating inequalities affecting young people over the last decade; other studies of disadvantage, for example of different ethnic groups, of the homeless, poor and of disabled young people really needed to be undertaken. Our work highlighted the need for critical social research and policy analysis but this ran against the contraflow of academic activity in the universities and polytechnics shaping up over the same period. The combined pressures of cuts, market forces, changing structures of accountability and intensifying individualism favoured more marketable projects. At the same time the wider political scene – the success of the New Right, the weakness of the Left, the enormity of the changes in Eastern Europe – caused us to halt in our tracks and examine our assumptions about what constitutes significant political action towards greater social justice. In the Introduction we consequently frankly and, we believe properly, state our current sense of impasse. Acknowledged uncertainty, rather than confident prescription, feels to us the appropriate tenor for debating the shorter and longer term steps to be taken towards more equal opportunities.

The academic debts involved in this book will be apparent in each chapter. Clearly we are particularly indebted to the other five contributors both for their sustained commitment to the book and for many discussions which have enriched our own thinking. We would like also to acknowledge the intellectual companionship and stimulus provided by all the researchers involved in the Initiative. Perhaps the most important contributions to acknowledge in this context, however, are the more invisible ones. Sue Martin undertook the laborious task of transcribing tapes and a great deal of typing. Carole Overall, Carolyn Medd, Janet Howatson, Pat Lee and Sally Moreton all helped in different ways to ensure the production of the final manuscript. John Skelton and Jacinta Evans were wonderfully patient and supportive editors. Dawn Harvey assisted with interviewing for the research on which Chapter 3 is based. Elizabeth Singleton helped with indexing and proof-reading. We are grateful to the ESRC for funding the research and particularly to Peter de Vries who facilitated crucial last minute financial support.

Finally our biggest thanks must go to all the young people who participated in the various projects represented in this book. This book is also dedicated to them and to their future.

Introduction

Deepening Divisions, Fading Solutions

Inge Bates and George Riseborough

This book begins and ends with our abiding general concern – inequality in all its nuanced complexity and, in particular, its manifestations in the lives of young people. It concentrates on inequalities associated with class and gender, which we know most about, and illustrates that these are not disappearing but rather reappearing in new forms despite increasingly modernized structures of education and training. Contrary to the Majorite thesis, a classless society is not in the making. The story of the reproduction of larger social inequalities through education has been richly told in many forms (Bourdieu and Passeron, 1977; Willis, 1977; Gleeson and Mardle, 1980; Ball, 1981; Griffin, 1985; Donald and Rattansi, 1992). This collection builds upon such work but does so in a radically changed economic, social and political climate. As a consequence, in exploring this terrain, we face a double problematic: the deepening of social divisions in the context of disappearing solutions. For whereas writers on inequality have traditionally headed towards a horizon of socialism, this prospect now seems increasingly clouded.

The Context of Writing

In this chapter, we begin by exploring the context of our writing, in particular the difficulty in writing about class, and more generally inequality, in the 1990s. A particular issue here is the silence gathering around class and its role in relation to other forms of social injustice. This is a complex phenomenon and it is beyond the scope of this Introduction to examine the issue in the depth it deserves. Nevertheless, since these circumstances affect both young people's understandings of themselves and our own meta-understanding of their position, they need to be taken into account. What is clear is that while political solutions to inequality may no longer be obvious, the problems posed by class, race, gender, sexual orientation and other forms of social oppression are not going away. While some youth researchers (see papers in Chisholm *et al.*, 1990) have suggested that young people are becoming freer from class-gendered constraints and can construct their futures in 'open spaces', the studies presented here do not support this. Surviving or luxuriating within the canopy of structured inequality remains the existential predicament of us all. In recent years, we have seen increasing divisions between rich and poor nation-states and between rich and poor within individual nations. In the UK, social class remains the major determinant of relative social mobility (Marshall *et al.*, 1988) and the labour market and labour process remain deeply gendered and racist. High levels of unemployment, the weakened position of organized labour, public expenditure cuts and the shifting burden of taxation have sharpened social divisions. Poverty, malnutrition and homelessness are increasingly commonplace – leading some writers to describe the emergence of an 'underclass' (Field, 1989; Mann, 1991). A recent analysis of Government statistics shows one fifth of the population living below the poverty line and an increase in these numbers of $1^{1}/_{2}$ million between 1987 and 1989.[1] Social protests have erupted in a variety of forms, ranging from youth riots on council estates and related spates of joy-riding and ram-raiding to the more peaceful candlelight gatherings in defence of the health service. For those in employment and in training, their labour is subjected to a tightening grid of surveillance and control, legitimated by ideologies of human resource management and constructed across an abyss of unemployment.[2] These changes at the level of labour process cut up collectivities, and individualize and pathologize the disablement which people experience in their working lives. In the absence of collective struggle, fright often becomes more usual than fight.

This is not to suggest that opportunity structures are not undergoing significant change. Claims that we are becoming a 'classless' society must resonate with some elements of human experience if they are not to ring completely hollow. De-industrialization, increasing social mobility and affluence among some social groups, together with the creative and empowering possibilities of youth culture (see Beck, 1987; Willis, 1990), are among the influences which have loosened class and gender categorization and multiplied the social and cultural bases for identity. In addition, as some of the studies in this book suggest, we are witnessing changing forms of social subjectivity of a kind loosely captured by the concept of 'individualization'. There are complex issues involved, however, in interpreting these changes and in identifying the aspects which are distinctively 'new'. Given growing inequalities and tightening social regulation, the forms of 'individualism' we have observed seem to reflect an erosion of former social bonds and an increasing *competitorization* and compartmentalization of self rather than a movement towards the emancipatory reconstruction of self and society.

Other social conditions remaining constant, deepening inequality and social fragmentation might have been expected to popularize socialism as an antidote, with its emphasis on community and equality. Instead, we find traditional socialist solutions have lost their purchase on the delivery of change. Most notably, class analysis, for over a century central to progressive social thought and political organization, has come to seem anachronistic. Thus, on the Left, writers such as Miliband (1991) have acknowledged doubts about whether 'socialism, as a project or even as an idea, has any future at all', and the Right have seized the opportunity to announce its demise: 'Socialism of course is dead and gone. Finished, past, out of the window. Nobody believes in it any more. Nobody. Not in this country, not abroad' (John Major, quoted in the *Sunday Express*, 19 April 1992). In contrast others have asserted, 'socialism did not die, because it had not yet been' (Galeano, 1990). The difficulties of Marxism, we would suggest, derive not from failing relevance as an important source of explanation of, and insights into, present troubles. As Jameson (1991) has argued: 'it does not seem to make much sense to talk about the bankruptcy of Marxism when Marxism is . . . the study of just that capitalism whose global triumph is affirmed in talk of Marxism's demise'. Rather, it is the credibility of Marxism as a total social theory and as a force for political change which has steadily been dissolving in a potent concoction of Thatcherism, Post-Industrialism, Nationalism, the collapse of communist experiments and accompanying changes in Eastern Europe, Feminism, Post-Modernism and the growth of new social movements. A central ingredient in this mixture is the critiques of feminists and post-modern thinkers. Once feminism unveiled the huge absence of women in Marxist thinking, its own historic specificity was clearly on the agenda. The emperor of Marxism-as-science had no clothes, or rather it had men's nineteenth-century clothes. After all, as Marx himself might have argued, it was 'produced in circumstances directly encountered, given and transmitted from the past'. Subsequent doubts and confusions over the status of Marxism as 'grand narrative', the privileging of 'class' over other forms of oppression and the depowering effects at the level of everyday political activity of non-relativized discourse, have brought further dispersion. In this climate of doubt, the collapse of communism could readily be seen as further vindication of fundamental weaknesses of its Marxist ancestry.

It is a climate in which Left vacillatory crisis has met New Right conviction. The Right have seized the social democratic notions of meritocracy, 'class' and 'opportunity' and proclaimed the coming of a 'classless' society. Part of this New Right project was what may be called a New Embourgeoisement Thesis. 'Despite economic retrenchment, we are all capable of getting on, becoming "middle class", if we have the talent, work hard in education and work.' This has continuity with, but is distinct from, the old embourgeoisement thesis of the 1960s, i.e. 'We are all becoming "middle class" because of increased affluence.' The new thesis of the Conservative Offensive characteristic of the 1980s was a vision of an 'open', 'classless' society, characterized by the new technologies and service industries, where, as Thatcher reminds us, 'Equality and opportunity cannot exist alongside one another. What is opportunity if your only opportunity is to be equal?' (speech in Eastbourne, 1981). Indeed, in such a 'classless' society, inequality is a *sine qua non* because 'Opportunity means nothing unless it includes the right to be unequal' (speech in New York, 1975). This conception of a moral society of 'just deserts' and 'you get what you deserve!', is homologous with the biographies of figures such as Margaret Thatcher, John Major and Norman Tebbit themselves. The new social prototypes, replacing the old 'Affluent Worker', were 'the Yuppies' and 'Essex man/woman' who had 'got on their bikes' and were in acquisitive possession of, or aspiring for, the icons of prosperity – the Porsche or Escort GTi, the Rolex watch and the mobile 'phone.

Nowhere was the potency of the New Right project and pallor of socialist alternatives as then constituted more clearly demonstrated than in the election of 1992. Considered in the light of the studies gathered together in this book, one of the factors underlying this success was the fact that the New Right rhetoric was finely tuned to a social context characterized by a lethal combination of growing injustice and growing individualization, a context which the Conservatives had themselves helped to create. The 'classless' society discourse incorporated and solved the problem of social injustice, combining a frank *recognition* of inequality with an apparently graspable solution at the individual level. 'I want a society where everyone can not only see the summit, but reach it . . . I mean a society in which everybody, wherever they come from, whatever their background, can go wherever they wish to go and wherever their abilities take them' (John Major, quoted in the *Sunday Express*, 19 April 1992). The barriers to opportunity would be lifted. Through talent, enterprise and hard work, individuals could create their own material and social success. They could climb, contribute to wealth production and best of all not feel guilty about it! In contrast the Labour Party, while claiming to care about inequalities, offered no unifying ideology and, in the short term, only ameliorative measures.

Education and training were a major superstructural terrain where New Right rhetoric was translated into concrete policy (see papers in *Education Limited*, 1991). The progressive educational solutions to the problem of inequality pursued from the 1960s to the early 1980s, from comprehensive schooling to curricular innovations such as the Technical and Vocational Education Initiative (TVEI), seem like fading history in the face of the new forms of pedagogy under construction. In comparison, even the much critiqued 'new vocationalism' now seems benign in the considerable scope which it offered for re-interpretation by teachers and curriculum developers (see Bates *et al.*, 1984; Bates, 1989). The incoming tide of market

pressures and related managerial approaches favour measurement of individual performance on singularized, nationally determined class-culturally
biased criteria, marginalizing more liberal approaches to the management,
organization and content of education. The new forms of curricular appar-
atus – the National Curriculum and the system of National Vocational
Qualifications – vastly tighten control over educational and employment
knowledge and reduce the 'relative autonomy' of the teaching profession.
Borrowing from Bernstein (1971), they also tighten the 'classification' and
'framing' of success and failure. The resulting intensifying competition is
no leveller; rather, it brings social advantage and disadvantage more forcibly
than ever into play, reinforcing broader trends towards widening and
deepening inequalities. At the same time, by undermining potential solidarity
within homogeneous groups, it reduces effective resistance; or, in Beck's
terms, 'community is dissolved in the acid bath of competition' (Beck,
1987).

In further education, while equal opportunities commitments are a
common feature of 'mission statements', the fundamental shift towards
employer-led training and labour market determination make it difficult to
enact these aspirations. The impact of the new corporate objectives is yet
to be researched, but there are certainly signs that there will be the usual
transformations in the course of implementation. To quote a teacher involved in one of our research sites, 'Our mission statement has its longest
statement on equal opportunities but its commitment extends to putting
a ramp up.' 'Access' courses and adequate resourcing for 'special needs'
students and the disabled are increasingly difficult to sustain in a market
economy (Corbett and Barton, 1992). These highly political developments
have been accompanied by the gradual erosion of social and political
education, which has been marginalized with the increasing emphasis on
employers' needs. In contrast with the rhetoric of mission statements,
at practitioner level it is increasingly difficult to sustain a sense of 'mission'
in the sense of moral commitment and integrity in the context of cuts,
market forces and reduced autonomy.

These wider circumstances have shaped the lives and perceptions of the
young people presented in this book and the interpretations and analyses
offered by the authors involved. While the inequalities which surround
them are glaring, the young people themselves were not, on the whole,
reaching for radical political solutions. One factor here is that the various
groups explored, from Youth Training Scheme (YTS) to public school, are
often fairly invisible to each other, being widely separated institutionally
and socially – an added reason for bringing them together in this book.
Consequently, they have no clear measure of their relative advantages or
disadvantages except in relation to groups they rub shoulders with daily,
for example in the same further education college. The more privileged
were actively pursuing the acquisition of the social and cultural capital

which would lubricate their careers and were relatively oblivious of the rest. On the middle rungs, some of the upper working class and lower middle class were struggling to transcend class-gendered boundaries and had launched themselves on various kinds of 'enterprise' careers. Many of these, for example Bates' fashion designers, imagined possibilities where there were in fact going to be none. A few, usually the socially and materially better-cushioned, were more successful. However, while social class background was a major factor affecting success and failure, this was not understood by young people themselves, who had no overview of the situation and experienced failure in terms of a succession of personal setbacks. Anger and overt resistance were most prominent on the YTS schemes, where vast creative energies, rendered superfluous by the narrow bounds of training, were channelled into constant entertainment and combativity culminating in the overthrow of any kind of classroom order. At all levels, many young people showed a notable degree of reflexivity, a capacity for creative reconstruction of biography in terms of personal progress and fulfilment. Ironically, at moments of critical adjustment to labour market realities, personal autonomy was often most highlighted.

From YTS Lads to Public School Girls

The following chapters fan out to cover a wide social spectrum of groups, though beginning and ending with those from the lower working class for whom upward movement seems most blocked. The initial chapter by Inge Bates on the 'care girls' develops an analysis of the transition into employment of a group of working-class girls involved in youth training. The chapter underlines the importance of, and interrelationships between, class and gender in shaping vocational identities. The fact that occupational destinations and training opportunities remain heavily class-gendered, despite two decades of 'equal opportunities' work, is confirmed by the survey evidence of the 16–19 Initiative, which Ken Roberts discusses in the final chapter of this volume. The point of Bates' chapter is to uncover some of the processes involved in reproducing these patterns. The young women's occupational choices at the start of training were well out of line with the opportunities available, a possible reflection of the impact of both comprehensive schooling and equal opportunities developments on aspirations. Underlying these choices, however, was a strong undertow of cultural preparation pulling these young women towards domestic employment. In the context of contradictory vocational socialization, the die was cast by the labour market. This was a buyer's market for labour, one consequence of which was that cultural preparation, in addition to suitable qualifications and training, gave them an 'edge' in the stiff competition for jobs. These young women's servicing roles within the family had furnished them with attitudes and skills which helped them to survive in 'caring' careers, while disqualifying them for more conventionally attractive jobs such as nanny and secretary. A related theme is the role of post-16 education and training in mediating between labour market opportunities and class-gendered cultural attributes. Through processes of selection, screening and occupationally specific socialization, post-16 provision is seen as performing an important labour supply function, which despite the egalitarian intentions of many teachers and trainers, is in tension with the delivery of more equal opportunities.

These arguments are explored further in subsequent chapters. In his study of a BTEC National Diploma course in Hotel Management and Catering, George Riseborough presents a more advantaged group experiencing much more promising occupational horizons. Congruence between cultural attributes forged in the family context and employment demands is again central in explaining both entry into and success within this course. Riseborough portrays a student sub-culture characterized by 'strategic compliance, impression-management and a sublimation of overt conflict' which draws upon a 'deferential and aspirational' parent culture and harmonizes with the occupational culture they are entering. It is the cultural consistency through tiers of experience in the family, vocational training and work which provides the necessary lubricant to success.

The experience of a different class fraction is examined in Bates' chapter on BTEC National Diploma fashion design students. This group came from upper working-class and lower middle-class backgrounds and entered the course with aspirations towards glamorous, 'post-modern' careers and 'jet-set' social lives. In fact, most students were destined for skilled and semi-skilled work in the garment industry and retail trade and only a small proportion entered the Higher National Diploma courses necessary for more specialized training for fashion design. The analysis suggests that specific material and social advantages played a crucial role in determining which of these directions students took and, indeed, in allowing their entry on to the course in the first place. For example, the emotional stresses and financial costs of training meant that students needed to be able to draw upon a supportive sub-structure of family life in which the career investment of two years' unpaid training did not impose an impossible toll. For families on low incomes and/or where young people themselves carried part of the burden of domestic problems, the dice were heavily loaded against entry into, let alone success within, the course.

As in the preceding chapters, a central theme is the 'snipping away' at aspirations through specific socialization processes within training as tutors struggled to persuade trainees to formulate more realistic aspirations and to prioritize the development of marketable skills rather than creative self-expression. This group is particularly interesting in the extent to which they perceived themselves as free to construct their own futures and resistant to messages to the contrary. In so far as their ambitions reflected the impact of growing 'individualization', this could be seen as dysfunctional from the point of view of social reproduction.

The floundering of 'enterprise' careers is a major focus in Robert MacDonald's work based on young people attempting to become self-employed in the North-East. The chapter develops a typology of youth experience (runners, fallers and plodders) which distinguishes different groups in terms of the degree of success which they enjoy. Most young people studied were working class and fell into the less successful categories of 'plodders' and 'fallers', whose experience of self-employment ranged from struggling along to gruelling and traumatic failure. For black young people, whose exclusion from decent jobs was often a motive for embarking on self-employment, the racism of the marketplace brought further trials. Overall, the study underlines the struggles endured by young working-class people in order to remain in employment rather than fall into the 'underclass' of the unemployed.

A more successful launching pad for social mobility than the Enterprise Scheme appeared to be the conventional sixth form. John Quicke focuses on a rather more privileged group studying for A-levels, hoping to enter higher education, and valuing their schooling. As with the BTEC students, however, their backgrounds were by no means solidly middle class. Their parents were mainly lower middle-class small businessmen and white-collar workers but had been upwardly mobile from the working class. Quicke argues that the experience of parental upward mobility was an important factor shaping these students' identities, career perspectives and moral and political attitudes. However, it evoked different types of response. On the one hand, there were 'nostalgics' who were 'socialists' uneasy about their movement into the middle class: this group was oriented towards careers such as education and social work. On the other, there were 'elitists' who would 'go for it', tended to be 'conservative' and admired aspects of Thatcherism. The groups differed, for example, in their attitudes to a group of YTS lads who used parts of the school building. The 'nostalgics' tried to explain the lads' rebellious behaviour as understandable and the 'elitists' to dismiss them as 'slobs'. The political perspectives of both groups were still presumably relatively volatile at this sixth-form stage. Nevertheless, given their own and their family experience of upward social mobility through educational opportunity and individual enterprise, we can see here an example of a constituency likely to be more than usually receptive to Thatcherism and Majorism.

Moving further up the social scale, Debra Roker and Patricia Allatt offer different perspectives on young people benefiting from the investment of substantial economic, social and 'emotional' capital in their careers. While these young people enjoy many kinds of privileges, it is their parents' capacity to buy and thus select and shape their education, which decisively separates them from the rest. Roker's study concentrates on girls from solid middle-class backgrounds, with parents in professional and managerial occupations who are quite explicit about their use of private education as a means of gaining 'the edge' for their children. Here again it is the consistency between home and school cultural values – both emphasizing academic achievement, individual responsibility and the importance of career planning – which reinforces the girls' success. Without such social–psychological support, students were on a precarious path through school, liable to run into difficulties in peer group relationships and ultimately to leave, as was from time to time the case with some pupils in school on the Assisted Places Scheme.

The analysis of sub-structures of privilege is the focus of Patricia Allatt's unusually detailed exploration of the social processes involved in family life, forms of capital and the contexts in which these are invested. Allatt's paper develops a conceptual framework which 'names the parts' of family life involved in the transference of privilege, laying bare the complex but nevertheless systematic processes of class maintenance. The major focus is on the reproduction of economic, social and cultural capital through parental management of the various arenas which young people inhabit: education, the family itself and the social context. In all areas, financial and socio-cultural advantages facilitate parents' promotion of their children's interests. Nevertheless, investing in these resources does not take place automatically, but rather involves a constant labour of surveillance, discussion, negotiation and intervention as parents seek to optimize the educational and social position of their offspring. While there is not, unfortunately, directly parallel material on the other groups studied, the evidence available suggests that such labour was strikingly absent or naively misdirected elsewhere. Typical, for example, among YTS groups were families where young people themselves were important props helping out in relation to illness, domestic crises and child care, at significant cost to their own education, training and social lives. Their YTS allowance was often crucial to family income. More poignantly, some of the families of young people pursuing enterprise careers, or the BTEC fashion design course, made substantial but poor investments through lack of a crucial form of cultural capital, good information about labour market opportunities or access to the social networks which would provide this.

The chapters considered so far emphasize the deep sub-structures of inequality and the ways in which privilege and disadvantage are ploughed into youth careers through family and education but most importantly at the interface between the two spheres. Young people climb into adulthood on slopes of differential gradient and the results show. Roberts' analysis of the 16–19 Initiative survey evidence in the final chapter confirms the insights emerging from the qualitative studies: social class background and sex were the major determinants of young people's career prospects. It is difficult from this evidence to see any sign of a classless society in the making, though we can observe some fluidity among the upper working class and lower middle class. Roberts' argument, however, puts this into a wider perspective, arguing that the proportion of social mobility revealed by both qualitative and quantitative studies was essentially a mirage, the consequence of changes in the structure of the labour market, particularly the expansion of professional and managerial jobs at the expense of manual employment. The resulting increase in middle-class occupations has bene-fited some of the working class but has also strengthened the position of the middle class. Meanwhile, 'top' and 'bottom' remain intact and gendered divisions, while looser among the middle class, cut across all levels.

More significant from the point of view of working-class career prospects is the increasing risk of downward mobility into unemployment, tempor-ary schemes and possible long-term unemployment. It was the risk of entering the growing numbers of unemployed which helped to explain the strategies and orientations of some of the young people we studied. Their determination to succeed, or preparedness to accommodate, and the levels of active parental sponsorship which we observed, were driven as much by fear of unemployment as by the expectation of upward mobility. So what was so alarming about life on the margins in the last decade? We have not been able to include material on homeless[4] or unemployed youth in this volume, but the fate awaiting those who 'failed' in education is suggested in George Riseborough's study of the 'lads', some of whom eventually became long-term unemployed.

The major power of this chapter is that it provides a unique and vivid portrayal of the vital and creative culture of a group of working-class lads, their forms of power and the limitations of that power as a means of radical challenge. Part of the meaning of the study is, as Riseborough (forthcoming) suggests elsewhere, that the 'tedium is the message'. Beyond this, the chapter provides a rich account of the constant, explosive combativity of the 'lads' within the confined spaces which they daily ex-cavate. Identity is salvaged through a dual strategy of creatively *blocking* all attempts by others, for example their tutors, to control them – and creatively *building* a sexist, racist and disablist hierarchy over which they have dominion. The latter practices underline the daily uphill struggles involved in developing an 'equal opportunities' ethos within post-16 education and training. Analysis, or even an account, of the author's perspective is deliberately left implicit and some readers will find much to concern them here. One effect, however, is to leave us working with the issues and contradictions with which the chapter starkly confronts us: the social structures which shape the lads' culture and practices; the role of training within these structures; the meaning of resistance; the inhumanity and potential for fascism among oppressed groups; the role of racism, sexism and disablist practices; the relationship between research and fiction;

the meaning of ethnography and more broadly of research and transformative writing. Perhaps, most importantly, this study reveals ways in
which oppressed groups become the oppressors of others, splintering
potential solidarities.

In Conclusion

This takes us back full circle to the problem of writing at all about social
inequalities at the present juncture. The studies included in this book,
through concentrating at the level of youth experience, reveal something
of the vastness of the gulf between the opportunities of different groups
of young people. Those studied by Patricia Allatt are worlds apart materially,
culturally and geographically from the 'Gobbo Barmy Harmy'. The chances
of shuttling between the two trajectories are virtually negligible. Comparison
across the various groups shows the extent to which their life-chances are
shaped by social class and family background and some of the means
through which this happens.

Family and education are important sites of reproduction but the key
site remains relatively invisible, having no institutional base: this is the
interface between the two. Family circumstances become linked with specific
levels of education/training and hence with occupational strata and sectors
through the circulation of *differential currencies of opportunity* in the form
of material conditions; domestic and emotional factors; cultural values;
gender codes; social networks; geographical mobility; access to information and occupational cultures. The resulting convertibility of these 'currencies' allows some to shop in private education and others merely to
survive on youth training schemes. In turn, routes within education and
training are not neutral to class-cultural factors. The social organization of
each route is premised upon class-gendered student or trainee types and
related assumptions concerning their material and cultural resources. Thus
student progress on the different tracks depends partly on how far they
conform to these types. Present government policies are tightening these
relationships and reducing education's already limited capacity to act as a
'leveller'. Significant reductions in youth inequalities would require measures
such as social and educational policies designed to reduce the gap between
the rich and poor; the abolition of private education; further development
of more genuinely comprehensive education at secondary and post-16 levels;
post-16 maintenance grants; the restoration of grants for higher education
to previous values; the introduction of really high quality training; and the
reduction of unemployment. In the last decade the tide has been going out
for social democratic reforms of this kind.

Herein lies some of our difficulty in identifying tangible solutions, relevant forms of praxis and, indeed, in writing about these issues. Moreover,
while in education and academia we are conscious of explosions of critical

theory, cultural production and new forms of personal politics, we are doubtful whether these do more than swirl like mists around a landscape of inequality and injustice. Given the history of attempts at socialism, what are the ways of working for more egalitarian, democratic and caring forms of social organization? *Quite simply, what are they?* In our view this is the fundamental question which needs to be frankly, openly, widely and urgently addressed. The acknowledgement of uncertainty – rather than confidence in understanding and prescription – seems to us to be a necessary step to take in debating and working on these issues. For between the absence of grand solutions and the presence of growing social injustice lies new territory, Arctic in its proportions but immense in its potential. Hopefully, if we can approach this in a spirit of discovery, imagination and creative sharing, we will find richer possibilities for debate, for learning and for social change than have yet been explored.

Notes

1. This study and the other Sheffield ethnographies (Chapters 2, 3, 5 and 8) were made possible by an ESRC grant (Banks, Bates, Gray and Quicke, Ref. C OS 25 0012) and conducted in the Division of Education, Sheffield University.
2. See David Piachand's analysis in *Guardian Society*, 30 September 1992.
3. For discussions of the application of the Foucauldian concept of surveillance in education and training, see, for example, Hargreaves and Reynolds (1989) and Bates (1991) and, more generally, Ball (1990). For discussion of surveillance in the context of 'Total Quality Management' and the consequences for industrial relations, see, for example, Sewell and Wilkinson (1992).
4. A further study arising from the 16–19 Initiative is Patricia Ainley's book *Young People Leaving Home* which includes discussion of homelessness.

References

Ainley, P. (1991) *Young People Leaving Home*. Poole, Cassell.
Bates, I. (1989) Versions of vocationalism: an analysis of some social and political influences on curriculum policy and practice. *British Journal of Sociology of Education*, 10(2), 215–31.
Bates, I. (1991) Closely observed training: an exploration of links between social structures, training and identity. *International Studies in Sociology of Education*, 1, 225–43.
Bates, I. *et al.* (1984) *Schooling for the Dole? The New Vocationalism*. London, Macmillan.
Ball, S. (1981) *Beachside Comprehensive*. Cambridge, Cambridge University Press.
Ball, S.J. (ed.) (1990) *Foucault and Education: Disciplines and Knowledge*. London, Routledge.
Beck, U. (1987) Beyond status and class. In W. Mega *et al.* (eds) *Modern German Sociology*. Columbia, Columbia University Press.
Bernstein, B. (1971) On the classification and framing of educational knowledge.

In M.F.D. Young (ed.) *Knowledge and Control: New Directions for the Sociology of Education*. London, Collier Macmillan.

Bourdieu, P. and Passeron, J.D. (1977) *Reproduction in Education, Society and Culture*. London, Sage.

Chisholm, L., Buchner, P., Kruger, H. and Brown, P. (1990) *Childhood, Youth and Social Change*. Lewes, Falmer Press.

Corbett, J. and Barton, L. (1992) Fears and expectations of special needs co-ordinators. Unpublished working paper. University of Sheffield.

Donald, J. and Rattansi, A. (1992) *'Race', Culture and Difference*. London, Sage.

Education Group II, Department of Cultural Studies, University of Birmingham (1991) *Education Limited: Schooling, Training and the New Right in England Since 1979*. London, Unwin Hyman.

Field, F. (1989) *Losing Out: The Emergence of Britain's Underclass*. Oxford, Basil Blackwell.

Galeano, E. (1991) A child lost in the storm. In R. Blackburn (ed.) *After the Fall: The Failure of Communism and the Future of Socialism*. London, Verso.

Gleeson, D. and Mardle, G. (1980) *Further Education or Training? A Case Study in the Theory and Practice of Day Release Education*. London, Routledge and Kegan Paul.

Griffin, C. (1985) *Typical Girls?* London, Routledge and Kegan Paul.

Hargreaves, A. and Reynolds, D. (1989) Decomprehensivisation. *Introduction to Education Policies: Controversies and Critiques*. Lewes: Falmer Press.

Jameson, F. (1991) Conversations on the new world order. In Robin Blackburn (ed.) *After the Fall: The Failure of Communism and the Future of Socialism*. London, Verso.

Mann, K. (1991) *The Making of an English 'Underclass'? The Social Provisions of Welfare and Labour*. Milton Keynes, Open University Press.

Marshall, G., Newby, H., Rose, D. and Vogler, C. (1988) *Social Class in Modern Britain*. London, Hutchinson.

Miliband, R. (1991) Socialism in question. *Monthly Review*, March, pp. 16–26.

Riseborough, G. (forthcoming) 'The Wolf Pack!': An ethnography of YTS classroom politics in a further education college. *International Journal of Qualitative Studies in Education*.

Sewell, G. and Wilkinson, B. (1992) Someone to watch over me. Surveillance, discipline and the just-in-time labour process. *Sociology*, 26 May, 2, 271–89.

Willis, P. (1977) *Learning to Labour*. Farnborough, Saxon House.

Willis, P. (1990) *Common Culture*. Milton Keynes, Open University Press.

Chapter 1

A Job which is 'Right for Me'?

Social class, gender and individualization[1]

Inge Bates

Why do working-class girls continue to enter working-class, gender-stereotyped jobs? Why do they still swarm towards traditional female occupations and rarely, for example, seek training as electricians, joiners, technicians or computer operators? Since the classic studies by Willis (1977) and Griffin (1985), we might have expected significant dislocation in processes of class and gender reproduction arising from post-Fordist production patterns, new systems of education and training, and the promised lifting of barriers to opportunity. Similarly, the supposed greater confidence and autonomy of 'late' modern youth might lead us to expect the emergence of new career paths more expressive of the growing impulse towards individual self-realization. There is increasing evidence, however, that these wider changes have so far done little to counteract the influence of class, race and gender on youth transitions (Cockburn, 1987; Jones and Wallace, 1990; Mirza, 1992).

This chapter explores the experience of a group of young women whose lives reflect ancient, but nevertheless apparently perfectly durable, patterns of oppression. It focuses on social class, gender and vocational training and their influence on entry into 'caring' careers. The chapter is based on an ethnographic study of a group of 16- to 18-year-old girls training for jobs in the field of institutional care. It begins by exploring aspects of the girls' experience of their training and work placements. These involve physically and emotionally stressful tasks such as coping with violence, dealing with incontinence and laying out the dead. The chapter then documents a gradual process of adjustment to this type of work, which ends with the girls positively seeking work in this field. This provides a basis for posing the central questions of the paper: Why do working-class girls continue to enter working-class, gender-stereotyped jobs? What role does vocational training play in promoting their adjustment? An explanatory framework is then developed which draws on theories of social reproduction and interweaves: the occupational culture of institutional care; aspects of gender socialization in the context of working-class families; vocational training; and the wider context of youth unemployment and job scarcity.

The 'care girls' who were the focus of the research were on a Youth Training Scheme (YTS: now YT) programme, training mainly for jobs as care assistants in homes for the elderly. On a hypothetical continuum from 'tough' to 'soft', the girls could be situated at the 'tougher' end of the spectrum, similar in many respects to the 'wenches' as portrayed by Davies (1984). Their training programme was regarded locally as an example of a high-quality scheme, with off-the-job training provided in a college of further education. The lecturers involved were experienced in the field of social care and the tutor in charge was a senior lecturer in the college. Work placements were mainly in homes managed and inspected by the local authority, where standards of provision and training are generally regarded as higher than in privately owned homes. Trainees worked towards a City and Guilds qualification, now ranked at National Vocational Qualification (NVQ) level 2. Training was based on a nationally recognized curriculum development scheme and organized around sets of 'modules' prescribed in terms of pre-defined competencies. The research was based on a year's participant observation with first- and second-year 'care girls' and follow-up visits over another year. Much of the time was spent with the group in college, during their off-the-job training, but numerous visits to work placements in homes for the elderly were also made.

The Work Roles of the 'Care Girls'

One entry point into the central problematic of this chapter is to begin with the jobs themselves. Posed most simply, when we ask why working-class kids get working-class jobs, what is it that they get? The usual generalized analysis of working-class occupations in terms of the mental–manual dichotomy, low pay, monotony and absence of intrinsic satisfaction slides over lived experience, particularly the experience of women. In so doing, such analyses neglect specific forms of accommodation which jobs require and the significance of these for the gender-stereotyping of occupations. So as to develop and test theories of social and cultural reproduction, it may be important to unpack the different occupational cultures which form the context of work. Working in homes for the elderly involves a wide range of domestic and nursing tasks, ranging from working in the laundry, generally regarded as boring and of low status, to going shopping for residents, which is seen as more rewarding. These various aspects of the job, while differently evaluated, were all broadly acceptable to the trainees. Routines and skills needed to be learned, but the tasks involved did not require major adjustments to individual identity. However, as I came to spend more time with the care girls, it emerged that their jobs involved some extremely stressful tasks which made entry into this field of employment potentially much more traumatic. Three such tasks are briefly highlighted here: coping with violence, coping with incontinence and coping with death.

A constant theme in the girls' discussion of work was the residents themselves, many of whom were senile and confused and could be physically violent. Hence violence, being 'whacked', 'smacked', 'given a belt', often featured in their accounts.

Coping with violence

Marie: I don't know, I never feel like hitting them. I must save it for when I get home 'cos everybody says that they drive them crackers and that, you know, when they – all keep going off. But they don't me. And like one, she keeps biting me, hitting me and grabbing hold of me hair when I'm trying to take her shoes off, and she's yanking me about, and I just laugh it off, it doesn't bother me.

Pam: I'll never forget the day Mary Smith whacked me in the stomach and I fell...I actually flew across the bed and I landed on the floor on the other side of the bed. And another time she punched me that hard I just fell into the wardrobe and slid down it. She were...well, she were senile, not confused.

I.B.: You fell into a wardrobe and slid down it?

Pam: Yes because she whacked me that hard.

I.B.: How did you fall down the wardrobe?

Pam: Well, she was stood up and she whacked me and I fell on to the wardrobe and then just slid down it.

Marie: There's one at our place and he's quite frightening really. He's ever so strong. And he gets high sometimes. He's on drugs to keep him low, but he had an accident, and it's not because he's old that he's in there, it's because he's got brain damage and everyone said he should be in a mental home, because he's not really safe to be there, and he just flings out. And he's hit me once or twice and it does hurt...I won't hit him back or anything, 'cos I just feel sorry for him...'cos once he was saying to me, 'Can you remember what I were like before this?', and he's always looking at his hands. He cries and I feel really sorry for him. And I can't hit him 'cos he's hurt me. I never really would have.

Pam: I've never hit one of the residents. I mean, that's why Mary Smith were like she were, she were that senile that the drugs she were on were making her lash out...It's when...the drugs are wearing off, that's when they start...lashing out at you. 'Cos the drugs are wearing off and they need to take some more drugs.

Marie: But I think they can be really frightening sometimes.

Pam: A lot frighten me. I used to dread it when somebody used to say 'will you get Mary Smith up?'. I used to think 'Oh my God, not Mary Smith, not Mary Smith please'. Because I knew that she hadn't took her medication and she's be in one of her moods, she were most likely to give me a good crack round the earhole – she used to say to me, she says 'You're only a child you', which is right, she's right, I am only a child.

In relation to such incidents, the girls typically reported mixed feelings of pity, fear, absolute dread of particular patients, the struggle to repress the urge to retaliate, their pride in not doing so and, occasionally, their own violence.

Interwoven with accounts of residents' behaviour are descriptions of their physical care, a significant proportion of which consisted of what the girls themselves sometimes called 'shit shovelling'.

Coping with incontinence

Wendy: But you're not only looking after old people are you? You've got all that laundry to take out to all them 40 or 50 bedrooms, do the beds and wash everybody when you get them up.

Sue: And when they get *tished* up to the eyeballs, and that, done it all over the carpet, and you've got to clean it up. You've got all them beds to make. All that laundry to give out, put clean towels out, do this, do that, even help out in the kitchens sometimes, set tables.

Wendy: You can't believe really how much you get done in one day. I just couldn't believe it.

Sue: You get so much done, when you look back on what you've done, you think 'God'.

Wendy: If you just go home and you sit down and you make a list of everything you've done that day, how many old people you've changed in one day, how many beds you've made.

I.B.:   How many might you have changed in one day?

Wendy: What, beds or residents? From top to toe?

Sue: Some people you change about six times don't you?

Wendy: You can change one person, the same person, three times in one day.

Sue: With us we can change the same person about six times. You sit down and they do it again.

I.B.:   A complete change of clothing?

Sue: We toilet them right often but they're still always wet through.

Wendy: We toilet ours often. We toilet them ever so regular.

Sue: And then there's turning one what's in bed.

Wendy: And like when we had that diarrhoea bug going around, if anybody were in a really bad mess, we had to bath them, so they
were bathed, three people getting bathed every five minutes.

Sue: If they were that *tished* up you can't just give them a strip wash,
they had to go in the bath.

I.B.:   When you say tished up, is that, you mean . . .

Sue: Messed up.

I.B.:   Tished up. I'd just not heard you use that word before.

Sue: Well it's better than saying they're shitted up to the eyeballs isn't
it?

Whereas being 'belted' was reported with anger and dread, coping with
incontinence appeared to be more readily accepted. Typically, the girls
commented when asked about these aspects of their job that: they 'didn't
mind', 'somebody's got to do it', 'you've got to see they're comfortable'.
The social taboo dimensions were dealt with in part through a humorous
language strategy: the reversal of shit to produce 'tish'.

The most distressing part of the job appeared to be the regular occurrence
of death and the processes involved in caring for the dying and dead.

Coping with death

Carol

Carol: . . . I've seen four people laid out. Second day I were there I saw
somebody die. She like died on me.

I.B.:   Holding you?

Carol: Yes, she were like holding me when she died so that really upset
me. I didn't want to go back after that. It really, really upset me.
[Trainee cries again, remembering.]

Carol: After that one I were alright, I just kept away when anybody died.
It were just seeing them being carried out on like a rug thing and
put into the black van. I'm alright about it now, it doesn't bother
me.

I.B.:   When you say that you saw somebody laid out, what did that
involve?

Carol: Washing them and cleaning them all up and that and changing
their clothes.

I.B.:   And were you helping or were you just present?

Carol: Well I were helping in like running water and that and passing that
but she didn't want me to like help lay out because I were so
young. So she just said I can stop in and watch if I want to . . . But
I think I feel now that I'm glad I watched. I'm glad I watched then
I know what it's like.

Fiona

I.B.:   Have you been with people when they're dying?
Fiona: Yes.
I.B.:   Actually dying or, you know, weeks off or . . .
Fiona: No, dying.
Diane: I haven't been with anyone when they're on like their death bed
          as you put it, but I've been when they've been really ill. It's the
          things they say that upset you, all their life comes out.
Fiona: Yes, they start talking about the past.
Diane: It's right upsetting.
Fiona: And how they used to enjoy their lives and they'd come out with
          when their parents died and then they'd come further up to their
          older life and they'd carry on and carry on.

The girls' distress about such occasions was a regular feature of college
life in the first year of training. Again, however, they expressed a pride in
what they did. In the context of coping with death, it was a pride in their
growing 'toughness', in becoming unflinching in the face of harsh facts or,
in the words of one trainee, not being 'a bleeding, whining Minnie' (see
Bates, 1990).

Another way of exploring the occupation of trainee care assistant was
through the reactions of others. While trainees themselves gradually learned
to 'switch off' from the job, they were reminded afresh of the awfulness
and the 'taboo' aspects of the job by the reactions of others. Girls reported
that friends outside the scheme, boyfriends and parents expressed surprise
and disgust when they heard stories about work.

People's reactions

Parents

Judy: Me mum sort of looks at me in disgust when I start talking about
        it. 'Shut up, I'm eating'.
Helen: Because there's some things you don't talk about when you're
        eating.
Judy: I mean it's like you're sat having your dinner in like the staff room
        and they'll just sit and talk about it and it doesn't really bother you
        because you're used to it and then you go home and you start
        while you're eating your tea and they feel like throwing up every-
        where.

Friend

Linda: No, she's not here, it's a friend out of college. You know, I grew
        up, I went through school with her, she stayed on. She's how can

I put it, she's clever, she works ever so hard and she's not so . . . like when you talk to her about old people (she'll say) 'oh shut up, shut up, shut up' and she'll cringe and she'll say 'I'm going home if you don't shut up'. She's, you know, all proper and don't like touching . . . I think that sort of personality.

Occupations would appear to vary in the extent to which their contents, in terms of lived experience, can be readily disclosed to wider publics. These trainees were commencing entry into a relatively closed occupational community, a feature of their training which appeared to intensify their identification with the role of 'care assistant'.

What, in summary, did the role of care assistant involve for 16- and 17-year-old trainees? They were essentially extended domestic careers, but extended to include the grimmer – to the exclusion of the lighter – sides of domestic life. The picture which developed was one of a physically back-breaking and emotionally demanding job, involving an altogether ancient tapestry of female tasks which ranged from: bed-making, food serving, bathing, lifting '18 stone women', sitting with the dying and laying out the dead. Swearing and being sworn at, getting a 'belt' and occasionally delivering one were taken for granted parts of the day's round. To the outsider, the 'caring' world may have appeared as one of pink overalls, cleanliness, jangling keys, 'Come along Annie', wheelchairs, walks around the grounds, trolleys, laundry, the ubiquitous institutional smell, dozing residents in television lounges. This was the re-presented, more acceptable face of an occupation, which in effect, in terms of contemporary cultural constructs, was a 'heavy', 'dirty' job, steeped in taboo subject matter such as the body, age, 'shit-shovelling' and death. These social responsibilities were transported from the wider society to a sub-society, staffed largely by women. Within this sub-society, a partial and truncated version of 'caring' was enacted, involving constant tension between caring for and processing people. The limits to 'caring', however, were ultimately determined not by women themselves, but by an occupational culture and levels of resourcing which reflected the priorities of capitalism and patriarchy.

Choice and Adjustment in 'Caring' Careers

The job of assistant in homes for the elderly presents a critical case for examining the scope for occupational choice in what has been termed a 'decade of opportunity'. Viewed in terms of dominant cultural values, the job can be identified as undesirable on a number of levels. The tasks involved are physically and emotionally demanding and stressful. Much of the job content is both dirty and distressing. The work involves long and often socially inconvenient hours and low pay. One obvious possibility which needs to be considered here is that these perspectives on the job reflect the more congenial and hygienic work values and experience of the writer *qua* academic. However, the perception of the job as exceptionally demanding, stressful and generally unattractive was echoed by the trainees themselves, their tutors and also reflected in the reactions of their friends and family members to 'stories' about work. These aspects of the job did not, however, discourage many of the trainees from seeking 'caring' careers. The seeming paradox which emerged from the data was that, despite the apparently gruelling nature of 'caring' work, many of the girls came to accept, and moreover became positively enthusiastic about, jobs in this field. It is a contradiction which takes us into the quicksands of the meaning of choice. How far could their decisions to enter these jobs be seen in terms of individual choice, in the sense of selecting from a range of alternatives the most personally meaningful course of action? Was there any sign of a lifting of the barriers to opportunity? Did they choose or were they pushed? If they were pushed, why did they think they had chosen?

One place to begin an exploration of these issues is with the girls' career plans in their last year of school. Of the twenty or so girls in the study, none had decided to work with old people while at school. A wide range of previous ambitions were recalled, e.g. beauty therapist, typist, working in big department stores, laboratory technician, working with people, particularly children. Many of the girls had applied for Nursery Nurses Examination Board (NNEB) courses to train to be nursery nurses. Most had been introduced to 'caring' at a careers exhibition and some had then applied for at least two courses (e.g. hairdressing and 'caring'). 'Caring' had been presented in terms of generalized information about 'working with people': children, the handicapped and the old. By the time they had left school, most of the girls had applied to join the 'caring' scheme, often as a 'fall-back' strategy, but occasionally as a first choice. When it was a first choice, it was generally perceived in terms of leading to work with children.

These initial 'choices' were interesting in that they were well out of line with labour market opportunities. Thus at the crucial juncture of school-leaving, the structures to which they had so far been exposed had not brought their aspirations into line with labour market opportunities. This is not to suggest that the work of reproduction had not been done. Rather, the reverse; it was simply not quite complete, the results were ragged and unstable. While oriented in the general direction of gender-stereotyped, working-class jobs, they were still seeking jobs a 'cut' above what was possible. In the context of the direct transitions from school to work more typical in earlier decades, this mismatch would perhaps be unusual. However, since closure in career choice tends to occur when labour market entry is imminent, in the absence of end-on transitions it is likely to be a more common phenomenon.

The girls' initial 'choices' were jettisoned because they failed to gain entry into the relevant courses or jobs and hence they found themselves on the YTS 'Caring' course. Most still hoped to work with children rather than the elderly but gradually discovered that, without an NNEB, secure jobs were much more likely to be found in homes for the elderly.

Once they had experienced, on work placements, the job for which they were now being trained, the girls typically expressed disgust, shock, considerable distress and more generally the experience of threatened identity. As one explained: 'I thought I was going to be a nanny travelling the world and look where I've ended up.' Individual autobiographies dissolved and the process was traumatic. At this stage, most of the trainees were perfectly clear that these were not jobs they had chosen:

> At first I dreaded it. I never stopped worrying. It gave me nightmares thinking this is what I would be doing for the rest of my life.

> It was really difficult, straight from school and into this, you know, very, very difficult to cope with the situations.

> When I started I got so depressed I didn't even want to go out.

> To start with I though it were horrible . . . all the smells and I were feeling sick all the time.

> I thought 'this is the pits, I'll never stick this'.

In the first term, reactions of this sort resulted in a few drop-outs, including the most sensitive girls and the only male trainee.

However, after about six months on the scheme, the majority had developed a pride in the job and were keen to find work in this field. In the analysis which follows, I shall suggest that the process of coming to terms with an 'awful' job involved two critical components: the reconstruction of individual biographies and adaptation to the occupational culture. In other words, the 'care girls' changed both their definitions of themselves and their approach to their job.

The example of Kay reveals elements of the process of reconstruction of self in the light of labour market realities:

I.B.: How did you feel about your friend going on to do A-levels compared with what you're doing? Has that ever been a problem to you?

Kay: At first, I mean I've said to you before, when you first came I said . . . *I were ashamed to say I worked with old people, because they sort of look at you and go 'Ugh, God, how can you do it'. And I say 'Someone's got to do it', but like now I say 'Because I enjoy doing it', you know, I'm not ashamed of it any more*, I were at first you see. When she [her friend] went back to do her A-levels, I felt jealous in a way because I knew I was never up to that standard. I could have never done A-levels, I mean I couldn't do O-levels. I can't do exams. And I'm not, I don't know, I'm not very good at exams and I could never have done any A-levels. *At first I felt jealous and then I thought, well, now I don't feel jealous at all, because she's happy doing what she's doing and I'm ever so happy doing what I'm doing.* So why should I feel jealous when I've chosen something and it's right for me as a course. At first when she were, you know, staying on, I did feel jealous, I felt envious that she could do that.

. . .

They [her feelings about her friend] like built up inside and we didn't see each other for a few months and then we got . . . I got to the point where I were bitchy with her, *I was envious that she'd got things that I hadn't got and I knew that I could never do it, but I turn the tables and think, 'well, she can't do what I'm doing, she couldn't do that',* so . . . you know.

Kay's account illuminates both her capacity for reflexive analysis of her own feelings and the way in which *this late/post 'modern' tendency may be harnessed on behalf of social reproduction.* She suggests that, at the beginning of training, employment as a care assistant was incompatible with her self-image. So as to cope with her emerging vocational identity, she had to undergo an inversion of her previous values, with the consequence that her emotional reactions to her work became more tolerable. Feelings of disgust and shame which, had they persisted, would have eventually made the job unendurable, were self-consciously recognized, challenged and converted into feelings of pride. In Kay's words, she reached a point where she could 'turn the tables'. Once Kay embraced the occupational culture of institutional care, she was able to overcome feelings of social shame and inferiority and moved to a point where she felt she had chosen something which was 'right for her'. Thus, in this case, reflexive individualism facilitated not the fulfilment of her 'original' ambitions (she had wanted to be a secretary), but a re-invention of ambitions in line with labour market prospects. In this way, the difference between her own and her friend's opportunities, initially experienced in terms of social *injustice*, was redefined in terms of appropriate *justice*, as something which was 'right for her', relieving her from feelings of anger and resentment and easing adjustment.

While the production of a sense of vocation lessened the stress of caring work, resistance did not disappear. If trainees could not opt out into other employment, they could nevertheless opt out psychologically. Successful trainees looked for ways of protecting themselves from the emotional and physical demands of their employment. Here adaptation to the occupational culture of 'caring' as practised in the workplace played a crucial role. Central to this culture was the management and control of empathy, the development of an impersonal, detached approach to the job and alienated social relations.

Although college tutors stressed the need for sensitivity and genuine caring in this type of work, this was at times overtly rejected and scorned by trainees, particularly as they became more attuned to workplace practices. Effective and sustainable performance in the field of institutional care appeared to depend as much on the absence as on the presence of sensitivity in the care worker and this was recognized in the way in which trainees came to resist the meaning of 'caring'. What they contested, however, was not the institutional constraints upon 'caring', but the quality of care which they were expected to offer within such constraints. Hence their resistance took the form of 'coping strategies', as discussed by Hargreaves (1978) in relation to teaching, and was essentially accommodative rather than challenging.

Examples of 'coping strategies' included 'keeping busy', 'keeping out of the way' and, more importantly, 'switching off'. 'Switching off' emerged as the dominant strategy for accommodating to the job of caring for the old *en masse* in an institutional context. It involved a style of 'care' in which the dying person was depersonalized, allowing the care assistant to control the extent to which she shares in the suffering she observes. Acquiring the capacity to 'switch off' was crucial to trainee survival and helped to explain why staff were encouraged to limit their personal involvement with residents and 'keep busy'. 'They'd have you cleaning the lampshades if you'd got nothing to do.' Gradually, caring careers came to be seen more clinically, in terms of a certain toughness as much as, or even more than, tenderness: 'You can't get attached to them', 'You can't let it get through to you.' At times, detachment threatened to degenerate into harshness and even brutality as other researchers who have investigated homes for the elderly have also noted (e.g. Stannard, 1978): 'You have to ram a wheel-chair behind her legs to get her to sit down', 'He were left all night and no-one went to him. They were just sat there in the kitchen chatting.' Thus while resisting their official work demands allowed the trainees a measure of control over their labour and could be seen at one level as subjectively emancipatory, it objectively contributed to the reproduction of a desensitized, truncated version of 'caring'. Moreover the irony of the contradiction was deepened by the fact that they were 'caring' largely for women from their own social class.

Returning to the broader theme of occupational choice, 'choosing' had both nothing and yet everything to do with the girls' employment as care assistants. In so far as this group formulated personal ambitions, these were repeatedly cooled out until aspirations matched labour market opportunities. However, belief in individual choice played a prominent role in the achievement of effective work adjustment, a necessary condition for which appears to be the maintenance of a sense of volition and personal agency. At critical stages, duress was rendered durable through the re-writing of personal biographies in terms of choice, for example through the 'discovery' of vocation. Within the job, agency was further strengthened through selective withdrawal from the emotional demands of this work.

The Social Context of Adjustment

It is difficult to escape the conclusion that it is a highly socially constrained form of 'wannabee' which leads 16-year-old girls to long for jobs working with the senile, the dying and the dead. The problem, then, is to explore the nature of these constraints, or in other words the material basis of what has been termed the 'inbuilt power' (Roberts and Parsell, 1988) of this career trajectory. How they accommodate to these jobs can partly be explained in terms of processes of social–psychological adjustment, as outlined above. We are still left, however, with our original problem of why it is *working-class girls* who end up in this job. In order to examine this issue, the research needs placing in a larger context.

At one level, what is identified here is a trans-historical, cross-cultural and now well-documented phenomenon – a consequence of patriarchy. The social construction of gender-based divisions of labour has for centuries depended upon ideologies and social structures channelling girls towards domestic, familial and nursing roles, which are accorded relatively low status and rewards. Family, mass media and education have been identified as strongly implicated in these processes, which are interwoven in complex ways with social class divisions (see Sharpe, 1976: Deem, 1980; Walker and Barton, 1983; Chisholm, 1987). These general analyses need developing and refining, however, through close examination of particular cases and specific historical contexts. In this final discussion, I shall suggest that the care girls' problematic needs to be explained in terms of the interaction between the *labour market, family background* and *vocational training*.

The basic parameters of choice were set by the labour market. In the context of high unemployment and job scarcity, the evidence of this study suggests that class-gendered divisions of labour may be reinforced. The intensified competition for jobs and courses brings both qualifications and underlying social and cultural attributes more forcibly into play in selection processes, with the consequence that the barriers of class and gender are more difficult to overcome. The care girls had at first wanted 'better' jobs than that of assistant in homes for the elderly but failed to gain acceptance because there were many others applying whose qualifications and qualities were deemed more suitable. It takes a context of labour scarcity, or very determined application of equal opportunities policies, for unconventional applicants to break through.

Given the conditions of a highly competitive labour market, we also need to explain why they were successful (where others failed) as care assistants. The explanation offered here concentrates on the interrelationship between their family backgrounds and vocational training.

Domestic careers in the family context

In the course of the college day, the girls frequently talked about their lives at home and their involvement in domestic work was clearly a source of tension. 'Family talk' revealed the well-documented, uneven distribution of labour between girls and brothers, mothers and fathers. It also suggested that the presence, rather than the absence, of physical violence was regarded as normal. 'Getting a crack round the ear 'ole', getting 'belted', 'smacked', 'pasted', 'beaten up' were frequently referenced, implicating mothers and boyfriends rather than fathers. Perhaps more significantly for the purposes of this research, 'family talk' revealed something of the girls' strategies for survival. (In the following dialogue the 'she' Kay refers to is her mother. Gavin is her brother.)

Kay: ... I try my hardest in that house. I'll do everything in the house. Yet she'll still have something to get at me ... I just count to ten, go upstairs to my bedroom and try and keep my calm ... If I can't count to ten, I have to, I hit the wall, I go mad.

I.B.: Can you give me an example of the sort of thing you're talking about which makes you absolutely furious?

Kay: Yes. Last Sunday, she's working full-time now and last Sunday I did the dinner. I mean there's Gavin in the house and he doesn't do a damned thing and he's not been to school since he were 13 and he doesn't even wash a pot. He brought a dog into the house and he won't take that a walk, he won't feed it, he won't wash it, he won't do anything for her and I had to walk the dog, I did the dinner, I washed all the pots and tidied ... and Sunday is my day to tidy round, do the polishing and that, I did all the house through and I hoovered up. And she come in ... and the night before she said 'I won't want any dinner, I'll have dinner at work', I said 'O.K., fair enough', and then she come in, there was some dinner left, I put it on a plate, 'it's up to you whether you have it or not', I said 'You don't have to have it because I know you said you didn't want none'. And she says ... she had it anyway, what did she say when she walked in? She said ... 'Oh this cooker looks a state', I says 'I've done the top, but I'm not scrubbing, why should I do that?' 'Well you could have scrubbed it' ... and then she hardly ever ate the dinner, she says 'I don't like the way you do your cabbage, Kay'. I said 'Don't eat it then', and then she says 'I don't like the way you do it', I said 'Don't eat it then, I like it, my dad liked it and our

Gavin liked it, don't eat it if you don't want it'. She says 'No, I'll eat it'. And I made her a cup of tea, 'This tea's too strong' and everything were wrong, and I thought 'Oh *you* do all this', I says ... and then in the end I'd got that mad, I didn't count to ten, and I turned round and said 'You haven't said thank you for everything I've done, you've contradicted everything I've done' I says 'and I've had enough of it'. She says 'Look at the state of the front room', I says 'I've tidied it, he's been in and messed it up again'. She said 'Why haven't you made Gavin's bed?' Oh I could have killed her, honestly.

While this incident explodes with Kay's overt resistance, it reflects high levels of accommodation both to domestic labour *per se* and to inequitable proportions of it, relative to her brother. She has taught herself to 'count to ten', then to 'hit the wall', as alternatives to open resistance, which it had emerged from other conversations could end up in a 'pasting'. She fights back only as a last resort, when her level of oppression has gone beyond the point she has schooled herself to accept.

It was noticeable that the domestic contributions of the 'care girls' extended beyond large amounts of housework to include care for younger brothers and sisters. For example, Jane explained her regular duty of looking after her 5-year-old brother when sick at night:

Tutor: Does Roger share your room?
Jane: No, but there's a spare bed in my room so if like he's not very well or he wakes up in the night, he usually comes in that bed, so like in a morning I'm creeping about ... so it sort of restricts you.
I.B.: ... You know you said earlier about your brother Roger? Does he come in your room every night then?
Jane: No, not every night. If he's, he suffers with ... he chokes a lot, you know, when he's laid on his back, he's sick most nights. So like rather than me mum taking him into her bed and disturbing me dad, he comes into my bedroom and he sleeps in the spare bed.

Domestic work also included care for babies of relatives and for grandparents. Thus one consequence of the extended family more typical of working-class communities was that it called for extended domestic contributions from its daughters, particularly when mothers were working.

It was beyond the scope of this ethnography to explore the family context in depth. The concern here was with the interface between cultural resources acquired through family experience and the process of becoming a care assistant through youth training. Clearly, the experience of domestic work, serving others, denying their own needs (e.g. for regular sleep at night, for time off on Sunday) were demands to which these working-class girls were well-accustomed by the age of sixteen. Possibly more important, given the

specific demands of the job as outlined above, was the characteristic stoic-
ism which Kay, for example, had clearly found it necessary to acquire for
the purposes of survival at home and which many of the girls exhibited.

The role of vocational training

Turning to YTS itself, an important latent function was the screening of
girls for possession of these cultural resources. The majority of tutors and
trainers who worked with the girls had a background in 'caring' or nursing
and were steeped in the associated occupational cultures. Central to these
cultures is the definition of what it takes to be a 'good care assistant' and
this appears to be partly defined in terms of a certain 'toughness' and a
capacity to be long-suffering and unsqueamish. Essentially, trainees need
to be able to accommodate to a brutalizing form of work without becoming brutal. Working-class girls, particularly those whose family life has
exposed them to experiences such as care of the young or elderly, crowded
conditions, demanding physical work, verbal and physical aggression and
related psychological stress, would appear to be ideal candidates. They are
hardened by their previous experience but, crucially, *constrained by gender*
from developing a pattern of violent response. Under the dual influence of
class and gender, they would typically 'hit the wall' in Kay's terms before
they hit back.

'Screening' for such qualities took place at several stages. On entry,
the girls were interviewed and enquiries were made about their previous
experience of the sorts of tasks likely to be involved. Previous successful
experience of looking after granny or nursing were likely to be advanta-
geous in securing a place on the scheme. During training, further screening
was carried out on placements, and in reviews on the course. The training
culture permeated the social culture and the girls also informally assessed
one another in these respects (see also Skeggs, 1989). There were strong
pressures not to be 'mardy', or 'a bleeding, whining Minnie'. Those trainees
who were too 'mardy' were likely to drop out. The least 'mardy' were held
in a certain awe within the group. Most crucially, 'care girls' are screened
on exit. At the point of being interviewed for a job, tutors' reports became
significant and tended to revolve around the extent to which the girls
fulfilled a 'good care assistant' stereotype. These processes of prolonged
screening would appear to pull girls from 'tougher' sections of the working
class through this particular system as assuredly as Oxbridge pulls public
schoolboys. Hence the long transition of vocational training, contrary to
hopes which have been expressed that this might prove an opportunity for
career exploration, tightened, through its sifting mechanisms, interrelationships between social class, gender, occupational culture of origin and
occupational destinations. This 'grounded theory' finds further support
in work by Lee *et al.* (1987), who, in arguing the importance of 'in-market

segmentation', have suggested that YTS makes possible a more refined evaluation of individual capacity than is available from traditional recruitment practices.

In Conclusion

The cycle of reproduction of labour turns upon a human axis and, in the absence of crude physical coercion, is in principle vastly vulnerable to volitional activity. But not in practice. The potential for disruption is not realized partly because it is bound by multi-layered cultural traditions which predispose us to 'come to terms' with the personal experience of inequality. Hence the production of processes of 'coming to terms' with, or 'finding the right attitude' towards unacceptable jobs, or unacceptable features of particular jobs, is central to the reproduction of labour, or indeed any system of oppression which seeks to enlist 'hearts and minds'. However, human agency is not an entirely malleable resource and people do not readily accept what they deem to be undesirable. It is this terrain which the 'care girls' study has attempted to explore.

Each time I have returned to the data from this particular ethnography, I have been struck forcibly by the radical transformation over a period of some nine months in these young women's attitudes towards jobs which they initially viewed with abhorrence. In various papers, I have developed explanations on different levels, focusing on different contributory factors (Bates, 1990, 1991). In this chapter, I have simplified the analysis to concentrate on what seem to be the major elements involved.[2]

Reversing the order of discussion, class-gendered cultural preparation in the context of the family appeared to be a crucial factor in explaining the trainees' adjustment to their jobs. Young women without these resources tended to react more sensitively to their working conditions and dropped out of training, as did any young men who became involved. In the context of direct transitions from school to work, employers themselves would have selected young women partly on the basis of what were essentially cultural criteria. However, in the context of the elongated transitions which are now normal, occupational sifting, screening and further socialization takes place in the context of training. It should be emphasized that vocational training is not an independent source of the pressures which bring about the 'care girls' adjustment', but simply mediates the gravitational pull from labour market segment to class-gendered fraction.

For social pressures to affect individual action, they must eventually be internalized. Individual capacities for adjusting their biographies in the light of labour market constraints played an important role here. A necessary precondition appeared to be for these young women to have come to the conclusion that there were no real alternatives to this job. Given a context of high unemployment, most trainees soon arrived at this definition of the situation. I have suggested that this flexibility was enhanced by aspects of current trends towards 'individualization'. The values of personal reflexivity and self-actualization facilitated the reconstruction of 'fate' as choice, or in one trainee's terms as 'a job which is right for me'. In this way, the binding agreement of personal commitment was brought to class-gendered destinations.

Notes

1. Parts of this chapter have also been published in the *British Journal of Education and Work*, 3 (1990) and in *International Studies in Sociology of Education*, 1 (1991).
2. The explanation of the 'care girls' adjustment developed in this chapter differs from the analysis in the two papers referred to above (Bates, 1990, 1991). The various analyses are not inconsistent with one another, however. Basically, I have been fascinated by this very clear-cut example of career adjustment and have developed explanations at different levels and focused on different contributory factors in different papers. No single paper yet integrates all the various elements.

References

Bates, I. (1990) No bleeding, whining Minnies: the role of YTS in class and gender reproduction. *British Journal of Education and Work*, 3, 91–110.

Bates, I. (1991) Closely observed training: an exploration of links between social structures, training and identity. *International Studies in Sociology of Education*, 1, 225–43.

Chisholm, L. (1987) *Gender and Vocation*. London, University of London Institute of Education PSEC Occasional Paper.

Cockburn, C. (1987) *Two-Track Training: Sex Inequalities and the YTS*. London, Macmillan.

Davies, L. (1984) *Pupil Power*. Lewes, Falmer Press.

Deem, R. (ed.) (1980) *Schooling for Women's Work*. London, Routledge and Kegan Paul.

Griffin, C. (1985) *Typical Girls*. London, Routledge and Kegan Paul.

Hargreaves, A. (1978) The significance of classroom coping strategies. In L. Barton and R. Meighan (eds) *Sociological Interpretations of Schooling and Classrooms: A Re-appraisal*. Driffield, Nafferton Books.

Jones, G. and Wallace, C. (1990) Beyond individualization: what sort of social change? In L. Chisholm *et al.* (eds) *Childhood, Youth and Social Change*. Lewes, Falmer Press.

Lee, D. *et al.* (1987) Youth training, life chances and orientations to work: a case study of the Youth Training Scheme. In P. Brown and D.N. Ashton (eds) *Education, Unemployment and Labour Markets*. Lewes, Falmer Press.

Mirza, H. (1992) *Young, Female and Black*. London, Routledge.

Roberts, K. and Parsell, G. (1988) Opportunity structures and career trajectories from age 16–19. ESRC 16–19 Initiative Working Paper. London, City University, Social Statistics Research Unit.

Sharpe, S. (1976) *Just Like a Girl: How Girls Learn to be Women.* Harmondsworth, Penguin.

Skeggs, B. (1989) Gender reproduction and further education: domestic apprenticeships. *British Journal of Sociology of Education*, 9, 131–49.

Stannard, C. (1978) Old folks and dirty work: the social conditions for patient abuse in a nursing home. In R. Dingwall and J. McIntosh (eds) *Readings in the Sociology of Nursing.* Edinburgh, Churchill.

Walker, S. and Barton, L. (eds) (1983) *Gender, Class and Education.* Lewes, Falmer Press.

Willis, P. (1977) *Learning to Labour.* Farnborough, Saxon House.

─────── Chapter 2 ───────

Learning a Living or Living a Learning?

An ethnography of BTEC National Diploma students[1]

─── George Riseborough ───

The Study

> ... when I queried colleagues ... about their reactions to mobility (and stratification) research, they have answered that the literature is boring. Why should that be so? ... The answer surely lies in the flavor of that research and in its limitations. Colleagues remark that the research is rather bloodless, rather statistical, often is concerned with elegant proof of the insignificant or the obvious, and rarely tells us much about the individual's experience as he [sic] moves up or down the social ladder.
>
> (Strauss, 1971)

This chapter focuses on a social class and gender-mixed 'conformist' group of mainly 17- to 19-year-old BTEC[2] National Diploma (Hotel, Catering and Institutional Operations) students in the second year of their course at 'Gastronomic Tertiary College'[3] in a heavy-industrial city in the North (cf. Fine, 1985). The fieldwork was conducted throughout the academic year 1988–89, the author being a participant observer with a group of about twenty students throughout their time in college. The majority were from working-class backgrounds, mostly skilled Social Class III (the traditional industry of the city has always had highly skilled, primary segments with an established 'labour aristocracy'), and the minority from Social Class II. The data are derived from recorded individual and group 'conversations with a purpose' (Burgess, 1985) held during the college day, together with field notes. Although unrepresentative in terms of curricular contents (a vocationalized track heading for a specific industry), the study is hopefully a critical case – an examplar of 'high status', 'new vocationalism' (Bates et al., 1984) in action, but also an attempt to describe and theorize what may well be a typical, majority student experience of schools, colleges and universities.

An Initial Problematization of 'Conformity'

... we can expect that much conformity to school demands is motivated as much by instrumental concerns, for example to get good
exam results and thus a 'good' job, as attachment to school values for
their own sake. In other words, conformity may be a calculated strategy rather than *simply* the product or successful socialization into school
values and norms.

(Hammersley and Turner, 1980)

In their considerations of students and educational outcomes, sociologists
have often 'taken their problem' (see Young, 1971). The 'conformist' is
'the "ideal" client'. For the teacher, there is no 'client problem' (Becker,
1971), and for 'respectable society' there is no morally panicking 'social
problem'. So, historically, there has not been a significant 'making of a
sociological problem' *vis-à-vis* the 'conformist' and the pro-school/college
culture (see Hargreaves, 1967; Lacey, 1970; Ball, 1981). Consequently,
sociologists have been more preoccupied with visible, intractable, 'non-
ideal', 'deviant' students at the expense of less visible, or invisible, tracta-
ble, 'good', 'conformist' students (see Hammersley and Turner, 1980;
Turner, 1983; Brown, 1987). By keeping the conformist relatively invisible,
sociologists have been guilty of a theoretical trivialization of the process of
their schooling. This 'conformist-blindness' is all the more remarkable
given the centrality of the concepts of *social* and *cultural reproduction* in
the armoury for understanding schooling and society.

Thus, there is often in the literature an implicit over-socialized assumption
regarding the 'conformist' who comes replete with 'Internalized adjustment,
in which the individual complies with the constraints and believes the
constraints of the situation are for the best. He [*sic*] really is good' (Lacey,
1977). In such a formulation, conflict, contradiction and cognitive dissonance all disappear. Even Willis (1977), the doyen of student proactivity
theory, is party to the conspiracy, taking 'the lads' stereotypical perspective and leaving 'the ear'oles' marginal to his analysis:

The term 'ear'ole' itself connotes the passivity and absurdity of the
school conformists for 'the lads'. It seems that they are always listening, never *doing*: never animated with their own internal life, but
formless in rigid reception. The ear is one of the least expressive or-
gans of the human body: it corresponds to the expressivity of others.
It is pasty and easy to render obscene. That is how 'the lads' liked to
picture those conformed to the official idea of schooling.

(Willis, 1977)

Given such phenomenological simpletons, reduced to the status of edu-
cable blotting paper, there is nothing apparently 'exotic' for sociologists to
'romanticize' or 'glorify' (see Hammersley and Turner, 1980). As Delamont
(1976) notes: 'It is very difficult to write vividly about such paragons of
virtue and make them come up off the page for the reader.' The consequence is that this over-determination deflects attention away from any

critical theorizing of the teaching and learning of 'the conformist'; and, thereby, ignores the contribution life in educational institutions may make to their social production and to wider social reproduction. In short, the few insights we do have into 'the conformist's' educational identity and career are usually inadequate at the level of meaning. Rarely do we find proactive student 'strategic compliance' (Lacey, 1977) – merely being seen to be good – represented in the theorizing of teaching and learning. 'Strategic compliance' is naively conflated into 'internal adjustment', negating the subtleties of the handling of everyday classroom life.

Background: The Economy, the Industry and Labour Market

Tourism and leisure is a dynamic, expanding sector of the economy and an important source of new jobs. Estimates vary, but, in the next four years employment is predicted to grow by nearly a quarter of a million new jobs. This will exacerbate the recruitment and retention problems which many businesses in the sector are currently suffering. On top of this, employers, in an industry which has traditionally been heavily dependent on young recruits, will need to cope with the ebbing tide of young people coming onto the labour market and the ageing of the available workforce.

(National Economic Development Office, 1989)

The traditional, primary-industrial base of the city has suffered severe economic destruction and reconstruction in the last decade or so. Vast heavy-industrial zones lay derelict and deserted with weather-worn 'For Sale or Let' boards hanging cock-eyed, and in abundance, on rusting wire and nails. General employment opportunities within the city for the working population, and for 16- to 19-year-olds in particular, are still dire. The present, official overall rate of unemployment is about 16 per cent. In 1989, only 9 per cent of 16-year-olds had a full-time job, 47 per cent were on Youth Training Schemes (YTS), 32 per cent were in other full-time education and training, and a further 13 per cent were not in full-time work or education and training. Overall, the city is contemporaneously a 'schooled-up' and 'tools-down' society.

Willis (1977) explored acutely 'how working class kids get working class jobs?' His 'question, in part, reflected the expanding educational opportunities and relatively buoyant labour market of the sixties and early seventies in which working class kids might have been expected to compete for "middle class" jobs' (Bates, 1990). This chapter looks at a late 1980s inverted travesty of this Willisian paradox: How, in a situation of increased educational selection and a retrenched labour market where 'many working class youths only obtain jobs at all if they are lucky' (Bates, 1990), some young people (including those from the working class) still manage to get 'middle-class' jobs?

Certain 'trades' within the food, catering and hotel industry have historically always provided 'respectable destinations' for the male working class, e.g. 'master baker', butcher, chef, etc. 'Getting on', 'being "deferential" and "respectable"' is as much part of working class culture as 'getting by', 'being "subversive" and "rough"' (see Hall and Jefferson, 1976). There are also 'citizens', 'ordinary kids', 'swots', etc. (Jenkins, 1983; Turner, 1983; Brown, 1987). Even Willis concedes 'the lads' are a minority, working-class student population 'in the "mix" of resistance and accommodation' (Hall and Jefferson, 1976). This chapter explores how despite and because of 'New Right' reconstruction, some youngsters, drawing upon a 'repertoire of negotiations and responses' (Hall and Jefferson, 1976), will manage a degree of 'middle-mass' social mobility, albeit in a manner that reproduces instead of the perfect 'middle-class' salaried employee in utter ideological subjection, much more the white-collar worker as a culture-carrier of characteristic contradictions and 'antagonisms of the social formation as a whole' (Johnson, 1976).

The growth of the hotel and catering industry has been antithetical to the overall economic trends of the 1980s. The Hotel and Catering Training Board (HCTB), together with the National Economic Development Office (NEDO) (1989), produced national figures that showed employment in restaurants and cafes had increased by 27 per cent, in public houses and bars by 22 per cent and in hotels by 28 per cent in the period 1983–88. Further, they forecast that in the period 1987–93, there would be an increase in employment of the order of: restaurants and cafes 34 per cent; pubs 13 per cent; and hotels 21 per cent. Admittedly, many of these are highly proletarianized exploited jobs – seasonal, casual, part-time, gendered, low paid, etc. – but the industry also requires white-collar career supervisors and managers. Indeed, the HCTB and NEDO were so concerned with the problem of staff recruitment and retention within these primary and secondary segments of the industry, that they mounted a series of regional conferences in 1989 in which this anticipated growth was set within a panicking national context of a reduction in the absolute numbers of 16- to 19-year-olds in Great Britain from 3,600,000 in 1985 to 3,200,000 by 1990 and 2,600,000 by 1995.

The above future predictions must be treated as highly problematic – indicative rather than definitive – especially in the light of the recession of the early 1990s. However, throughout the Thatcher decade, the hotel and catering industry was relatively buoyant, a paradigm of 'the new service industry' in the 'new service economy'. Certainly, employment growth in the industry outpaced the economy as a whole, and is expected to do so into the next century. Indeed, BTEC promotional material disseminated in 1992 continues to insist that 'The hotel and catering industry, like the closely connected leisure industry, is a fast growing business', which offers '... good long-term career prospects to people with the right qualifications and training' (BTEC, 1991). A BTEC major national newspaper advertising campaign was headed with the slogan 'Learning a Living'.

The Ethnography

> ... respect for authority is still alive and well in the North and is vital as kitchens are still notoriously hierarchical. In turn, good old Yorkshire grit and hard work play their part ...

> ... what the head of catering and all his lecturers determinedly instil into their students is that with a good catering degree in their pockets, ... and with a set of knives, the world is their oyster ...

> (*Financial Times*, 5 August 1990:
> *Cordon bleu, made with black pudding*)

Gastronomic Tertiary College

The college has a modern split-site campus and offers a gamut of provision, including community health, hairdressing, art and design, science and technology, motor engineering and management, 'special needs' and 'access' courses, together with traditional GCSE and A-level ones. It is at the heart of the city and the students commute from throughout the surrounding environs. The college also has a large Department of Food Technology, Catering and Hotel Management which gives the main site on which it is based a distinctive ethos. Unlike the typical smell of many educational institutions (that unique synthesis of disinfectant, warm bodies and 'school-dinners'?), Gastronomic College reeks of saliva-inducing, freshly made bread and high cuisine. Among the amenities, there is a large space set out and furnished like the reception area of a 'plush' hotel together with a bar, wine cellar and an *haute cuisine* restaurant where students daily serve to the general public other students' culinary delights. Symptomatically, the menu is in French and French commands are shouted in the kitchen.

Elsewhere, the corridors, kitchens and refectory are filled with students, some in mufti, others dressed in *de rigueur* institutional clothes, chef's uniform – starched white tall hat, apron and jacket, blue gingham trousers and pot towel hanging over the rear-end from apron ties; or waitress/waiter's uniform – crisp white blouse or shirt with black bow-tie and spotless white jacket (males only), back trousers/skirt and shoes, etc. They appear to be 'cleanwork' and 'cleanworkers' in every sense. Students look freshly scrubbed and 'presentable', their hair at a 'suitable' length. Among these students there are no sartorial, bejewelled or hirsute symptoms of any distinctive 'youth culture'. Ostensibly, they are replica reproductions, they conform to all the traditional requirements of five star hotels and restaurants:

G.R.: Don't you find the white duds and black skirts stifling? What would happen if you came in here grubby?

Jane: I don't know, it's all part of the job, isn't it. You just don't, do you?

There are no visible manifestations of non-conformity or teacher coercion. The lecturers are also 'appropriately' dressed for their *maître d'hôtel* or 'chef' role. Indeed, YTS lads studied elsewhere in this volume had no difficulty in identifying the college as a 'fuckin' poofters' palace', albeit complete with some 'reet smart tarts'. Meanwhile, bourgeois restaurant customers are normatively at home, impressed by the courtesy, confidence, articulateness, demeanour and accomplishments of the students.

The hotel and catering courses at the college have a high local reputation and a positive image is regularly beamed via the local media. For example, local politicians, city administrators and educationalists wine and dine visiting dignatories to the city. Annually, the college students and their teachers completely take over a major local, chain hotel for two weeks, culminating in a 'disco-buffet' for the students given by the Company Chairman in thanks for the 'superb work done', etc. This is followed by a plauditory letter to the Chief Education Officer. All this is fully covered by the local media.

Thus, prima facie, the students are the epitome of a so-far successful educational career – a vocationalized 'ear'oles' (Willis, 1977) trajectory. If the Secretary of State for Education made a flying visit, even before a fine four-course meal and bottle of the college's own label wine, he would indubitably eulogize that Gastronomic College was an outstanding prototype for the forging of the nexus between college and industry; honing excellent 'square' pegs for 'square' industrial holes, demanded by the 'Conservative Educational Offensive' (CCCS, 1981) on behalf of Capital.

College recruitment and the labour market

The BTEC National Diploma course is advertised primarily as a vocational A-level equivalent intermediate qualification for those going on to a degree-equivalent BTEC (Higher National Diploma) or a degree in a university, polytechnic or college with a view to entering the hotel, catering and leisure industry at a managerial level. It is also advertised as a terminal qualification for those who intend working at a supervisory level. Approximately 80 per cent of course finishers go on to higher education. The official entry requirement for this particular course was that students must possess proven ability in literacy and numeracy and have a minumum of 4 GCE O-levels at grades A, B or C (or their equivalent). Although having a broadly based, modularized, vocational curriculum, the BTEC course had some characteristics of traditional academic curricula – it was formally assessed, and taught to 'able' students in homogeneous ability groups (cf. Young, 1971).

There is considerable competition for places even though the college recruits three BTEC classes with 50–60 students in total. Given the demise of the traditional local economic infrastructure, the BTEC course is in a very strong 'buyer's market' for students. Simultaneously, it is able to 'market' its courses to would-be students on open days, in the media, in visits to schools, in course literature, career conventions, etc., by stressing high employment and career prospects in the industry. The following conversation took place with the senior tutor, Mr Fivestar, in 1988 before the NEDO Report (1989) referred to above was published:

Mr F.: There is a shortage of skilled labour. The labour market is very good in the industry. It is one of the most rapidly growing areas but being a service industry, the wages are lagging behind. But that is going to change due to a shortage of skilled labour especially with the 16–19 dip in the birth rate. This is one area that is going to thrive because they have always taken in young people, it is a young person's industry. By that I mean young people, skilled young people, can get on quickly. And pay is going to be driven up. The world is their oyster really, they can go anywhere, cruise boats, airlines, abroad, anywhere.

Thus, the dominant ideological fantasy, arguing education/training make their own employment opportunities, can be apparantly translated into reality by the College on behalf of its students. Students are told that once well-qualified they are in a 'sellers' market' regarding their labour power both locally, nationally and internationally. This at a time when the majority experience and prospect is unemployment. For this reason many students elected to do the vocationally orientated BTEC course in preference to a traditional academic sixth-form experience.

Harry: So I thought, I might as well have done this course. I might as well do a two-year course, get a degree and get a job out of it. I could have stayed at school, done three A-levels, Geography, History, or whatever, and what would I have had at the end? At school I enjoyed Home Economics in the 4th and 5th year and fancied working with people. I really am interested in the cheffing side.

Strategically, the college, in terms of recruitment, has a powerful insidious mechanism of selective control. Most students were recruited by the college with qualifications considerably superior to the minimum requirement, presumably together with the appropriate behavioural and moral attributes (cf. Becker, 1971). The selective recruitment procedures ensure a continuity of the student's 'presenting culture' with the 'official' college and work requirements.

G.R.:   I've noticed your students are highly ambitious and mobile?

Mr F.: It starts at selection on the marketing side. When we market courses
we do selection interviews with parents' evenings which is how we
generate places. We affirm that in order to get on, you have to be
prepared to move. So it is chicken and egg, if you like. We encourage it and the kind of kids we select want to get on and move up.
They really know that 'If I have got to move, I've got to do it.' But
of course the industry does encourage it because they provide a
house and home. In fact one firm has suggested that one of the
causes of high turnover is the staff were using them as hotels
themselves. A couple of years in one part of the country, then
fancy Scotland for a couple of years. So they get jobs without
having to buy or sell houses or anything like that. So there is a
high turnover. I worked in a hotel where the annual turnover was
300 per cent. It's like no industry I know. That's why some firms
now have long service awards and payments.

The students' orientation to the labour market

In terms of self-selection, when asked why they had initially chosen this
particular course and the future career trajectory, there was a spread of
explanations, from deliberative career decision making to the plain aleatory.

Ben: I knew I wanted to go into catering, anyway. I knew what I
wanted to do, to be a chef. I've been wanting to do it since the
3rd year in senior school, anyway. I don't know, it was one of
those things, I've always wanted to do it, like I help me mother
with the cooking.

Tansy: I didn't know what I wanted to do, not really. It's the Careers
that helped me, told me there were jobs, so I phoned the college
and got a prospectus and came and had a look and applied.
The college were very helpful. I was lucky. The course is dead
popular.

Anne: I did a YTS in catering first. I didn't want to go on the dole I
knew I wouldn't get a job so I just did the YTS because there
were nothing else. After that you could get on to the BTEC
after the first year and by then I wanted to do catering.

G.R.:   What about you Stan?

Stan: I knew some people on the course, so I went straight into it.

Charlotte: I went to work at the Grand Hotel, casual like, my brother
works there and got me in and I had a real low-level job but
I was fascinated by it. Still am. But you have got to have some
qualifications if you are going to get on. So I came here.

Against the backdrop of economic depression in the city and the concomitant limited occupational horizons, many stressed the excitement, glamour and romance of their chosen occupational field. The students affirmed that Catering and Hotel Management would enable them to leave the city and home with relative ease, to adventurously travel around the country and world, to meet 'interesting' and 'important' people, to eat well, always have comfortable accommodation provided and have 'a good time'. Few mentioned the traditional 'low status' of the industry in the occupational hierarchy and the boring, unglamorous and unromantic aspects of the work. Their general perception was the 'Anyway, "anything" in the way of *real work* was better than "nothing".'

Den: The job situation is easy now if you are willing to move. You've always had to travel for hotels and that. You always have a home with a hotel and food is found as well. It comes out of your wages but you're always able to move even if you couldn't afford to live on your own. So I'm willing to move, oh yeah. Anywhere, around the country if a good job came up.

Ronnie: Me, when I leave poly I'd like to work on board ship for a while. Chief steward type stuff. I'd travel anywhere for the right job. This city is boring really. I don't want to spend the rest of my life in this hole. There are only two good hotels to choose from anyway. I wouldn't work just anywhere, I want something 'classy' not any old place.

Eddie: I want to get on boats as well. Go around the world on cruise liners. I'm hoping to get a job on the QE2, it's the Ferrari of cruise liners, isn't it? I like catering, it's exciting, I don't know, it's exciting. It's hard work but I like it.

Pat: I'm working behind the bar at the Red Cow so that I can get enough money to go to the States, Miami. I'm going to work there when I've finished here. I've been to this agency, they're getting me a visa, get me a card, work permit. I've got the phone number somewhere [looking for it, to show it]. They do all the work for you. Fix up the job for you. It'll be great, I'll have a good time for a couple of years. Yeah, I can do anything once I've finished here. I know somebody who is already there and she knows a lot of people there and she is helping me out.

So strong was the ultimate desire for good employment, prior to going to college, some students were already into cynical, strategic compliance – being 'merely seen to be good' (Lacey, 1977) at the interview stage. They were fully competent at impression management techniques in the face of the selective recruitment by the college. Nevertheless, all of the students insisted on a high level of commitment to the course as a highly valued means to a highly valued end – work and a career.

Greta: They interview you and you've got to say the right things. It is stiff, depending on who you have. It took me half a hour and you've got to say the right things.

G.R.: Like what?

Greta: Like I've always wanted to do it [laughter].

G.R.: So you've not always wanted to do it?

Greta: No, but afterwards, everybody says they have always wanted to do it.

Underpinning all the conversations was a realization by the students that there were real career opportunities in the hotel and catering industry (cf. Fine, 1985). Whether the origins for this were in a pre-existing common-sensical awareness of the labour market, or given by the college, or the School's Careers Service, or by actual experience in the labour market (see below), or a complex permutation of all these, was very difficult to disentangle for many individuals. As can be seen in the data so far presented, different students gave salience to differing informational sources.

Olive: I didn't know what to do when I finished school but I think it's just that I know I'm guaranteed a job when I finish poly. I mean what-ever happens I'll be able to get something, employment. That is initially why I chose the course. I think a career is an issue to bear in mind, you've got to get to the basics. I know it's an industry where I'm guaranteed a job and that is very important these days, isn't it?

G.R.: Did someone tell you that or did you just know?

Olive: No-one told me, but just looking around you can tell, can't you?

When asked why they chose to do the course, many replied, 'I don't really know what first gave me the idea.' Notwithstanding, one thing, however, was stressed continuously by all the students, 'There are jobs in this in-dustry' and 'You need qualifications nowadays to get them and to get on.' Further, they moved in a social world where this was never disconfirmed (dominant culture, 'parent culture', peer group, work, college, etc.). In the interstice between school and work, in the paradox of mass unemployment, the students belonged to an amplification spiral of warmed-up expectation. Commonsensically, they knew they were ultimately entering a very favour-able labour market. Thus, their primary orientation to the course was that they were *learning for earning*, an awareness that the course and its cre-dential, together with further qualifications (HND, degree, etc.) would lead inevitably to 'a very good job'.

Freda: Catering is always there isn't it? It isn't going to die, catering is a trade that will never die, will it? It's an expanding industry, yeah.

Most people find jobs alright. The pay's getting better, you can get £2, £2.20 an hour waitressing. Some jobs are atrociously paid but I know one place where you can get £20 an hour as a waiter.

Olive: Yeah and the big companies like THF, Grand Met, major companies pay more, have good rates of pay and a ranking due to age and experience and you get rewarded on merit. So it's alright, you can get on.

Neil: There are a lot of jobs, isn't there? And I want a job, its expanding. It's management and I like catering. The college came around with the video showing the whole thing. My uncles and cousins are in catering. I want to run my own restaurant and manage it. I've always wanted to. If I had a choice, I'd still go to college, rather than a job first, to get the training.

All of the students were at some time or another during the course employed in the industry's secondary labour market in the city, that is, they had part-time jobs. Indeed, among themselves they informally ran a 'Job Shop' specializing in 'job hopping', as they managed their progress through the course. There was no paucity of such jobs and generally being hotel and catering students they were favoured in the marketplace. Indeed, the college, emphasizing the social utility of their student output, facilitated 'job shopping and hopping' with a well-used 'situations vacant board' and the encouragement of contacts with and visits by would-be employers.

The main reasons given for this involvement in part-time work were to provide a material means to see them through college, to win some considerable space from total financial dependence upon their parents (especially for fashion clothing), and for the enjoyment of their 'social lives' (mainly pubbing, clubbing and cinema-going). Indeed, there was no visible signs of material deprivation despite no state finance to undertake the course except in very exceptional cases. Further, they justified the part-time work in terms of their curriculum vitae, showing evidence of a considerable variety of work experience to any future employer.

G.R.: What's your part-time job then?

Anne: Waitressing. Its not too bad, it depends when I finish. I work Wednesday and Thursday every week and like when there is a dinner dance, they want me Friday and Saturday but I like Saturday off. And I work on the buffet on Sunday. Its good. I get £10 a night but it can be for about 5 hours. Like it's a long night because I have to stay until the guests go when it is a dinner dance, sort of thing. So it is £10 no matter what hours I do really because it is a private club. They say 'Oh, you'll finish 10 or 11 o'clock', but it can be 12 or 1.

Greta: You want to try one job I had. It was great, hospitality box waitressing at the Football Ground. Fifteen minutes at half time, an hour before and an hour after, £16. Watch the match and have as much booze as you want because it is all paid for, it's hospitality, whoever's paying for it. Get pissed, it was great. And the people are great 'cos it's costing them nowt. The only problem is like now, it is the end of the season and away matches but it could be Saturday afternoons and midweek. They ask you if you want to go back like but I've got another job. It was great but there wasn't enough of it. It is alright with something else like after the match on Saturday I'd work at the Grand. But you could drink as much as you wanted because whoever it was coughed up the bill. You could put a bottle down your stockings. Not very often [laughter].

During the course, the students operated a sophisticated 'pick and mix' calculus regarding work, college work and 'having fun and a social life'. Depending upon the differing demands, at particular times, differing emphases were given to each. The most common pattern was all students worked, usually full-time, during vacations, often away from home; most 'retired' or went on 'short-time' during examination and revision periods; and all combined work and college during 'normal' college time.

Obviously, work experience gave practical expression to the students' aspirations, amplified pre-existing commitments to the course, and kept current their knowledge of the subtleties of work practices and the labour market. Indeed, many could have left the college and worked immediately full-time. Offers of work were constantly being made by employers, but the students were aware of the distinction between 'job' and 'career' and wanted the latter.

No matter what their social class background, all of the students subscribed to the dominant conceptions of the social order which have been ideologically fortified and invigorated in the last decade. They subscribed to 'the notion of a social ladder that all have an opportunity to climb' (Goldthorpe *et al.*, 1969). They saw their chosen occupational and wider social world as a relatively open hierarchy which, given the appropriate determination, educational achievements, geographical mobility and hard work, people could 'get on' and climb. Aspirational regarding the structure of opportunity and reward, they possessed a moral framework which promoted an 'endorsement of the existing social order' (Parkin, 1972). All of them saw the BTEC course, usually followed by an 'advanced' course, as ultimately making for bourgeois occupational openings.

Ian: I've got offers so far, I've got Newcastle, Liverpool, Trent and Coventry Polys for HND and Cardiff have offered me a degree place. I really want to go to Nottingham, it's a nice area. I want to specialize in hotel management so I want to be a hotel manager definitely. After poly I'll get about £6500 plus everything found, room, food and clothing, so that's worth at least £10,000. After a couple of years I'll be an assistant manager on £8000–£10,000 which is like £15,000 and then well we'll see. The industry is one of the biggest for taking in people. So in about 15–20 years I want to open my own hotel/restaurant or something.

G.R.: How did you get into this game in the first place?

Ian: I don't know, it just happened. I was going to be a dentist. But at the end of O-levels I came here. I don't know it was just one of those things. I was sat at home and I thought I don't want to be a dentist. So I decided I wanted to get into hotels and I came here and got on the course and I'm here two years. I think the reason I came in, is the work is so varied and I like meeting people and I do, I do want to be my own boss. And I do want to own my own hotel/restaurant. So I don't know, it is just one of those things isn't it? I mean you don't wake up one morning and say 'I'm going to do it.' It was one of those things wasn't it, you drift into it. But I've got no regrets, I'm enjoying it, it's so much more interesting than something else.

G.R.: Don't you find it stifling, the conformity?

Ian: I don't have to conform. You just have to think 'If I am going to be a manager and serve people, I can't have my hair all over the place or stroll around in a dirty pair of trousers.' But what you do when you get out of the hotel is your business.

G.R.: Won't you find the unsocial hours too much, what about 'fun'?

Ian: It depends doesn't it, if you're enjoying the industry, you're going to work the hours aren't you? So I mean I am quite prepared to work hard simply because I know, because it is something I enjoy. Like I can see a light at the end of the tunnel when I have my own hotel, my own car, a beautiful house and everything, a wife and kids, you know. Mr Sierra Ghia with two kids, sort of thing [laughter].

G.R.: You can see all that for yourself can you?

Ian: Well in diluted form. I don't want to be totally conforming, but I wouldn't mind the 2.2 kids or whatever it is, a Cosworth and a hotel.

G.R.: Where are you going to get the 250 grand to buy the hotel?

Ian: I'm going to work for 10–15 years and get it together. There is no way I'm going to secure that much capital but hopefully there must be something like a bank. I mean I shall have to start small, buy a small place or something but I mean everyone has to start somewhere, haven't they? Look at Charles Forte, he started up in a confectionary shop and he's well away! You've just got to get on and do it.

This typical case of Ian illustrates how some young people have ideologically incorporated hegemonic assumptions. He accepts fully the educational paradigm's basic exchanges – 'Knowledge for qualifications, qualified activity for high pay and pay for goods and services' (Willis, 1977). Incidentally, Ian's father is a redundant steelworker living in a council house, who in all probability will never work again. His mother works in the home. Ian sees in the future a more enhanced material basis to his existence. He has an elaborate conception of his future life trajectory which is underpinned by a highly individualistic work ethic and associated deferred gratification pattern. Both of these, he believes, will ultimately and inexorably, *via* exploitation of educational opportunities, lead to a promoted social status – upward mobility characterized by conspicuous consumption.

The students' orientation to college

On the curriculum load

The BTEC course is an example of a nationally agreed syllabus, locally interpreted, translated and bureaucratized by the college, then validated by the awarding body and moderated externally. As such, the course comprised definitive curricular modules which were continuously assessed and formally examined. No elements of the course were voluntary or unassessed. The students were on an 80 per cent college timetable and lesson attendance was supposedly obligatory, class registers being kept (cf. Fine, 1985). They had to prepare a large number of assignments mainly of the project variety which were an assessable course requirement. Also, there were 'phase tests', examinations during particular curriculum modules, and 'end tests' given at their termination. All assignments and tests had to be successfully completed, but the students had an apparently infinite opportunity to resubmit or resit in the case of failure. Marks were awarded at the pass, merit and distinction levels for the various course elements. These were not without significance, being a powerful cultural currency, because polytechnics, colleges and universities specified minimal entrance requirements premised upon them.

Being a public qualification with validated written syllabi and set assignments, for both teacher and learner the course in everyday practice was perceived as an objectified reality which in the manner of any external examination 'had to be done'. Although the teacher may have done some initial 'conceptualization' work on the agreed syllabus and assignments, once written and reified, teachers were into a 'one-way transmission' and 'execution' mode (cf. Braverman, 1974; Ozga, 1987). The result was that the formalized course protocols represented a technology of control over both teacher and taught. As such, the externalized workload was considerable for the students and proved too exacting for some who simply dropped out of the course.

Michael: It's hard work. It's homework, more homework, assignment, assignment, test and test, isn't it? And you've got to get merit and distinctions if you want to go to poly. Most of the work is phase tests, so many week's work and then you have a test on that and you have end tests as well. There are about 30 assessments of work to do. I'll give you an example, we had a Food Service project this year and we worked on it for months and months and months. Would you believe you have to design a diner, do the interior decor, do the costing of all the dishes, you've got to write a cocktail and bar list and price all that out and say how you would prepare and store the food and what hygiene regulations and fire regulations and it's just, you know, unbelievable for just Food Service. The load really, it's too great. It gets too much for loads of people.

G.R.:   Why don't the pressures become so great that it becomes explosive?

Michael: People do say 'we are not going to do that and we are not going to be treated like that' but people just leave. They don't complain but they just leave. They just give up because of it all. Attendance starts to suffer. It was bad to start with anyway and it builds up and they eventually leave. You have got to have a load of determination to finish this course no matter what and not let things get you down.

Indeed, the pace of pedagogy often irked. Some teachers felt obliged to teach with considerable momentum in order to cover a prescribed syllabus load with their students in the allotted time.

Greta: And then there's Miss Motel, she's nice enough but she just relies on hand-outs and rushes on and says 'Now move onto the next one' and 'Move onto the next' and you're still struggling with the first one. And it makes you feel awful because you can't do it because she loves it [i.e. her subject].

Further, the students criticized not only the sheer quantity but its uneven distribution, resulting in peaks and troughs in loading. They could make little sense of why this should be so and, as such, it was interpreted as inefficiency and the teachers showing scant respect for the pressures upon them as they managed their journey through the course, work and social life.

Tansy: I don't know, I think it is something to do with bad organization. We do piles of projects in the second year. We have Catering Theory, Reception, Food Service, and Catering Theory and Food

Service are enormous subjects and Reception wasn't so bad but even so people have been panicking, have had four projects on the go all at once. Unless you pace yourself you get snowed under. Some people have trouble pacing themselves. I mean you are doing a project and you are loaded down anyway and it is too long for a start and people switch it off and then they only have a week left to do it. And people are finishing it off quarter an hour before it is due it. It's too much of a rush. They don't seem to take account of what other teachers are giving you, it doesn't bother them. If they feel like giving you an assignment, they will even though ... The teachers don't pace it, badly organized, they don't do it properly. I would have happily done a lot of the easier projects in the first year.

G.R.: Why are they so badly organized?

Tansy: Which they are basically! I don't know. Yes like Mrs Cleansheets, don't tell her. She has said to us that she thinks the college is badly organized. She has said they give the work all at once and that the communication in between the departments is terrible. So the student is not given a fair workload, you know.

G.R.: So why don't students complain about it then?

Tansy: They do do but they don't listen. Sometimes in exceptional cases if the student is under a lot of pressure and got a lot to face, they give them an extension in fact but if they had organized it in the first place, it's stupid.

The quantity of work might not have been onerous if the students had been morally involved and committed. However, the students were merely instrumentally involved in the college course. It was a means to an end, not a gratifying end in itself. As can be seen above, the general impression they conveyed in discussions was a weariness, a realization 'they were "shovelling away at a giant slagheap"' (Woods, 1978).

Liam: All you have to do is be prepared to do your work as soon as you get it and it is no problem at all. If I could do this year again, not that I want to [laughter]. If I could then I know exactly what I'd do, as soon as you get the work, just start it and do a bit a week and then you do it and get top marks for that. But there is only one who has done that, she's in another class and has got distinctions. She works every hour God sends. Pillock! I'll be OK though.

Part-time work and 'having some sort of social life' amplified this college workload into overload (cf. Becker, 1961). Many students were physically fatigued in college, particularly after a busy weekend or an evening's work. Sometimes, students could be combining the equivalent of a full-time job with college attendance and a meagre kind of social life.

G.R.: How do you manage a social life?

Den: You just have to work around it, don't you. I'm in college 9 to 5
and work at the hotel so the hours are a bit heavy. I have trouble
getting up but once I'm here that's it. I must confess I'm often not
in the land of the living.

Liam: I'm so tired, I'm knackered. I've been up all night, you know. I
worked last night and then went to the Zombie Club.

On the quality of the curriculum

The students also questioned the quality of the curricular provision in
tandem with the sheer quantity. This was despite it being a vocational
course and qualification, which in terms of the hegemony of common
sense is supposedly intrinsically practical, relevant and utilitarian. However, in the context of student instrumentality, college workload and work
experience, much of the course was perceived as impractical, unnecessary,
irrelevant and of doubtful utility. 'Common sense' and work experience
led many students to view certain course contents as 'job-orientated' rather
than 'career-orientated'.

G.R.: What kind of questions did you get asked in your Housekeeping
exams?

Eddie: I answered one on contract cleaning.

Ben: How to use a duster? [cynical laughter]

Eddie: The procedures involved in the operating of a buffer. [officious and
sarcastic tone, more laughter]

G.R.: You're joking!

Eddie: No! That was early on.

Such banal curricula were seen as 'a total waste of time'. All the more
so when course components recapitulated pre-existing work experience.

Michael: I got a distinction in 'Waiting'. I am a waiter at the Imperial. I'm
a good waiter but you are bound to be after about 18 months
doing it, aren't you? I mean Christmas time last year I was
waiting 60 hours a week! So you are bound to be good, two
or three nights a week. So who needs more! So that aspect of
college is a waste of time really, isn't it?

As such, their teachers were seen to be responsible for a 'Great Training
Hype' in which menial and boring work-related activities were inflated,
'academicized' and reiterated within the curriculum. Curriculum contents
concerned primarily with everyday 'skills', with 'jobs', were perceived
as irrelevant to future 'careers' to a point where they were paradoxically

' "at odds" with daily life and common experience' (Young, 1971; cf. Gleeson and Mardle, 1980). The students felt they were not appropriately learning for earning. There was a gulf between 'college theory' and 'work practice'.

Jenny:	Truthfully, on the whole, a lot we learn is relevant but what happens is you have one particular teacher who whines for about two weeks solid, how to wipe a table, or use a squeezee. You don't need to know all that, I'm quite sure. Same with Social Skills, we go over them again and again and again when we have already done them before. There is a hell of a lot of time wasted by the teachers. There is a lot of overlap. One teacher doesn't know what the other is doing. I would say that what teachers do is not relevant.
Neil:	In Housekeeping we have to clean up. We have to learn that and even have a little test on it, a test on cleaning the sink! They fill a morning on cleaning the sink, that's right. You could do that in 10 minutes. Same with making beds. God we've spent all morning doing that because we've got beds in the Housekeeping room. It's really boring after a while, when you go over it again and again. We were unfortunate in our group, we had three different teachers and they all did the same thing, making beds, washing dishes forty-nine times.
G.R.:	Is that just housekeeping or other things?
Charlotte:	I would say other things. You can learn things quicker. I got a job behind a bar to get some money and you learn how to survive in three days flat and you either learn quick or get sacked. You don't need a term's lessons. In college you don't get things that can only be learnt in college. If you get a job as a chambermaid, they give you a mop and bucket, give you a floor to do and leave you to it. And if the sinks are dirty and your lavs are grotty someone will have a word with you and you quickly learn how to clean a bath with the minimum of fuss and effort, don't you?
Neil:	Besides I've not come here to do that, it's irrelevant. I want a better job than that. A lot of it is just time serving for the sake of it. But you've got to do it and when you've got it [the Diploma], you are a lot more, they [employers] will look at you with different respect. Because you have got the qualification but I would say 50 per cent of the time is wasted and 50 per cent you actually learn something. You know, you think 'Oh, God', here we go again, we're going to do something we actually did last week and over and over again.
Charlotte:	You just have to grit your teeth and get on with it. I think you

could actually learn as much actually out working your way
up. But the only thing like is that in hotels and catering, you
do actually do need the qualification.

Neil: But you could do without a lot you do at college, but I think
it is a lot more relevant than what you do at school but still it
is not relevant. I don't know, I don't think any place of learning,
any course of study can be relevant to real life. It is good that
you learn the theory behind things, but it is when you are
taught what you already know and you go over it again and
again and again and the teacher is doing something you'll never
use, you know.

Other course requirements were just seen as essentially irrelevant, the
students finding it impossible to make an intellectual connection between
a course component and their chosen vocation.

Freda: We had a Housekeeping project on about a building structure. We
had to label and draw a map and plan, do about wet rot, damp rot
and all that and all sorts and how to do the roof and all sorts and
how to do the insulation, how to do the foundations. Everything
except build the damn thing. Housekeeping!? [exaggerated questioning tone]

Further, given the breadth of the course (covering all and every aspect
of catering and hotel management) and as students' career interests developed, different students gave different meanings to what was relevant. For
example, what was relevant to a would-be hotel manager was not relevant
to a would-be chef or would-be personnel officer. Yet all were doing a
common syllabus.

Kate: What we are taught is sometimes not really relevant, like learning
the wines of Bordeaux unless you are going to be head wine waiter
or importer. Sure you've got to have some knowledge but you get
that when you go into it but we have too much of it in some ways.
Week after week after week on Bordeaux wines. You see you get
interested in one thing, like I want to go into personnel, you get
fascinated. But to other people they just don't want to know that,
they want to be a head wine waiter.

Paradoxically, aspects of the course, although manifestly in daily use
within the industry, were experienced by students in a manner not dissimi-
lar to traditional 'academic' curricula. This was because their teachers did
not 'apply' their curricular expertise to the industry and treated the BTEC
students as 'non-ideal clients' because they were instrumentally involved
generalists, not 'ideal', morally involved specialists of their subjects. As

such, these supposed applied subjects were experienced by BTEC students as unrelated, as abstract, as compartmentalized and 'external' to the learner (cf. Young, 1971).

Pat: Honestly, some of the teaching is bloody appalling.

G.R.:   Like what?

Pat: Computing Studies, right. You've got to think for yourself, up to a point but you need help. And he used to piss me off saying 'You've got to think for yourself' and he would completely ignore you. Yeah, alright but when you couldn't find something on the menu, he wouldn't find it. His attitude was 'You are not computer students, you're not becoming programmers, you're not really interested in that way, I'm not interested in you. Others are doing computers for a living, who want to go into computing, want to do computers and know what is happening to computers. So, therefore, I have not got no time for you. Get on with it and don't bother me.' It's frustrating and it gets you mad, really mad. Harry said, di'n't ya, he felt like going through that computer room with a chain saw and see if that makes any difference to him. The plonker!

Harry: He was so sarcastic, he'd carry on like that and let you get behind. He was that type of person right, where if you get behind they will not carry you. But he is the reason you are behind. They don't think they need to. He has never tried to discuss your work. The students, he never tells what standard you are at. I mean the lecturers then turn around and say 'You have been slacking this year.' And you just didn't because they leave you to it. They just do not let you know. Why didn't they tell me that earlier? I could do something about it, do you know what I mean? Their attitude is 'Sod you, you are not doing computing proper' or whatever.

Pat: Same with Bookkeeping. I wag it. I hate it and you get a lot of people having time off because he's a funny man. Mainly he just doesn't give you time, he doesn't make it relevant, he doesn't make it interesting. Bookkeeping is relevant because you have to do it in a hotel but the way he does it. He never mentions hotels or catering, he doesn't apply it in any way. He's mad about bookkeeping and he can't make sense of anyone who isn't. I've been resitting it because I keep on failing it. I failed last week so I got Ken to teach me. I passed with 83 per cent but that's not due to the teacher but Kenny. And I teach other people like I'm good at Personnel. So it all works out. Mr Ledger says to me, 'That revision went well' and I said 'Yes', lying through my teeth because it's Kenny who did the teaching, who explained it to me. I learned more from Kenny in half a week than from him in a year.

On the teaching

Thus, the students were disgruntled with the vocational curricular messages, which were not perceived to be 'really useful knowledge'. However,
they were equally disgruntled with the pedagogical styles of teachers. As
already noted, the course was characterized by one-way transmission of
a pre-ordained curriculum, combined with an emphasis on individualized
written products and never-ending assessment. In order to acquire the
valued qualification, the students had to regurgitate the appropriate teacher
'deposits'. The teachers had 'control over knowledge' and, therefore, control over students (Delamont, 1976). In short, the students were in a
classic 'banking' scenario (Freire, 1972). The course 'was a strange activity,
at times difficult, tortuous, and much disliked, not at all involving the
ingredients of "fulfilment" – opportunities for choice, decision, acceptance
of responsibility, self-determination and growth' (Woods, 1978). Peda-
gogically, this banking was a legitimate piece of 'teaching for survival'
(Woods, 1977), given the overall situation of formal validation demands,
workload and student instrumentality. Without any student moral involvement, it was an effective way for the teacher to ensure that course requirements were met. Indeed, although such banking and 'spoon-feeding'
was experienced as boring, paradoxically, 'a good set of notes' – 'learning
for survival' – was always appreciated in terms of passing the course.

G.R.:   What would make it more interesting for you?
Harry: The style of teaching. You know Mrs Hygiene, its the overhead
        projector! Here's a transparency, copy it down, here is another one
        copy it down, here is another one copy it down, here is another
        one copy it. You are there for like an hour and a half and you
        come out like 'Uuuarrr'! [Zombie-like imitation]. You get totally
        pissed off, week in and week out. Just building up a set of notes
        and revising those for the test and that's it.
Eddie: Why don't they just give us the complete lot at the beginning?
Harry: I mean you can teach a monkey to teach how to change sheets
        with the overhead projector, can't you? [laughter]. A monkey can
        do that and that's it, put one down, take one off. A monkey can
        do that. I used to think teaching was an interesting job but it is
        boring. It's a right cushy job teaching. OHP Number 1, Number
        2 and on and on to the end of the year. And its 'Oh bollocks' if
        anything goes wrong. One week the OHP was broken. 'Oh dear,
        what am I going to do?' Fluster. They don't know what they are
        going to do with themselves. It's disaster, 'I don't know what we
        are going to do. I had better dictate!'

The biggest source of complaint was 'the teachers just do not care about
us'. Of course, the students had no understanding of the occupational

culture of teachers – 'what teaching does to teachers', and especially what it has done to them in recent years (Ball and Goodson, 1985). There was no reason why they should, but the students in reponse personalized the teacher indifference.

Freda: They don't care about anyone. They are not involved and don't like teaching and they don't talk to you.

Anne: We have about one good teacher who is interested in our problems but he's too busy. But the thing is I think it is really boring, they don't like teaching and they're not very good at it, then what the hell are they doing it for! And most of them are like that. One of them said to us yesterday, 'I don't want to teach you anyway' and gave us our marching orders. It is bad enough he feels like that without him telling us.

Den: It is relevant, it is interesting, but they should teach ya and advance ya, but they don't give a shit. They don't give a damn, to make sure you pass the exam, to make sure you go to poly. That's just it, they don't bother to come up to you and ask if you are alright. There's only Mrs Metropole, she always asks. You just get pissed off and don't want to do it anymore. Honestly, that's how you get.

Jenny: I mean Miss Motel and Costing, she doesn't hide the fact that she's bored to tears in her lesson and she can't wait to get out of it and let you go. She couldn't wait, she'd let us out early, 'Finish that at home'. We needed to go through things carefully and slowly but she can't wait. She always arrives 20 minutes late and lets you go early. Now some who are good at maths can pick it up anyway, where the rest of us haven't a clue but nobody blames the teacher. People like me who can't pick it up quickly fall behind. And it is 'If you can't do it, I'll not talk to you and bother with you. If you can't do it then I'm not bothering with you.' Its awful.

By way of mitigation, although very little contact was maintained with the teachers, this particular year the city had just 'gone tertiary'. Generally, this had wrought massive organizational rationalization, together with considerable redeployment of staff and suggestions of future teacher redundancies (cf. Riseborough, 1981). However, this had not directly affected the accommodation, structure and staffing of the BTEC course, but as Miss Motel observed:

Tertiary has made a great deal of difference. Although tertiary is obviously, perhaps ideologically, a good move, the methodology that has brought tertiary about is a load of crap and they have brought in high disaffection among the workforce. It's demotivated everybody. Some people have spent years working here and then to turn around and say that what you have done in the past, and what you

are doing, is rubbish, is very upsetting. And then ask you to do this
and that with the resources they provide is ridiculous!

Small wonder the students in reciprocation experience college 'as being
treated like schoolchildren', that teachers cannot have 'a laff' and that the
course is basically dehumanizing. In the dialectic of BTEC teaching and
learning, it is theoretically erroneous to assume it is a non-problematic
transfer of knowledge from a morally involved, committed teacher to a
morally involved, committed student. However, 'the war within classrooms
was so cold that its daily battles were not evident' (Dumont and Wax,
1971).

Tansy: They don't treat on a level. That's wrong. They should treat you
all equal and be on a par with them but they are teaching us. Do
you know what I mean? But still have that sort of relationship
where you can have a laugh and that. Sometimes they are snooty
and put you down and that. When you get down to it, you are still
a kid. And you think, 'Oh, shit'. You just don't learn, they don't
talk to you, they talk to you as if you are thick, especially Mrs
Cutler. She gives you that sort of feeling that she knows everything
and you know nothing and why should you know anything, sort
of thing. They don't treat you on a level. They treat you as if you
are further down from them which we are, we are not as qualified
as them but we are still human beings, you know what I mean,
and you are still treated like a kid.
Liam: I think if you have a 'laff' about the subject, it helps you to absorb
more because you will think about what you have been laughing
about and you'll apply it, you know what I mean. You'll remember it. I don't know, they just sit in their office and that's it. They
don't even bother to have a laugh with you. It's the fact they don't
talk things out with you and discuss things. They don't bother, do
they? They'll tell you when you have failed and got to resit and
that's it. I've never known anyone call me in and tell me where
you have gone wrong.
Tansy: We've been told by one of our sarcastic lecturers that we are the
'Cream Team', that our course is crappy, you know. They can't be
bothered, the lecturers' attitude is we'll get them out of the way,
that'll be it. I've been going on all year about how demotivated
I am. I can't get up in the morning.

Spoon-feeding and regurgitation may be boring but the students were
particularly bitter towards those 'idiosyncratic instructors' (Becker *et al.*,
1968) who did not make the appropriate connections between their
proffered curriculum, their teaching and their eventual evaluations. The

students were very critical of the 'autistic' situation in which teacher inputs and examination demands were not commensurate.

Anne: She's a real bitch, she rips into you. Hostile, she really is. She makes it really hard. Easy notes and then in the exam the question has some relevance to what could have been taught but she has a different way of putting it sort of thing, know what I mean? You've got to think in depth to grasp it and she doesn't give it you in class. The way it is taught, there is no connection.

Stan: About 50 students did an end-test and a dozen passed. Yeah, honestly. I got 53 per cent, that's not brilliant but that was good.

Anne: And really bright students, people you'd pick out and say are really bright, who work hard, a couple of them struggled on the resit. June sat that exam three times. She's bright. She knows a lot about catering. She knows what she is doing. She revises a lot. She does not work during revision times and you don't understand why she fails. But it is the teacher's fault.

Stan: People don't understand what's happened when they failed. You don't know what she is thinking. Her questions are so ambiguous, so out of this world. Whereas other lecturers just set questions on what they give you and you know where you are but her . . .

Anne: When you sit down and she tells you what she is doing, you say 'Oh, shit! Yeah, I can see what you mean.' She ought to do that before the exam, do you know what I mean?

The students were also highly critical of the apparently arbitrary and random nature of teacher differentiation and evaluation of them. This was seen to be premised upon ascriptive, diffuse, particularistic and affective labelling criteria, when they felt it should be premised upon achievement, specific, universalistic and affectively neutral criteria.

Olive: I think the lecturers are very biased. They are really biased. Definitely, they just have their favourites. Oh, they have honestly!

Ronnie: They are bound to. Like at O-levels, you weren't a name you were a number. And they were sent away to people and you were a number and just another paper to read and mark. Where here like, you've got your name on the paper, it is the first thing they see. They get a picture of who you are and it is just natural to have people you like and get on well with and people you don't like. And I think personally I would prefer it was externally marked, they are not marking on who you are but it is what you have written, how good you are, that's why an exam should be externally marked.

Olive: Like that with Eddie, that time with that assignment and he failed

that assignment but he gave him a pass. The lecturer turned around
to him and said 'I want to give you a good mark on this because
of all the hard work you did for me last time.' Yeah. After that
I said why bother! It's bloody pathetic! One student did a lot
of work on the Book Project, a recipe book. So like for his next
project, the next project that he failed the lecturer turned around
and said, 'I'll pass you anyway because you did a lot of work on
the Book Project.'

On attendance

Given such an overall severe student critique of the course, its curricular
provision, its teachers' practices and evaluations, it would be surprising if
there was not a high degree of absenteeism, especially since students were
invariably working part-time in the evenings and weekends. Daily attendance ran at barely 60 per cent. However, given the student instrumentality,
such absenteeism was calculative and strategic. Sustained absence obviously
would have been counterproductive in terms of passing the course and
peer support was necessary to keep up with the missing work. Further, as
well as using it to win respite from the rigours of work and college work,
paradoxically absenteeism was also used to do college work in the peak
overload situation, as this was considered the best and only time to do it.

Olive: Working at the Grand that two weeks were great. I did laundry.
            I learnt quite a lot. It is more like a real professional situation,
            like in real life, I think. After I did that, its funny I hardly had
            time off college for four or five weeks. It gave me my enthusiasm
            back, but after five weeks into it I was back battling on and the
            attendance just went.
Neil: A lot of teachers have a lot of trouble with attendance.
Michael: Bookkeeping is very bad, isn't it? Its late in the afternoon and
            there is nothing to do all day except hang around for it. So most
            people go home, don't they? Sometimes there's hardly any one
            there. I should say two-thirds of the time in college is just spent
            hanging around.
Neil: So you just put the attendance in and then people start to take
            time off. People don't disappear for four or five weeks on end.
            They say I've been three weeks, I'll have a week off, or when
            work is heavy and you get a friend to give you notes. Then
            others do the same, so it's your turn this week, then someone
            else next, sort of thing. You don't tend to take the whole week
            off, you can do, but what usually happens, you take two or three
            days off and you come back with a good excuse otherwise you
            get a bad name. But a lot of the time they don't miss you. They
            take registers but it don't matter.

Michael: People are off in droves just before assignments are due in. That's noticeable because that's the only way they can get it done. Which is a bit silly really.

Resolving the contradictions: passive resistance in active accommodation

'Grades are the currency with which the economy of campus social life operates' (Becker *et al.*, 1968). However, grades are also cultural-capital passports into higher education and work – into the economy, into wider social life itself. It is hardly surprising, therefore, in a situation of contradiction, of overload, of instrumentality, calibrating 'making the grade' (Becker *et al.*, 1968) with the minimum of effort became important. Expediency in production of work was the student norm (cf. Becker, 1961).

Harry: The only thing that gets me to college is to get that grade basically because you want to do whatever you want to do after college, basically, you know what I mean? The lecturers are only bothered about that one hour you are with them in the classroom and that is it. I mean they turn up late and I think sod that I'll turn up late.

Greta: 'What have you got?' '89 per cent'. That's all people talk about around here. When you meet one another, all the time is spent worrying about whether you have passed, whether you have got to resit, what the result was, is it a credit or distinction mark. That's the preoccupation a lot of the time.

Ian: Or 'I only took two days, how long did you take, two months honestly? And you got the same mark as me and only took two days.'

Harry: It causes some real aggro that. Some people go off complaining about it isn't fair, don't they? Why bother sort of thing.

Greta: Yeah! Or it's, 'Mr Croissant have you marked our work yet.' You have to keep pestering all the time to find out how well you've done. You can wait ages sometimes. Eight weeks, I think is the longest.

Harry: Yeah! And you can see they don't mark it proper. Ticks on the bottom of the page. They don't take it seriously.

Given the students could resit their various tests and given their other out-of-college commitments, many delayed a successful completion to a personally more convenient time. To the effort/grade calibration was added a temporal dimension.

Ben: A lot of people have a lot of problems with Reception, end-tests and everything. I think it's because of notes after notes after notes and there is that much to revise.

Stan: It's really boring. You've got to do it to pass. You've got to pass
everything. If you fail one paper or test you have to resit. And you
can go on and on resitting. There is a certain stage where they say
that is it, you've failed. But no-one's ever reached that stage. You
just go on, on and on and on with these bloody boring resits.

Ben: Yeah, but 'cos you know that you don't bother sometimes do you?
Because you know you can do it again later when it suits you.

Given this fixation on 'making the grade', classrooms were observed to
be always orderly. Teachers normally had no overt disciplinary problems.
To anybody passing the room, 'It seems that they are always listening,
never *doing*; never animated with their own internal life, but formless in
rigid reception' (Willis, 1977). However, conflict was latent to the situation. Indeed, we can expect the students' minimalist instrumentality and
concomitant resistance to some of the official curricular and pedagogical
provision to impact upon the teacher's life and career (cf. Riseborough,
1985). It can be perceived as a threat to 'the authority of the teacher' for
the students are not 'miniature versions' (Hargreaves, 1979) of their teachers. Some teachers learn to 'swim' in such a situation by a reassertion of
the teacher paradigm with a 'domination mode of adaptation' (Hargreaves,
1967) towards what are often assumed to be 'lazy' students with the
'wrong attitude'. 'Teaching for survival', in a situation where clients are
not totally ideal and where a teacher is not morally involved, ends up premised upon a socially distancing dialectical unity of instrumental teacher
and learner opposites. In such a situation, 'Teacher-as-examiner' masks the
'teacher-as-survivor' (Woods, 1977). As Mrs Silver-Service noted:

These BTEC students are shocking! They will just not use their initiative. So they are not a good class to go by. They have had months
to do this work. Give me City and Guilds General Catering anyday
[i.e. 'lower status' students], they've got four times the common sense
they have. The BTEC is the better qualification but it doesn't mean
they have common sense. I'd rather work with first-year General
Catering than second-year BTEC personally because at least they see
the importance of what you are doing and how it is worthwhile. But
BTEC students come in with the attitude 'We've got a few academic
qualifications' without seeing that they have to start at the bottom.
It's a continuous battle because their attitude is all wrong. They think
the world owes them a living and they want everything put on a plate
which is what you end up doing. I've said to them 'Look, I've got
first year General Catering who can leave you standing in attitude,
in the effort that they make and also in academic ability in some
cases.' Just because they've gone on a BTEC, they come with this
superior attitude. It is bred into them from day 1. They think they
are the bees-knees. They're pathetic, they really do think they are the
superior to City and Guilds. They've been in this restaurant, one day

a week for the last two years, off and on. They know the state tables should be put back in. It is only a minor thing but if they were hotel managers and they allowed their staff to do what they do! Yet I'm all the villains under the sun because I say it has to be done properly. Look you can't put the silver away, you can't put the china away because how they've thrown the furniture in. They are not a good example of a group to study. Give me City and Guilds every time.

The conflict between teacher and taught, when it became manifest, was usually focused upon teacher assessments. Generally, popular teachers were the generous markers, unpopular the parsimonious. Marking was the visible point of tension in the contradiction between the aspiration for qualifications and in-college dissatisfactions. The usual manifestation was frustrated student emotionalism. This was especially so when the student felt relatively deprived when failing to make the grade when other students were making it with ostensibly far less effort.

Kate: People start getting really emotional about it, you get upset with the pressure, not getting a good mark. Crying and crying at home. Another girl did loads of project work, she couldn't handle it, she did really well in the end. I don't know why she gets upset but she does. She can't handle it. But then again no-one gives a damn. Me, I just think well, never mind, otherwise you'd get really depressed and some do. I can't talk like this to any teacher here, getting it off your chest. You never tell them what you are thinking and feeling. They don't know you after two years and they don't want to know.

Thus, it was only around marks that there was a very explicit 'site of struggle' between teacher and learner. In the only example observed of major overt conflict, it was straightforwardly resolved in favour of the teacher. Broadly, in the conflictual bargaining process (see Becker *et al.*, 1968) there was no contest. In the data below, the whole year group were asked to display publicly a particular project, the teacher walked around the room and marks were given there and then for 'visible presentation'. The 'intellectual' content was to be assessed later.

Jemma: Mr Pastry, Mr Pastry! [tearful and distraught]. I put a right load into that, and John got 85 [Mr Pastry ignores her and carries on with his clipboard assessing work]. Mr Pastry!! [even more distraught]. I put a right load of work into that and I get 60. Look, he won't even look at you, will he? [addressing other students]. The plonker! It's a pointless exercise, pointless, a waste of time. Honestly. He just hasn't looked. He just strolls up and mutters something. This is a big mark, if you don't pass, you don't pass sort of thing. It's a joke. A mockery of the whole thing.

Ronnie: I've passed, three days work [laughing and stirring it up].
Jemma: Mr Pastry, Mr Pastry! [crying] . . . I put a right load of work
             into that! [at last gaining his attention].
Mr Pastry: I'm very sorry about that!
Jemma: So am I after all the work I have put into it. And Harry's only
             put three days into it.
Mr Pastry: Look the only reason you've seen the mark is you've looked
             over my shoulder.
Jemma: Isn't it right we should see the mark?
Mr Pastry: No, not until I decide, now go back to your place, young lady!
             Go back to your place! [shouting] . . . Otherwise you'll get a
             lower mark still [Jemma retreats].
Ian: [To G.R.] . . . She's done a massive project. She's every reason
             to be pissed off actually. It's a joke. She's done a big thing on
             'Food in Space', OK and obviously, you can't get many posters
             about that but she's done a massive project for it. She's only
             got 60 and the lad next to her has done 2 hours on his and he's
             got 63 [Jemma has left the room in frustrated tears with sym-
             pathizing peers]. The guy's a fool, he really is. Everybody's
             getting agitated about it.
Mr Pastry: Now come on now. Get back to your displays. Compared with
             last year's lot, it's an absolute disgrace. You're shocking! You're
             as idle as anything, most of you. You really are. Now come on!

From the perspective of her peers, Jemma was 'a slow learner'. There
was much covert sympathy for her but no overt support. Everybody else
had learned long ago 'to keep your nose clean'. They knew that being
labelled 'deviant' could bring considerable consequential retribution from
important career mediators. They knew, way before Mr Pastry reminded
them, 'that the grade is a source of power, and they understand that it may
be used as a weapon against them' (Werthman, 1971). In such a situation,
'impression management' becomes critical. Deferential 'apple-polishing' and
'brown-nosing' became legitimate student strategies, although few admitted
engaging in them (cf. Becker *et al.*, 1968). Needless to say, this student
sycophancy confirmed the aura of conformity. Further, in this context,
favouritism was perfectly acceptable if one was a beneficiary of teacher
largesse.

Anne: Where here it is reflected in the marks. I mean Douggie actually
         turned around on one lecturer and now they are all against him.
         One lecturer, I want to strangle her, I do but I don't because, you
         know, you can't. So you don't, you smile and keep 'em sweet.
         People don't rebel. They'll go up to a certain mark but they'll not
         shout and scream and put their career on the line.

Pat: Yeah. We don't, I mean we don't open our mouths because after all we want to get references and the Diploma. Some of these college lecturers, it is a big mistake to get on the wrong side of one of them, you get on the wrong side of everybody. They make your life hell. They do. You just shut up. Like Anne said, Douggie shouted 'This is crap and boring' and his future is now ruined. They are dead against him from then on. They just ignore him, he gets rotten marks, he's a dead duck, isn't he? It just pays to keep your mouth shut.

Anne: Yeah. They never let it drop. They have it in for you for ever after. You've got to keep your head down. 'Yes sir, no sir, three bags full sir!' That's it, it's the only way.

In such an overall situation, 'the students withdraw any "authentic" learning' (cf. Willis, 1977) and 'go through the hoops', ritualistically appearing to learn. There are few occasions when learning is valued for itself. The students are largely deaf to the curricular and pedagogical message systems but obsessed with the evaluative one (Bernstein, 1971).

Charlotte: You get into a situation where jumping the fence is more important than real learning. You lose your enjoyment. You learn to jump the fence. After you have jumped the fences, you have learned nothing and then you have to get on to the next one. You don't learn, you don't take it in. Your learning does not have the impact, once you get over that one, there's another. Yes, you get into the Grand National where jumping the fence is more important than learning about it. I mean three weeks ago I did an end-test and if you asked me the questions now I would not be able to answer them. I can't remember anything we did last year.

Greta: That's it, that's what you have got to do. And you get certain difficult teachers who take a sadistic delight in ensuring you don't get there. The trouble with BTEC is you don't get the qualification until after two years, whereas with City and Guilds you get one after a year, so that keeps you going like. You get brassed off with the course but that's life isn't it? I don't expect anything better.

Beyond Gastronomic College

At the cessation of fieldwork, the majority of students had been provisionally accepted for an HND or degree course in a related field (e.g. Management, Tourism, Food Science, Leisure, etc.) at a college of higher education, polytechnic or university. They were positively encouraged to do so by the college, it being an obvious symbol of the success and status of the course.

Neil: Their attitude is poly, poly, poly. 'Everybody goes to polytechnic.' Sod the rest of you who don't want to go to polytechnic. That's always been stressed, poly, poly, that's all they talk about. Sod them that want a job, you know. They said when you first started on the course that they will give you a lot of help finding a job but they don't.

However, the majority of students required little college encouragement, they knew a higher qualification was vital. The students' experiences of Gastronomic College did not represent an impediment to continuation on their educational career trajectory. They also knew that they possessed all the cultural competences required to survive as a higher education student. After all, their experiences of Gastronomic College had provided or developed many of them!

Eddie: I'm going to poly because that's what I need to get the job I want. I could get a job but you need the qualification. I've learnt one thing and that is there is a lot of people who stand in the way of a young person getting on, so you can't start at the bottom and work your way up. You have to start above them with your qualifications. Otherwise, they are an obstacle to you getting on. So I'm going to Manchester Poly to do Hotel Management. I wanted a northern city, didn't want the south. I wanted a place with a good football team and social life. I'll get a grant and work as well, have a bloody good time. Then settle down probably and have a good job.

The major motivation of the minority who chose to go straight into the labour market was usually a combination of 'being sick and tired of college and learning', work availability and career opportunity.

Neil: I've got this assistant manager's job working for Bass Brewery in the West Country. Anywhere is better than here. I hate it. I start on August 1st and I'll stay as long as it takes. They are open all day through the summer season and in the closed season it is old hours. It is part of Bass so I'll be able to go anywhere with them. I'm living in. Anything for a change. It's my old boss at the Cat and Fiddle where I work at the moment. He's moving down there and needs an assistant manager down there and like it's easier for him to get one up here. The pay will be more than OK. Anything to get away from here. Its live-in accommodation anyway. All I need is pocket money. The pub I am going to is the best in town. I'm pissed off with here and you've got to leave some time. My ma and dad are getting rid of their car at the moment and they are wanting to give it me. So I am off. I'll get the BTEC, I'll do my BII which is the British Institute of Innkeeping, and then one more qualification. The firm will help you do day-release and all that and then one day I'll have a pub of my own then. No problem. Its a nice trade to get into. It's better now with the new hours, there's no split shifts. Not far from Bristol and only $2^{1}/_{2}$ hours from home.

Interestingly, with Neil above and Tansy below who had chosen to enter the labour market, there was no wholesale rejection of education, training and credentials. Tansy is equilibrating the current intermediate qualification against present career opportunities and postponing a decision to go on to higher education. This postponement will probably be indefinite if there are real career pay-offs in her future work.

Tansy: I've got a job, trainee manager at the St Andrews. It is really a good job. Really nice manager. £90 per week for four and a half days. There's a restaurant and hotel. He wants me to start on Monday. He was ever so nice. That's why I am ever so smart, can't you tell? He wants me to start on Monday, just like that now that I have finished all the exams and that. But I've got another job interview in Nottingham on Thursday and I'm going to go to see what it is like. If there are better prospects, I might go. If it isn't but better money, I'm not taking it. The job I've got is with Trust House so it is a big national firm. I want a place with more prospects, not better money. When you have worked with them two years they give you shares in the company, profit sharing. You get a weekend about three times a year in a hotel of your choice, 25 per cent off meals, cheap holidays. Ever so good, my hotel is number two in the group. Your pay will be reviewed in October. He didn't ask me any questions, he just told me about his lad and wife and the family atmosphere of the hotel. He's French. It's got a good reputation the hotel. He obviously decided he wanted me. He said some of it is split but if you work in the evening, you'll not work in the morning. He's right open. It is ranked number two in the group. I was going on to poly but I started looking at the areas where I could get a job. I'm tired of college work. I was all set for poly but I just changed my mind. I thought I'm 19 now, I'll get a job and if I feel I am not achieving anything I can go back to polytechnic. It is always going to be there. I can always go back to it.

The college experience as a preparation for work and life

Smile you are entering a public area!
(Backstage sign on hotel doors.)

The student subculture at Gastronomic College, characterized by strategic compliance, impression management, a sublimation of overt conflict, the exercise of covert manipulation, etc., forms a cultural circle with the occupational culture the students have already entered, or are about to enter, and with the wider deferential and aspirational parent culture. The public behavioural and private attitudinal college repertoire, the outer-life and inner-life dissonance, corresponds with the front and back regions of hotels and restaurants, etc.:

> In service trades, for example, customers who are treated respectfully during the performance are often ridiculed, gossiped about, caricatured, cursed, and criticized when the performers are backstage . . . Thus, in the Shetlands Hotel kitchen guests would be referred to by belittling code-names; their speech, tone, and mannerisms would be imitated accurately as a source of fun and a means of criticism; their foibles, weaknesses, and social status would be discussed with scholarly and clinical care; their requests for minor services would be met by grotesque facial gestures and cursing, once out of sight and hearing.
> (Goffman, 1969)

Paradoxically, the negotiated hidden curriculum of the course often manifested by backstage grotesque facial gestures and cursing (the students' lived experience), provides a practical, relevant, vocational and utilitarian preparation for the realities of work and life. Informally, the BTEC course is engaged in 'economic socialization', handing on and accentuating a range of 'transferable "life-skills"' in occupational and moral career trajectory survival. Indeed, they are so transferable, if and when the opportunity structure widens, the hotel and catering industry may well find great difficulty in retaining some of these students.

Thus, informally, Gastronomic College provides the students with a powerful exiting culture, 'a dramaturgical discipline' (Goffman, 1969), which in turn becomes an enhanced presenting culture in a new college or work arena. There is no 'stress and strain' (Roberts, 1984) in the transition. The students are well equipped for the presentational aspects of their industry, they have all the cultural competences to handle both clients and superordinates.

Jenny: On Saturday afternoons I work on in the restaurant at the Jerusalem Artichoke. Sometimes you can get people who are so sarcastic, and you can get customers who are great. You get some! There was a woman last Saturday, she sat down and said, 'Can you change this tablecloth.' 'Can you do this and I want that.' I could have bloody hit her. 'Can I have some vinegar', went and fetched it. 'Can I have some salt as well, please', went and fetched it, brought it back. She says 'Have you any pepper as well, please?' Go back and fetch it. I was that close [finger and thumb gesture]. Oh, I was nearly . . . that close [gesture]. It's not what you want, there are ways of asking.

G.R.: But did you do or say anything?

Jenny: No. You have got to get used to it working in a public service industry, to deal with the public sort of thing. I can't imagine doing anything else, me because I love working with people. I say something to them, that makes them relax, make them come off their high horses, do you know what I mean? Nice people make your day. People like that make you stay in it. It's not money, its job satisfaction that attracts me to it. If I am enjoying the job, I'll stay there. If you are pissed off, it makes it a really long day.

Discussion

School and the possibility of college were viewed by all the boys solely as steps to jobs. None was interested in learning for the subtle pleasures it can offer; none craved intellectual understanding for its own sake. The most common phrase in the entire body of interviews was 'nowadays you need a high school diploma (or a college degree) to get a good job'. Often a distinction was drawn between the diploma and the education it symbolized; the boys wanted the parchment, not the learning. In this pragmatic approach toward schooling, the boys reflected the views of their parents (and most of their teachers). All the boys who were convinced that a college degree was the basic essential for a job were seeking middle class jobs (*sic*).

(Kahl, 1953)

It has been argued that the learning for earning instrumentality, 'getting a ticket' (Gleeson and Mardle, 1980), provided the important key for understanding the lived experience of the college course. The students' orientation to the labour market was the source of a powerful 'presenting culture' through which the course was mediated. As Bates (1990) notes: '. . . curricula interact with, filter and are further shaped by the cultural backgrounds and resources which students themselves bring to classrooms'. As such, the students attached major meaning to the *extrinsic* rewards of their course, rather than any *intrinsic* ones. Student concern, centred around the work-related products of schooling (i.e. parchment for careers), shaped teacher–student interaction in the classroom (i.e. the process of schooling). As such, they were contradictorily alienated but satisfied. As Jenny eloquently stated, 'I don't regret doing the course but I am just sick of doing it!' The irony was that the students had penetrated this alienation and desperately sought some in-college satisfactions. Inasmuch as these were not forthcoming, they limited themselves to making 'the best of a bad job', 'gritting their teeth', 'grinning and bearing it' and 'getting it over with'.

This contradiction was resolved publicly with their teachers by being deferential 'conformists'; privately in their peer group they were 'non-conformists'. Strategic compliance was a cultural handling of 'college work for credentials' and 'credentials for work'. As such, the students in the classroom were labouring to learn. They were engaged in a severe critique of the college provision, but there was nothing but apparent conformity to its demands. Classrooms were characterized by manifest order, conflict remained latent. There was a discrepancy between the students' words and deeds. The students were engaged in a proactive passivity to the contradiction between their instrumental orientation to the course and its credentializing power, and the processual realities of the course's social organization and realization. They actively accepted the necessity of doing the course in order to obtain a good job and yet were engaged in a minimalizing resistance to its classroom rendition. Their major coping stategy was accommodation through ritual, their resistances were contained within an ultimate accommodation. Their 'rebellion' was 'privatized' within the subordinate student sub-culture; their conformity was 'publicized' within the dominant institutional order. *Vis-à-vis* their teachers, the students subculturally 'surrounded themselves with a wall of silence impenetrable by the outsider, while sheltering a rich emotional communion among themselves' (Dumont and Wax, 1971). 'Outsiders' observed only student acquiescence in which teachers always remained significant others and powerful critical reality definers.

Conclusion

> One walks automatically, and at the same time thinks about whatever one chooses. American industrialists have understood all too well this dialectic inherent in the new industrial methods. They have understood that 'trained gorilla' is just a phrase, that 'unfortunately' the worker remains a man and even that during his work he thinks more, or at least has greater opportunities for thinking, once he has overcome the crisis of adaptation without being eliminated: and not only does the worker think, but the fact that he gets no immediate satisfaction from his work and realises that they are trying to reduce him to a trained gorilla, can lead him into a train of thought that is far from conformist (*sic*).
>
> (Gramsci, 1988)

If Willis' lads' adaptation to schooling is 'guerilla warfare', then these BTEC 'ear 'oles' ' adaptation is 'passive resistance'. It is not 'rigid reception'. The BTEC students are in reality not much more 'ideologically incorporated' into the college than the lads into 'Hammertown Boys'. In the case of these BTEC students, 'institutional incorporation' is more effectively achieved via ostensible conformity and a commitment to credentialism. The reproductive paradox is that the college-constructed overt and hidden curricular agenda *apparently* is 'highly efficient in creating a docile and subservient workforce' (Bernstein, 1977).

As Delamont (1976) notes in her study of a girls' private school, the pupils' cardinal stategy was 'to find out what the teacher wants and give it to her – assuming that they can see a pay-off for themselves, in terms of grades [and] eventual jobs'. This chapter extends this insight, arguing that the BTEC workers' eventual strategy will be 'to find out what the customer and the employer wants and give it to them – assuming that they can see a pay-off for themselves, in terms of work and career'. As Delamont further notes, the girls would only play the game in so far as it suits them. Where no discernible benefit is forthcoming, by giving the teacher what she wants, 'disruptive behaviour' becomes the major strategy. Similarly, with BTEC workers, who will continue, in the politics of everyday life, to support the *status quo* so long as they continue to be prime career beneficiaries.

This chapter is a study of social reproduction – the economic and political socialization of students for the middle/higher rungs of the occupational ladder in a capitalist service industry and society. Although the concept of correspondence has been invoked, unlike Bowles and Gintis (1976), it has been argued that the dynamics of reproduction take place on contradictory cultural terrain, characterized by contestation and conflict, no matter how latent and corporate. The rhetoric of the ' "new" industrial trainers' is not being immaculately achieved among 'high-status' vocational students. We do not yet have a new model army of over-socialized trained gorillas. As the contradictions of work and schooling continue to unfold, 'transformative pedagogues' can still labour to translate their emancipatory fantasies into realities, even within 'the "new" vocationalism'.

Notes

1. This study is part of the national ESRC 16–19 Initiative (see Banks *et al.*, 1992) and was made possible by an ESRC grant, Sheffield University. Grateful thanks are due to the students, lecturers and principal of Gastronomic College for their kind participation in the research. This chapter is a revision of a paper which first appeared in the *British Journal of Sociology of Education* in Vol. 13, No. 2, 1992.
2. BTEC is the acronym for the Business and Technology Education Council. It was established by the Secretary of State for Education and Science to oversee and monitor a system of full-time (Diploma) and part-time (Certificate) non-degree vocational courses in England and Wales. BTEC has strong industrial representation on all its decision-making bodies. Its remit covers a wide range of industries in addition to Catering and Hotel Management, etc. It offers qualifications at three levels, roughly corresponding to GCSE, A-level and pass degree. This chapter is a study of a second-level course:
   • *First level*: General Certificate or Diploma (no formal entry requirements);
   • *Second level*: National Certificate or Diploma (NC or ND) (entry requirement: 4 GCE O-levels or equivalents or BTEC General);

- *Third level*: Higher National Certificate or Diploma (HNC or HND) entry requirement: 1 A-level and 3 O-level equivalents or BTEC NC or ND).
3. All names are, of course, fictitious. Certain details have also been changed to ensure total anonymity.

References

Ball, S.J. (1981) *Beachside Comprehensive*. Cambridge, Cambridge University Press.

Ball, S. and Goodson, I. (eds) (1985) *Teachers' Lives and Careers*. Lewes, Falmer Press.

Banks, M. *et al.* (eds) (1992) *Careers and Identities*. Milton Keynes, Open University Press.

Bates, I. (1990) No bleeding, whining Minnies: the role of YTS in class and gender reproduction. *British Journal of Education and Work*, 3, 91–110.

Bates, I. *et al.* (1984) *Schooling for the Dole? The New Vocationalism*. London, Macmillan.

Becker, H. (1961) *Boys in White*. New Brunswick, NJ, Transaction Books.

Becker, H. (1971) Social-class variations in the teacher–pupil relationship. In B. Cosin *et al.* (eds) *School and Society*. London, RKP.

Becker, H. *et al.* (1968) *Making the Grade*. Chichester, John Wiley.

Bernstein, B. (1971) On the classification and framing of educational knowledge. In M.F.D. Young (ed.) *Knowledge and Control*. London, Collier-Macmillan.

Bernstein, B. (1977) *Class, Codes and Control*, Vol. 3. London, RKP.

Bowles, S. and Gintis, H. (1976) *Schooling in Capitalist America*. London, RKP.

Braverman, H. (1974) *Labour and Monopoly Capital: The Degradation of Work in the 20th Century*. London, Monthly Review Press.

Brown, P. (1987) *Schooling Ordinary Kids: Inequality, Unemployment and the New Vocationalism*. London, Tavistock.

Burgess, R. (1985) Conversations with a purpose? The ethnographic interview in educational research. Paper presented at *BERA Annual Conference*, September. Sheffield.

Business and Technology Education Council (1991) *BTEC: An Introductory Booklet*. BTEC.

Centre for Contemporary Cultural Studies, Education Group (1981) *Unpopular Education*. London, Hutchinson.

Delamont, S. (1976) *Interaction in the Classroom*. London, Methuen.

Dumont, R. and Wax, M. (1971) Cherokee school society and the intercultural classroom. In B. Cosin *et al.* (eds) *School and Society*. London, RKP.

Fine, G.A. (1985) Occupational aesthetics: how trade school students learn to cook. *Urban Life: A Journal of Ethnographic Research*, 14(1), 3–31.

Freire, P. (1972) *Pedagogy of the Oppressed*. Harmondsworth, Penguin.

Gleeson, D. and Mardle, G. (1980) *Education or Training? A Case Study in the Theory and Practice of Day Release Education*. London, RKP.

Goffman, E. (1969) *The Presentation of Self in Everyday Life*. Harmondsworth, Penguin.

Goldthorpe, J.H., Lockwood, D., Bechhoffer, F. and Platt, J. (1969) *The Affluent Worker: Industrial Attitudes and Behaviour*. Cambridge, Cambridge University Press.

Gramsci, A. (1988) *A Gramsci Reader* (edited by D. Forgacs). London, Lawrence and Wishart.

Hall, S. and Jefferson, T. (eds) (1976) *Resistance Through Rituals*. London, Hutchinson.

Hammersley, M. and Turner, G. (1980) Conformist pupils? In P. Woods (ed.) *Pupil Strategies*. Beckenham, Croom Helm.

Hargreaves, D. (1967) *Social Relations in a Secondary School*. London, RKP.

Hargreaves, D. (1979) Durkheim, deviance and education. In L. Barton and R. Meighan (eds) *Schools, Pupils and Deviance*. Driffield, Nafferton.

Jenkins, R. (1983) *Lads, Citizens and Ordinary Kids*. London, RKP.

Johnson, R. (1976) Notes on the schooling of the English working class, 1780–1850. In R. Dale (ed.) *Schooling and Capitalism*. London, RKP.

Kahl, J.A. (1953) 'Common man' boys. In A.H. Halsey *et al.* (eds) *Education, Economy and Society*. London, Collier-Macmillan.

Lacey, C. (1970) *Hightown Grammar*. Manchester, Manchester University Press.

Lacey, C. (1977) *The Socialization of Teachers*. London, Methuen.

National Economic Development Office (1989) *Recruitment Challenges: Tackling the Labour Squeeze in Tourism and Leisure*. London, NEDO.

Ozga, J. (ed.) (1987) *Schoolwork: Approaches to the Labour Process of Teaching*. Milton Keynes, Open University Press.

Parkin, F. (1972) *Class Inequality and Political Order*. St Albans, Paladin.

Riseborough, G.F. (1981) Teacher careers and comprehensive schooling. *Sociology*, 13(3), 352–80.

Riseborough, G.F. (1985) Pupils, teachers' careers and schooling: an empirical study. In S. Ball and I. Goodson (eds) *Teachers' Lives and Careers*. Lewes, Falmer Press.

Roberts, K. (1984) *School Leavers and their Prospects*. Milton Keynes, Open University Press.

Strauss, A. (1971) *Contexts of Social Mobility*. Chicago, Aldine.

Turner, G. (1983) *The Social World of the Comprehensive School: How Pupils Adapt*. Croom Helm, London.

Werthman, C. (1971) Delinquents in school: a test for the legitimacy of authority. In B. Cosin *et al.* (eds) *School and Society*. London, RKP.

Willis, P. (1977) *Learning to Labour*. Farnborough, Saxon House.

Woods, P. (1977) Teaching for survival. In A. Hargreaves and P. Woods (eds) *Classrooms and Staffrooms*. Milton Keynes, Open University Press.

Woods, P. (1978) *The Sociology of the School*. London, Methuen.

Young, M.F.D. (ed.) (1971) *Knowledge and Control*. London, Collier-Macmillan.

Chapter 3

'When I Have My Own Studio . . .'

The making and shaping of 'designer' careers[1]

Inge Bates

In this chapter, I move away from the themes of violence, incontinence and death, which characterized the world of the 'care girls' in Chapter 1, towards the more glamorous setting of sequins, silver foil dresses and fashion shows. The chapter is based on an ethnographic study of a group of students on a BTEC national diploma course in fashion design.[2] The study extended the exploration of class-gendered female careers, begun with the 'care girls' research, by shifting the focus of attention up the social scale of vocational training and towards a more attractive, high-status career. Again the terrain this work explores is the magical 'black box' of labour supply, the social factors influencing entry into different occupational strata and critical moments of socialization at the level of lived experience. However, whereas in the 'care girls' research the labour supply problem was one of 'warming up' the trainees' commitment to a job they initially disliked, in this study the focus is upon 'cooling out' of an over-supply of would-be fashion designers. For, contrary to their expectations, very few students were likely to become successful fashion designers with their own companies. Most would, however, find employment, at least for a spell, somewhere within the garment industry as assistant designers, pattern cutters or machinists. The chapter begins by discussing the factors which draw students to fashion design as a career, concentrating on the role of gender. It then examines the further filters of social class and family background. Finally, the chapter explores the students' experience of vocational training, central to which was a latent 'running battle' over course priorities, with students emphasizing the importance of individual creativity and tutors prioritizing marketable skills.

The Gendered Appeal of Fashion Design

Although leading fashion designers have generally been men, the world of fashion and the garment industry has always recruited women, particularly as assistant designers and in the skilled and semi-skilled roles of pattern cutter and machinist. These gendered patterns of employment were reflected in the composition of the BTEC national diploma course – of some thirty students on the course, twenty-four were young women. From our research with these young women, it became clear that the gendered appeal of this sphere of work was particularly complex and multi-layered. Most basically, fashion design drew young women because it utilized what have traditionally been female skills in sewing and making clothes. Many of the young women involved in the course talked of their mothers' involvement in various kinds of sewing and craftwork and the ways in which this had fostered their own interest. For example: 'I was always making clothes and outfits for my dolls, then later I started borrowing my mum's machine and making my own clothes – if I wanted something different.' However, this student's explanation introduces a further dimension of female interests in fashion design. These young women wanted to develop their sewing and designing skills, partly so that they could make their own clothes in interesting designs and at low cost, thus enhancing their stakes in the all-important sphere of sexual and social relations.

I always wanted to look different and not just like everyone else.

Boys are always dead impressed you're a fashion designer.

We can dress like we've got our things from an exclusive clothes shop – that's why some of the other students hate us.

In other words, the investment of traditionally female skills in training as a fashion designer was partly an investment in social, sexual and ultimately marital capital. Fashion design training provided opportunities to develop resources which could tilt the balance of their power relations with men a little in favour of themselves. This was, of course, a deeply contradictory form of self-empowerment, reflecting and reinforcing female dependence on 'attractiveness' as a route to success, in the broader context of deeply gendered sexual relations.

Nevertheless, female entry into fashion design was not entirely a gender-conformist career move but involved elements of 'resistance' within an overall pattern of 'accommodation' (see Anyon, 1983). The social advantages accruing from a fashion design career were regarded as a bonus rather than a major reason for taking the course. Most students viewed a career as a fashion designer as a serious proposition affording them independence, mobility and even emancipation from child-care: 'I want to go to a London

College of Fashion and then set up my own studio . . . I know it'll mean
working long hours . . . I want to travel . . . I want a flat in London . . . If
I have children I want my own nanny.' Thus, out of the traditional female
domain of dress-making they were making post-feminist, 'cosmopolitan'
woman, blending sexual power and career power, and magically free from
child-care. Unlike the working-class girls studied by Griffin (1985) or,
more recently, Gaskell (1992), they were at this stage determined to avoid
a conventional career. They emphatically did not want to be 'stuck in an
office' and wanted to do 'something different not just work in Kwik Save'.
In contrast, the world of fashion promised: glamour, scope for individual
creativity, the prospect of 'loads of money' and the appeal of owning a
business and 'my own studio'. In other words, it offered all the attractions
of a post-Fordist, individualist, enterprise career path which could be carved
out in an international arena, transcending the generally more fettered
forms of female labour. It was a high-risk step into the future, reflecting
ambitions formed in the context of a mélange of interrelated late/post-
modern social influences: individualization; the cult of the 'designer'; youth
sub-cultures which centre their creativity on dress; ideologies of equal
opportunities and 'post-feminism'. As a career move, it was in step with
many current cultural trends, but out of step with labour market prospects.
Arguably, the students' susceptibility to what might be termed 'career
myopia' was also gender-related, reflecting the different status of 'careers'
in women's lives which results in different orientations towards the hard
practicalities of career planning.

Social Class and Family Background

The impact of gender on young people's career paths varies dramatically
between social classes and, more subtly, across class fractions (see Anyon,
1983; Aggleton, 1987; Brown, 1987; Chisholm and du Bois-Reymond,
1992). The distinctive, but on the whole unrealistic, career aspirations of
the fashion design students, raised the question of what sorts of social
backgrounds had nurtured their aspirations. While gender operated as a
general influence on the 'care girls' (see Chapter 1), the private school girls
described by Debra Roker (see Chapter 6) and on this group, in each case
it intermingled with other social factors. First impressions of fashion
design students suggested they came from rather more comfortable homes
than Youth Training Scheme (YTS) trainees. However, details of parents'
occupations revealed that both groups recruited largely from the working
class, although the fashion design group was more socially heterogeneous,
drawing students from 'upper' working-class and 'lower' middle-class
backgrounds. In one student's words: 'There are no roughs and no really
brainy ones. We're sort of in-between.' Or, as another explained, 'we're
not loaded and we're not scrubbers'. Typical examples of fathers' occupations were fitter, plumber, clerk at the town hall and garage owner; if

mothers were employed, they were mainly in secretarial work. There were occasional students from wealthy families whose fathers owned or were employed in larger companies but no students with parents who had higher education or were in professional careers. A large proportion of students' fathers were 'self-made' small businessmen, e.g. a joiner, a garage owner, an owner of a small firm selling suspended ceilings. The range of family backgrounds considered here suggests that this was a group originating in the working class but upwardly mobile over one or two generations. In this respect, there were similarities with the hotel management and catering students discussed by Riseborough in Chapter 3 and with the sixth-formers who are the subject of John Quicke's chapter. In all groups, but particularly the BTEC groups, there was a significant proportion of students aiming to develop their own business, suggesting the possibility that enterprise values may be distinctive to and transmitted through 'enterprising' class fractions.

The most crucial difference, however, between the YTS 'care girls' and the fashion design students was the extent to which they enjoyed particular forms of material and psychological support from their families. To risk overstating the case, in the words of one student, life at home was typically 'fairly hunky-dory'.[3] It was this factor which enabled these students to contemplate the several years of training which it could take to become a qualified fashion designer and which also cushioned them from the need to compromise their ambitions in the face of labour market realities.

The most basic form of support was financial and it was effectively a precondition to entering the course that students' families were at least 'comfortably off'. At sixteen, few were able to claim grants and the grants which were available did not by any means cover maintenance. Consequently, families had to be willing and able to support 16-year-olds for at least two further years for them to be able to contemplate entry into a vocational course in further education, as opposed to YTS with its allowance. This clearly discriminated against families where there were financial difficulties and a need for young adult members to begin contributing to the family income. The costs of supporting students in further education did not stop with their upkeep. Costs of equipment and travel which were part of the course were estimated by these students as being in the region of £500:

They paid for both my London trips and any other day trips we had. The initial kits at the beginning of the course came to about £100 ... When you add up all your books and things like that, fabric and stuff its probably nearer £500 than £250 ... It is a lot.

The extent of financial support available from parents could also be a factor in work performance during the course and could influence students' attitudes to carrying on, for example, into higher education. Work performance could easily be affected by the need to take part-time jobs, as one student with three such jobs explained:

> I used to start back at Baltimore at 6, then I used to get home again at 4 [a.m.] and I used to get up again and go to the Pizza Hut for 11, and I used to work at Pizza Hut from 11 to 6, come home for an hour and then go back to Baltimore and then get home at 4 [a.m.] and then get up again for college! Every evening I worked and I ended up not doing my college work . . . and falling asleep at college . . . My tutor says to me 'you're gonna have to do something' and I said 'well I need money to do the course'.

The availability of physical space at home for college work was an additional, perhaps less obvious, condition for successfully undertaking the course. The quantity of college work meant that much had to be done at home which, for fashion design students, entailed laying out patterns and materials for making up. Some families gave up a dining room or spare bedroom especially for this purpose. It is difficult to imagine, however, how such work could be regularly undertaken within the cramped space of a council flat or small house where there might be shared bedrooms and one main living area. One student on the course described such difficulties:

> I can't work at home. There's nowhere to work 'cos me bedroom's too small, it's not got a desk in it so any sewing I've got to do . . . is on the dining room table and it's awkward because my brothers come in at different times so only time you can start really sewing is after 9 o'clock at night if they've gone out.

This particular student eventually overcame this problem by working at a friend's house where there was much more space.

While material factors were important, psychological support and a stable family context were also major influences on entry into this trajectory. Comparison between background data on the fashion designers with similar data from the 'care girls' study vividly highlighted the reasons for this.

Care girls' home background example

I.B.: And your dad works shifts in the steel works?

Anne: Yes. Twelve hour nights, five nights a week . . . He's so tired. I don't know how he can do it . . . Saturday he sleeps in, he's up at four and he can't do it. He's too old now, he's 53. It's too much.

I.B.: Can he do anything about it?

Anne: . . . me and my mum get upset when we see him crawling in . . . you know if my dad's upset, I'm upset. If my dad's poorly, I roar [cry]. I right worry about him . . .

I.B.: So things aren't easy at home?

Anne: Sometimes I think, I feel like crying, I hate myself and I hate mum
but then I think well I'm luckier than a lot of people, there's child
abuse, there's kids getting beaten up, there's husbands battering
wives ... My brother, he'll say why don't you leave home? You've
got all these pressures on you, just leave, just turn your back and
leave, and I says to him, I says, 'I can't turn my back on my family,
it's alright for you'.

I.B.: So you won't leave home very easily?

Anne: No. Turn my back on my family no.

Fashion designers' home background example

D.H.: Have your parents supported you then while you've been at college?

Nancy: Well, they've always been there if I've needed to talk, if I've had
any problems and they've helped me a lot with money, you
know ... they paid for my first college trip to London ... They've
just always been around to help me ... And they've took me to
places to do questionnaires and surveys and things [for BTEC
projects].

D.H.: They've helped you practically?

Nancy: My mum's helped me out with me work, you know she's done a
bit of hand-sewing for me or whatever and cut out me fabric for
me when I've been really pushed. Everybody's helped in fact. You
know ... even little Dale's stapled things together for me ... we
have a really good time.

D.H.: Where do you do your work at home?

Nancy: Everyone just helps out and I've had me fabric laid all over the
floor ... it's been good. They've always been quiet when I've been
working or just helped me out ... They've moved all the furniture,
took everything up and just let me have all the space. They've
been great.

The two young women were in quite opposite family situations. Anne
was burdened by problems linked with her father's need to carry on with
shift-working to avoid redundancy, his ill-health and associated family
tensions. The problems were such that she also felt trapped, needed by the
family and unable to 'turn her back' on them. Her accounts were typical
of those given by the 'care girls', which were frequently laden with descriptions of unemployment difficulties, ill-health and conflict, leading the girls
to a position of feeling desperate to leave home or alternatively bound to
stay. In Nancy's family, dependency relations were completely reversed.
Nancy felt that her parents and family assisted her both psychologically
and practically in her training and her career. Whereas Nancy's success in
going to college floated on a supportive sub-structure of family life, Anne
suffered the worry that her family would 'sink' without her.

While Nancy was perhaps a little exceptional in the degree of support she drew from her family, the majority of students on this course indicated that their parents were on the whole encouraging and helpful and took a definite interest in their college training and their careers:

'And so I had a talk with my mum and dad, they said, look it's up to you, we want what's best for you, we don't mind if you're not going to get a grant at college you know, we'll support you in whatever you do . . .'

Well I come from a family where me mum and dad *are* bothered about what I do, they don't just say 'oh go away and do whatever you want'. That's why they wanted me to do A-levels 'cos they knew it would stand me in good stead.

But they're like behind me all the way. You know like they know it's what I want to do and I want two years experience and saying that, 'you've just got to go wherever education is'.

I think mum and dad are happy about it really 'cos like everybody else they just went into a job, you know, and me dad always said, 'get as much qualifications as you can 'cos there's better jobs and things'.

What their parents appeared to offer was generalized, unconditional support for further education and training. They wanted their youngsters to get 'as much qualifications as you can' but were undiscriminating about the related career prospects. Further questioning of the students suggested that their parents had little knowledge of career opportunities in fashion design and could not assess the realism of their children's goals. In this respect, they contrasted sharply with the parents described by Debra Roker in her study of private education (see Chapter 6), who were well-informed about the routes to high-status careers.

These perspectives also had a class-gendered dimension. There was some evidence that in these families realistic career prospects were considered a less significant issue for girls than for boys;

My brother's doing computing . . . I don't know what they would have said if he'd wanted to go in for fashion design . . . but he wouldn't have wanted to.

My dad thinks I'd have been better off doing a secretarial type course, but he thinks I'll get married anyway.

On the whole, intrinsic satisfaction figured more prominently than extrinsic rewards in parents' assumptions about what was most likely to prove important in girls' careers.

In summary, social class and family background influenced entry into fashion design training both through the transmission of enterprise values and through their capacity to raise what would otherwise have been financial, spatial and psychological barriers to extended vocational training in this field. The particular quality of family supportiveness which the students tended to enjoy was, however, a mixed blessing, particularly in the context of the gendered 'career myopia' mentioned above. While these students' parents were keen to encourage their youngsters to continue their education and struggled in various ways to support them, they were culturally naive and not overly concerned about the value and status of different types of qualifications and different forms of education and training. Partly as a consequence of this, their daughters' ambitions developed in a 'greenhouse' environment, which fostered career dreams far removed from labour market realities.

The Role of Vocational Training

'Snip, snip, snip she goes all day long, snipping away at us ideas. She's like a pair of scissors herself.' This comment expressed the reactions of a student on a BTEC fashion design course to one of her tutors. It records graphically a fairly typical feeling among students on this course, that the course tended to deflate their aspirations and constrict their approach to design, or, in other words, it reflects the experience of occupational socialization through vocational training. The tutors, on the other hand, presented a different perspective, inversely related to that of the trainees.

> They think they're going to be fashion designers and illustrators work-
> ing on magazines and so on. They turn their noses up at Marks and
> Spencers and Littlewoods. Not glamorous enough. You can't get them
> to be realistic and put in the effort . . . you've to nag them all the time.

The tutors perceived the students as, on the one hand, holding on to unrealistic aspirations, and, on the other, failing to channel their efforts towards acquiring marketable skills for employment in the garment industry. These conflicting definitions of the situation underlay a latent running battle within the BTEC course. At the classroom level, this was a struggle over appropriate course content, pedagogy and careers guidance, necessitating appropriate 'negotiation'. Viewed within broader sets of social structures, these grumblings can be seen as the noise of struggles over processes of 'cooling out'.

The basic problem was the gap between student orientations towards individualistic career success and labour market prospects. These were mainly students with about four GCSEs or a BTEC first certificate who would find it difficult to be accepted on to the higher education courses

necessary for more specialized training in fashion design. On leaving the
course, about a third gained entry into such courses but after a year some
of these dropped out without completing. Another third entered work
within the garment industry, finding low-paid jobs as pattern cutters or
machinists. The remainder became unemployed or entered quite different
jobs, mainly in offices, shops and garages. Those who became unemployed
sometimes attempted to become self-employed with the help of an Enterprise Allowance. Essentially, they were dressmakers, working from home,
with luck making wedding dresses, and perhaps hoping one day to open
a shop. This was probably the least lucrative and least secure outcome.
Two years after the course had finished, two students had been in almost
continuous unemployment. One was still hoping that she would eventually
become a fashion designer and insisted, 'I shall be trying as long as I live'.

Consequently, the tutors' goal was to provide a realistic introduction to
opportunities within the garment industry and to develop marketable skills
which would increase students' chances of gaining employment as pattern
cutters or assistant designers. This resulted in the underlying tension
throughout training between work disciplines, on the one hand, which
emphasized coping with pressure, working to deadlines, presentation and
practical skills, and, on the other, student values, which emphasized creative
design, aesthetic enjoyment and a good social life.

Student complaints revolved around four related themes: the industrial
emphasis within the course; the amounts and standard of work expected;
'crits' – the evaluation of course work by tutors; and the impact of the
course on social relationships and social life. The industrial emphasis was
seen as limiting the scope for creative design: 'Industry, that's your whole
thing, you can't do anything one off. Its just for industry, you've got to
do everything, even a lay like you would do it in industry.' The curriculum
was indeed explicitly industry-led, as is increasingly the case in the 'new'
further education. The course involved industrial placements, visits to
manufacturing units and considerable involvement of industrial repre-
sentatives in course provision and assessment. The tutors placed constant
emphasis in teaching on encouraging awareness of the constraints of the
market and production processes. The students characterized them as only
caring about the 'three p's': punctuality, presentation and pattern cutting.

A closely related issue was the volume of work which the students were
expected to produce: 'I didn't expect anywhere near this amount of work'.
The course was based on continuous assessment and the completion of
assignments was a constant source of worry. 'You could work 24 hours
a day literally and never finish everything that needs to be done', one
student complained. The tutors' emphasis on keeping to deadlines was
justified as a form of preparation for work within the garment industry
and this rationale was to some extent recognized, at least by some students.
Nevertheless, they felt that work demands were at times excessive: 'I've

learned a lot about working to times . . . especially in my final major! That was terrible. That must be the worst time ever, honestly, I worked so hard. I never slept for weeks to get that thing done.'

Work pressures were also a source of inter-group tension. Projects were undertaken and assessed on an individual basis and there was much peer group surveillance of performance. Students failing to keep up sometimes fell 'ill' on deadline day, a strategy held in much contempt, presumably since it negated the point of the efforts made by others.

The other major concern focused on 'crits' and tutors' evaluation of students' work generally. 'Crits' was the term used for critical evaluations of student work, which tutors carried out regularly and often in public. Such 'crits' were considered unnecessarily harsh and destructive.

> When they saw my first design they said the designs were wrong for the inspiration, the inspirations were wrong for the season and the fabric was wrong as well . . . they just tore it all to pieces and they did this with quite a few people.

This approach to evaluation was again justified by the tutors on the grounds of teaching students 'the ropes':

> In industry they can be quite cruel. The woman I worked for thought nothing of showing you up in the middle of the design room, pulling things to pieces and throwing them at you . . . It can be quite horrible . . . there's no nice cushioned welcome and showing you what to do. You have to be very tough to get anywhere.

By the end of the course, the students were more habituated to the ritualistic public denigration of work which was not up to standard. Vera enlarged on this:

> To start with I was thinking 'Oh God' and getting really worked up about it and the more I got worked up about it, the worse I did . . . now it doesn't bother me as much. If you think, 'I am not going to get upset no matter what they say about this', you don't really get upset.

The students continued to object, however, to their tutors' constant 'nagging' over the quality of their work and related warnings that they would never get a job in the industry.

The sheer number of college assignments, particularly when combined with the need for part-time jobs to earn money, inhibited the girls' social lives, caused boyfriends to be dropped ('I had to choose between him and me work.'; 'I had to fit him into two nights a week.') and generally tended to divide the group into workers and socializers.

Tara: You can either be one of these people that are all for yourself, not
bothered about college work, 'Going out tonight? What shall we do
this dinner time? Let's skive this afternoon', you know, *you can be
one of these people that everybody loves* but you never get nowt
done or you can be like a person that like *works, works, works,
works.*

The pressure of work generated considerable competition and rivalry
within the group of students. Cliques formed which tended to reflect both
work attitudes and home background. There was a tendency, by no means
consistent, for the most studious and committed girls to come from more
affluent backgrounds and the 'socializers' to come from less prosperous
homes. This led to typifications of different students as for example a
'snob', 'lazy cow', 'spoiled brat' or, more appreciatively, someone who
could 'muck in'. The tension within the group was characterized by one
student as like the 'North–South divide' and at times 'close to open warfare'. 'Some of them I could just hit.'

Friction was exacerbated by the shortage of equipment, particularly
sewing machines, which would provoke responses of possessive individualism. Nancy explained this with a vivid example.

There's some people who just took theirselves too seriously and
thought they were actually in London, you know, being top fashion
designers . . . They thought they were in their studio and all the
equipment was theirs . . . like we'd just muck in and help everybody . . .
but they'd take over one machine.

Galina, she'd like come in and get on a machine and she wouldn't
let anyone else use it and it became like her machine and one day
there were her machine except it weren't her machine, it weren't
threaded up, it weren't plugged in or anything. I went and got on it
and she come and stood in front, looking at me – '*What do you think
you're doing on my machine?*' . . . and she went on and on about it
for the rest of time, honestly . . . Everybody were under a lot of pressure but some people just took it too seriously.

However, it tended to be the students who took it 'too seriously' and were
most effective in laying claim to technical equipment who were the most
successful on the course.

This raises a further function of vocational training which I have discussed
more extensively elsewhere (Bates, 1990a, 1991): screening for material
and cultural resources. Such screening took place through three types of
process. First, the entry qualifications for BTEC of approximately 3 O-
levels filtered out the most educationally and socially disadvantaged students. Secondly, having reached the interview stage, aspects of the assessment

process could be seen as likely to screen prospective entrants for specific social and cultural advantages. For example, the tutors looked for young people who were presentable and 'well-turned out' and preferred the confident and articulate. They also asked specific questions at interview about family support, such as 'What do your parents think about you doing this?' From their own point of view, the tutors were simply attempting to identify young people who were likely to complete the course and to reduce drop-out rate. Their experience of the course and the industry itself has led to an underlying conception of the ideal fashion design student which guided their selection and rejection. The third stage of screening occurred more dynamically. This was the experience of the course itself. Through the simulation of occupational requirements, mediated through BTEC curricula, the course screened entry into fashion design and filtered the majority of young women towards lower-level occupations. At this stage, it was evident that family background continued to play a part. The students from the most privileged families almost invariably tended to carry on to higher education and those from the least privileged families tended to drop out or look for employment even though they might persist with the idea of becoming a fashion designer.

To summarize, the BTEC fashion design course performed a variety of roles in relation to vocational training. It both worked upon students' aspirations, attitudes and skills and filtered them towards different strata within the garment industry. It was experienced as a highly pressured form of vocational training. The combination of design and making up of clothes draws on both artistic flair and practical skills but most students seem to prefer the artistic elements of their training to gaining experience in the practical difficulties of cutting out and making up clothes. The course had a strong industrial emphasis which was greatly resented. There was an associated tension between tutors' and students' conceptions of good design, the former being typified by students as reflecting 'Marks and Spencers', in contrast with their own more exotic individualistic tastes. The coursework involved considerable amounts of homework, which limited the students' social lives, and expensive equipment. Continuous assessment added to these pressures, generating tension and competition within the group and encouraging the formation of cliques. Such cliques tended to solidify as the course developed and different sub-groups began to identify with different career paths.

Further Issues

In order to explore the further possibilities and limitations of theories of social reproduction, it is important to examine both the considerable diversity which exists in youth transitions and the consequences of recent social change. On the whole, it has been the more typical young people whose career paths have arrested the attention of researchers – the 'lads' (Willis, 1977), the 'ordinary kids' (Brown, 1987), the young women who enter office work, factory work or caring (Griffin, 1985; Skeggs, 1988; Bates, 1990a; Gaskell, 1992). It is in part the very predictability of their career trajectories which many of us have sought to explain. This chapter is based on the study of a group with more unusual ambitions, keen to pursue a more individualistic, artistic career path. Given their geographical and historical location – the North of England at a time of recession which was causing contraction within the garment industry itself – their sense of personal autonomy and belief in self-made opportunities was striking. The majority believed they could 'make it' as fashion designers. Some were extraordinarily persistent in sticking to their ambitions, despite their tutors' constant advice to adjust their aspirations. A few still clung to their original ambitions, even after lengthy unemployment ('I shall be trying as long as I live').

It is suggested here that these aspirations were in part a product of an unusual confluence of factors; in particular, gender in the context of lower middle-class and upper working-class families, backgrounds which were educationally supportive, trends towards 'individualization' and the enterprise culture of the 1980s. It was the *combination* of these factors which inflated these young women's aspirations and cushioned them from making the more rapid compromises typical, for example, of the 'care girls' (see Chapter 1).

Such compromises would eventually be necessary, since a career in fashion design was not the most likely outcome for more than a minority of students. For students such as these with the equivalent of four GCSEs, more realistic options would have been clerical or secretarial careers, computing or nursing. However, since they had not taken the appropriate training for these kinds of employment, many of these young women were more likely to end up in shops or even factories once they failed to gain employment in their chosen field.

This overall pattern of social class, gender and broader cultural trends combining to dislocate, rather than lubricate, youth transitions into work is not readily reconcilable with either structural or social reproduction theories as currently formulated. Family, educational experience and media influences had not successfully settled the score between human agency and social structure. Even vocational trainers were having a struggle to recast these young women's dreams. There were signs here of the impact of 'individualization' as discussed, for example, by Beck (1987), with young people 'becoming compelled to make themselves the centre of their own life plans and conduct' and losing a sense of social ties and traditions. Further work will be needed to see quite how ambitions such as those recorded here are sustained or burst in their further, inevitable encounters with opportunity structures.

Notes

1. This chapter develops an analysis which was published initially in the *British Journal of Education and Work*, 4(1), 1990 (see Bates, 1990b). Some material is also included in Banks *et al.*, *Careers and Identities* (Milton Keynes, Open University Press, 1992), the main report of the ESRC 16–19 Initiative.
2. The research took place over a year, mainly in one further education college with additional comparative work being undertaken in another college. I am particularly grateful to Dawn Harvey, then an undergraduate on work placement with me, who provided assistance with interviewing.
3. There were a few students in more difficult circumstances at home as a result of financial or domestic problems or both. Such students constituted a much smaller proportion of this group than the YTS 'care girls'. They were also more likely to do badly or drop out.

References

Aggleton, P. (1987) *Rebels Without a Cause*. Lewes: Falmer Press.

Anyon, J. (1983) Intersections of gender and class: accommodation and resistance by working class and affluent females to contradictory sex role ideologies. In S. Walker and L. Barton (eds) *Gender, Class and Education*. Lewes: Falmer Press.

Banks, M. *et al.* (1992) *Careers and Identities*. Milton Keynes, Open University Press.

Bates, I. (1990a) No bleeding, whining Minnies: the role of YTS in class and gender reproduction. *British Journal of Education and Work*, 3, 91–110.

Bates, I. (1990b) No roughs and no really brainy ones: the interaction between family background, gender and vocational training on a BTEC fashion design course. *British Journal of Education and Work*, 4(1), 79–90.

Bates, I. (1991) Closely observed training: an exploration of links between social structures, training and identity. *International Journal of Sociology and Education*, 1(1), 225–43.

Beck, U. (1987) Beyond status and class. In W. Mega *et al.* (eds) *Modern German Sociology*. Columbia, Columbia University Press.

Brown, P. (1987) *Schooling Ordinary Kids*. London, Tavistock.

Chisholm, L. and du Bois Reymond, M. (1992) Youth transitions, gender and social change. Working paper.

Gaskell, J. (1992) *Gender Matters from School to Work*. Buckingham, Open University Press.

Griffin, C. (1985) *Typical Girls? Young Women from School to the Job Market*. London, Routledge and Kegan Paul.

Skeggs, B. (1988) Gender reproduction and further education: domestic apprenticeships. *British Journal of Sociology of Education*, 9, 131–49.

Willis, P. (1977) *Learning to Labour: How Working-class Kids get Working-class Jobs*. Farnborough: Saxon House.

———— Chapter 4 ————

Running, Plodding, Falling
The practice and politics of youth enterprise[1]

———— Robert MacDonald ————

The last decade witnessed the proliferation of a host of schemes, agencies and courses designed to deliver the gospel of enterprise to depressed areas of the country. As Frank Coffield (1990) has put it:

> ...thousands of millions of pounds of public money have been invested in this ideological project and ... few people are likely to escape the tentacles of enterprise education – whether they are children in primary schools, students in higher education, unemployed miners or redundant executives.

Remedies directed at education and training tended to be to the fore in these programmes for national economic rejuvenation and, thus, school leavers and young people became prime targets of the Conservative government's enterprise policies, particularly if they lived in the areas of industrial decline and high unemployment. In this chapter, I aim to do two things. I will examine the successes and failures of young business people and develop a typology of their experiences: running, plodding, falling. Following this, young people's political interpretations of enterprise will be explored. First, though, I must describe the research upon which this chapter is based.

The Youth Enterprise Study

Until recently, there existed few in-depth assessments of enterprise policies and schemes (see Finn, 1986; Shilling, 1989; Burrows, 1991) and much of the activity of the mushrooming enterprise movement of the mid-1980s faced little independent scrutiny or critical evaluation. Certainly it proved hard to identify many qualitative studies of the outcomes of enterprise initiatives. The Enterprise Allowance Scheme (EAS), introduced by the government in 1983 to encourage unemployed people to 'become their own boss' with the provision of a £40 per week allowance (provided certain criteria are met; see Unemployment Unit, 1990), has largely been evaluated through statistical surveys. Additionally, academic research on young people and youth transitions has largely ignored enterprise and small business. Perhaps the main reason for this is that the period usually targeted by youth researchers (i.e. 16–19 years) tends to cover a time in people's lives when self-employment is not a realistic option. As studies within the 16–19 Initiative show (e.g. Roberts and Parsell, 1988; Banks *et al.*, 1992), the vast majority of people in their late teens are usually employed in jobs, training on schemes, studying in education or unemployed on the dole. Few are self-employed. However, I would argue that starting new, small businesses becomes of more interest to young people in their early twenties (as they leave training schemes, experience post-scheme unemployment, become eligible for bank loans, etc.).[2]

This lack of serious academic and 'official' consideration of the personal, political and policy outcomes of enterprise initiatives provided one of the main spurs to a study undertaken by Frank Coffield and myself. We felt it was necessary to cast a steadier eye over the busy world of the enterprise industry and to take a more critical look at the considerable amounts of time, effort and public money that were being spent in the name of enterprise. In the autumn of 1988, we thus embarked upon a short investigation of youth and enterprise in Cleveland, funded as an associated study of the ESRC's 16–19 Initiative.

The heart of Cleveland, in the North-East of England, is Teesside: the industrial towns of Middlesbrough, Stockton and Billingham which sprawl along the banks of the River Tees. Throughout the 1980s, the county had some of the highest rates of unemployment in mainland Britain, vying with Merseyside for the unhappy title of the country's unemployment capital. The impact of the recession of the early 1980s was severe. The manufacturing giants which breathed economic life into the area and upon which Cleveland had come to depend – chemicals and steel – shed over 50,000 jobs between them in the thirteen years to 1988 (Teesside TEC, 1990). And the boom times of the mid- to late 1980s were slow to reach the North-East. By March 1990, the jobless figure, despite many months of falling unemployment, still stood at 11.4 per cent (with the Great Britain average being 5.6 per cent; Department of Employment, 1990). Just over a year later, by April 1991, this figure had risen again (to nearly 13 per cent) as the new 'classless' recession that marked John Major's early premiership began to take hold (Department of Employment, 1991). The county was just starting to recover, albeit in a partial kind of way (Robinson, 1990), when the shock waves of the second recession started to break; many people lost jobs in the first recession and were still to find one as the second hit home.

This, then, was the economic context for our study of youth and the enterprise culture. We argued that given the notorious levels of unemployment in Cleveland, and a local culture of work which has historically depended upon employment in a few very large firms (ICI, British Steel), the locality provided a critical test for the government's philosophy of enterprise. Furthermore, early inspections of the enterprise scene in the county revealed a quite astounding level of activity. At the time our fieldwork began (late 1988), we counted over 100 agencies in Cleveland alone claiming to be involved in the youth enterprise field.

At this point, I should provide some details of our research methodology. Our study was a short one, but I was able to hold over 100 qualitative interviews with young men and women who were involved with small firms or cooperatives.[3] They were roughly equally divided by gender, their average age was 21, four were from the British Pakistani culture, the majority were from manual working-class backgrounds and had left school at the age of sixteen.[4] The majority of our informants had experienced considerable unemployment before starting up in business and this negative *push*, together with the positive *pull* of entrepreneurship, caused people to start their own businesses (see MacDonald and Coffield, 1991).

One of the most basic 'findings' of our research was that we witnessed a reinforcement of the gender divisions of the local labour market even when people had an active role in creating their own jobs. Congruent with national trends, this sample tended to form service sector businesses and traded on their own, for instance, as graphic designers, beauticians, car valets, hairdressers, photographers, mechanics, landscape gardeners and clothes designers. It is perhaps not surprising that these 'young entrepreneurs' tended to work *with* the grain of a sexually divided local labour market. Setting up was hard enough in itself, let alone trying to establish a business which challenged gender stereotypes. Young people traded on informal skills, previous training or childhood/teenage interests. These themselves tended to reflect gendered 'preferences' and influenced what forms of businesses were established. A boy's interest in computer games became a new computer programming firm at the age of 19; a girl's hobby of dressmaking was transformed into a clothes design and retail business when she reached her early twenties.[5]

Aspects of ethnicity also impinged upon the processes leading people to embark upon the enterprise path. I was only able to interview a very small number of British Pakistani people and, while not wishing to draw any hard and fast conclusions, their comments about starting in business were remarkably similar and drew attention to one overriding factor. Racial exclusion from decent jobs in the locality was said by all to be one of, if not *the*, main reason for starting in business (see Ward and Jenkins, 1984). They were not offered decent jobs, so they created their own in self-employment. Ranjeet, a 19-year-old from Middlesbrough, for instance, estimated that she had applied for nearly 150 jobs with no luck whatsoever.

Success and Failure in Youth Enterprise

The task of adequately defining success and failure is a tricky one; what counts as success to one informant might count as failure to the next (or to an outside observer or an enterprise professional). In sifting the experiences culled through discussions and interviews into broad categories of 'success' and 'failure', I *initially* paid attention to the criteria deployed in *official* assessments, for instance by the Department of Employment and Training and Enterprise Councils (TECs).

The 'numbers game' proliferated in the training and enterprise world during the 1980s, partly owing to the funding arrangements instituted by the Manpower Services Commission (MSC) and others. This led many training/enterprise organizations to employ the most basic, quantitative sketches of success (and failure). Some agencies in the county claimed quite staggering (and really quite dubious) *numbers* of successes, in terms of people benefiting from their services. Thus, how many clients had been advised, how many people had started up in business, for how long these businesses traded and how many jobs had been created became the criteria for judging the success of youth enterprise. Quantity, rather than quality, became the measure of success (Coles and MacDonald, 1990).

For how long did *our* informants stay in business? Were they successful according to official definitions? Of the 104 people I interviewed, 50 were self-employed in small firms or cooperatives at the time of interview. These people were followed up early in 1991, about eighteen months after the fieldwork had been completed. Were these businesses, after all, going to be the little, entrepreneurial acorns from which mighty commercial oaks were to grow? I was able to follow the fortunes of forty-seven of the fifty. Of these, twenty-five were still in business but twenty-two had, for whatever reason, closed down.

Our methodology was of course not designed to provide answers to statistical questions of 'success' rates in the long-term. Having said this, we can see from the limited data above that even for those trading at the time of interview, youth enterprise proved to be a risky business and brought mixed fortunes over this longer period. We deliberately tried to find young people who were 'successful', who had been trading for a number of years and had built up sound, small firms. This was a difficult job and we only located a handful of such people. Even some of these have since gone bust: examples of the many thousands of striving small firms to go to the wall in the recession of 1990–91.

The impression that we gained is confirmed by the National Audit Office's (1988) survey of EAS participants. It found that only 57 per cent of the scheme's participants still traded two years after the scheme had finished. Even these questionable levels of success must be placed against what is called 'deadweight' (those who would have set up in business anyway without the help of the scheme) and 'displacement' (the amount of existing jobs which are lost through competition with EAS participants). The National Audit Office estimate deadweight to be 44 per cent (that is nearly half would have set up without the help of the scheme) and that about half of all the jobs created simply displaced already existing jobs.

Our data also paints a rather sorry picture in respect of the number of jobs created in these new firms. The vast majority of our informants started up on their own, had not employed anyone else and did not intend to (see Hakim, 1988, 1989). Only a handful of small firms go on to employ significant numbers of workers (Storey, 1982; Storey and Johnson, 1987) and our sample was no different from the general population. In the next section, I will move away from 'official', quantitative criteria for judging success and failure to discuss some of the issues that played a part in informants' own evaluations of their failures and successes.

Running, Plodding, Falling

There was no one overall experience of youth enterprise. Of course, there were the 'horror stories' of going bust and the quite dire human consequences of business failure. At the other extreme, there were a small group of interviewees who seemed to be doing very well in business. In the middle fell the largest category – those who could not easily be classed as either successes or failures, but people who struggled to keep their business afloat on a day-to-day basis. Consequently, I developed a three-fold typology to categorize the different types of experience related in interviews. I have called these types of experience 'running', 'plodding' and 'falling'.[6]

Running

Caroline was first interviewed in the spring of 1989 and I revisited her in the summer of 1991. She worked in a partnership with her husband running a three-year-old firm which provided publicity, promotion and marketing services to local companies. Between the two visits, Caroline's business had grown to employ seven people in all and had moved to more sumptuous premises. She said:

> Well, since the last time we saw you we've obviously increased in size. The number of people that we employ is in direct proportion to the business that we are bringing in so that we can service that business. Our clients have increased in number – mainly on a referral basis. So we've had to change premises and get something a little bit bigger, which we are currently bursting at the seams already. So our next step is to have possibly more prestigious offices, hopefully to buy somewhere so that we can have a more tangible asset for the company . . . if you're successful it grows from there. We're going from strength to strength.

Caroline's firm had 'a good image' and fostered credibility and contracts with the largest local companies and organizations – chemical
firms, the health authority, the local TEC, the county council – and so
was clearly operating on a 'real', commercial basis. Targeted next were
even more lucrative accounts with national companies like Marks and
Spencer and Sainsbury. Perhaps, needlessly, I asked whether she was
successful:

It depends on how you translate the word success really. What does
it mean? At the end of the day we are in a position where we earn
a reasonable living from our business. We probably manage to support ourselves to the point where we're earning more than we would
earn in our jobs previously. We have a car each. We have a nice
house. Got married. We are able to employ people at reasonable
salary levels and that is what I would call relatively successful in
the current climate. But in terms of being wildly successful we're
not multi-millionaires or anything like that. But we're working on
it!

Caroline's vision of the future was one of continued success. She intended to expand into other areas of the country, to take on more employees,
to steer the firm on to even firmer ground and to be able to semi-retire,
with her husband, in her thirties. While it is not my intention to attempt
to account *fully* for the differential success of informants, some possible
explanations did emerge from the data. Caroline herself pointed to two
background factors (which distinguished her from the majority of people
in the sample). First, she had been to university and had a degree and
professional training in the exact area of her present business, which was
coupled with broad and relevant work experience gained in a number of
non-manual, salaried jobs. Many of our informants had left school at the
age of sixteen and most did not have formal training or certificated skills
in their chosen area of enterprise. Secondly, Caroline had been able to
inject a large amount of her own capital into her embryonic business,
again separating her from the more common experience of the sample.
She was able to rent suitable premises, recruit staff, advertise services and
establish contracts and contacts at the earliest stage. This sort of launch
provided a great headstart for a new firm like Caroline's and was able to
set them up and running when many others were struggling to get off the
ground. Caroline's broadly middle-class background had operated in these
two ways (in terms of material and educational advantage) to help set her
successful business apart from the majority.

I present Caroline as an example of a 'runner'. However, only about 10
per cent of our sample shared a similar experience of youth enterprise. The
majority, probably about 70 per cent of the people I talked to, were less
successful and 'plodded along'.

Plodding

The first person I interviewed was a working-class, 21-year-old called Ronnie. He ran his own small business as a motor mechanic. He lived in a local authority rented flat with his father. Ronnie concluded his interview by conjuring up the image he held of his personal enterprise path:

Ronnie: Well, I've got a way of looking at it. It might sound funny this, the way I see it, it's like this. Self-employment is like a corridor, like a tunnel, and I've made the decision to step into that corridor and I'm just at the start of it. It's pretty dark, but you know, there's light at the end of the corridor. There's loads of doors off the corridor, but, you know, if you can just keep going, like, one day you'll get to the end.

R.M.:   And what's at the end?

Ronnie: Well, I don't know, you know, success. Maybe a pot of gold! [Laughs].

Nearly two years later, I was able to revisit Ronnie. Had he found his pot of gold? Though he had had his share of 'sticky patches' he had also managed to move into more visible premises nearer the centre of town. These were more expensive but trade had picked up a little and he was earning more money. Perhaps most significantly he was still *in business*, in itself perhaps the most immediate sign of 'success' given the riskiness of youth enterprise. I asked him how things had been going, referring back to the first interview.

Ronnie: 'Light at the end of the tunnel?' ... Mmm [pondering]. Like I say – you start in the station, just explaining how I see it, the station was like you starting off in business, on the Enterprise Allowance or something. So you have got a little bit of advice. Enterprise Allowance finished and you come to your first station. Then you've got no back-up money and your money is running out on you. You come to the next station – there's someone waiting on the platform – customers. So that builds you up for the journey ahead. Like I say, the light at the end of the tunnel is when you've got bags of money in your pocket. You jump off the train and you can afford anything you want ... I want to put it some way I can actually explain it to you. I would say that now I'm just near the end of the tunnel – about to come out. I would say that I've gone through all the stations, for instance. In the tunnel, coming through. I like to be modest about what I'm doing, I'm not a brag, but with me being in business for coming on five years, for me to break, I think it would have happened.

Ronnie was slightly unusual in that he had started his business (unofficially) before his eighteenth birthday and had been trading for longer than most. Perhaps for these reasons he was more able and willing than most to take a processual view of his times in self-employment. Success for him had been a slow train coming: he still had plenty of 'bad times' but he could glimpse the light at the end of the tunnel. A 'good week', when I first talked to him, earned him £50. A good week now was £150. He had lived on 'bread and butter jobs for absolutely years' (by this he referred to basic, run-of-the-mill tasks which earned him little) and this meant that often he was still 'pretty skint'. His trade, though, was getting better, becoming more solid, improving.

What emerges primarily from Ronnie's account is a feeling of perseverance and doggedness; the archetypal qualities I have described elsewhere as characterizing the majority experience of youth enterprise (MacDonald and Coffield, 1991). He 'plodded along' through hardships and disappointments with the goal of 'success', in the long term, keeping him on the rails. For him, the long hours, low pay, hard work and trials of youth enterprise were not shocking or surprising. This was what he expected. This was the ordinary life of youth enterprise. This was not success nor failure in any obvious sense but 'plodding along'; simply a way of working which became more widespread during the 1980s as the numbers of non-traditional entrepreneurs swelled the ranks of the self-employed (Hakim, 1989).

Falling

I first met Trevor in the week that he had closed down his business. He was revisiting an enterprise agency in order to re-draft his initial business plan. It seemed he wanted to work out for himself where his entrepreneurial plans had gone wrong and, if only for his own sake, 'to get it as it should have been'. The closure of the firm hit Trevor hard. He was depressed to the point that he was receiving medical attention and his personal finances were in an extremely dire state. He participated in the interview because he wanted to 'help some other poor soul' and to 'show the other side of things'. Trevor was 22 years old when I first talked to him. He lived at home with his father, a retired bus driver, and mother, a voluntary worker for a local charity.

Trevor left school when he was sixteen, with '. . . great joy and great hope for the future. I found out it wasn't quite as easy. I came out at the start of the great unemployment boom [in 1983]'. His labour market experiences during the years 16–19 revolved around government schemes (Youth Training Scheme, Community Programme), lengthy periods of unemployment and very occasional temporary jobs. Following a particularly long spell without work, he decided to start up a car valet/repair business: '. . . I just realized there was no other option. I was getting no interviews. I had to start something up otherwise I would just be sitting there turning into a vegetable.'

He developed a business plan, secured a grant from the Prince's Youth Business Trust, joined the EAS, moved into premises on the outskirts of Middlesbrough and started business. Things started to go wrong almost immediately. He took on a couple of 'friends' as employees on a casual basis; these people, in his view, did much to harm his business in the early days, by working on other friends' cars instead of those of customers, by stealing parts and by generally causing trouble. Also, the premises which Trevor had finally leased proved to be quite unsuitable and far too expensive, despite its off-the-beaten-track location.

These early problems were compounded by others which quickly came over the horizon. He branched out into the buying and selling of used cars; the idea being that the valeting and basic repair work that he did on the cars would increase their value and he could then resell them at a profit. However, this also proved quite a disastrous step. To cut a long and gruelling story short, he lost several hundred pounds on the cars he attempted to sell and drove himself to mental despair and physical exhaustion. For instance, he sold a car bought for £150 for £450 after six weeks' intensive labour and spending nearly £300 on parts and repairs. He was taking out further bank loans to finance his deals and he was living on his parents' goodwill, often unable to pay himself any wage, ploughing any 'profits' into the next job.

These disheartening experiences combined to cause Trevor to close the business after a year. Business never picked up from these early mistakes and he spent much of his time and effort simply trying to keep abreast of his debts; working incredibly long hours in order to complete jobs, the profits from which went straight to pay off new debts. He never took a whole weekend off during his year in business. His 'pay' never rose above £40 per week and often he came nowhere near this amount. To an outside observer, Trevor's tale might seem almost laughable if it was not so tragic. He was clearly not a 'businessman' and many of the problems he encountered could be argued to be of his own making. Trevor would be the first to agree with this; indeed, he was amending his business plan for this reason.

I was able to talk to Trevor a year and a half later. He had been unemployed for most of this period, interspersed with a casual job working in the Lake District and a few weeks on an ET course. I asked him again about his business. Perhaps time had healed some of the emotional wounds? Did he see any positive sides to his experiences?

I failed miserably, though it gave me a taste for management rather than working as somebody else's idiot. No, it was a big bloody mistake. Looking back if I known I'd much rather have signed up for a ruddy year on ET and ended up with a certificate at the end of it. £10 a week extra and no bloody debts . . . It practically killed me. I came out of it and I was at rock bottom, mentally and physically. I would much rather have avoided all that. If I'd known I would never have started it. There was no real pluses to it.

In all, Trevor owed somewhere in the region of £6000 to the Prince's Trust, the bank, suppliers, British Telecom, and in unpaid rents and rates. Trevor was unemployed again, receiving income support of £28 per week from which he was gradually paying off his debts. For Trevor, business failure was unequivocal. Of interest to us, though, in our assessment of youth enterprise in general, are the issues and themes which are common across such cases. A number of factors which unite Trevor's story with those of other 'fallers' can be identified.

First, he had no formal training in the trade in which he became self-employed. He 'knew a bit about cars' and had worked, casually, on motor vehicles through his teens. Like many other 'young entrepreneurs', a teen-age hobby or leisure interest had been transformed into the explicit means through which he was to earn a living in his early twenties. Commitment was high but, in this case, effort was not matched by sound business practice. Secondly, Trevor, like many other failed business people, had received little business training. He clearly lacked shrewd business acumen and he could have perhaps benefited from more detailed, systematic advice and closer guidance *over time*. While he did attend some training sessions and an Enterprise Awareness Day, much of the help he received was in the start-up phase. Given the high failure rate of all new firms, I was surprised that I did not come across anybody who had received advice about how to *close* a business. Thirdly, Trevor took on poorly located, poor-quality and expensive premises. Again this was a common reason given by informants to explain (in part) the collapse of their firms. From shabby offices and shops hidden away in the backstreets (or tucked away in enterprise units) they had to do economic battle with other companies already established and often occupying much more lucrative locations in the town centres and on busy high streets.

This takes us to the fourth and perhaps most basic point. Virtually all the informants interviewed faced quite severe competition from large companies, from other new, small firms, from the 'fiddle economy' and/or from the next EAS participant to establish a business similar to their own. Moreover, they were disadvantaged in this capitalist competition by their age, their class, their locality, by their marginal market location and they faced, in some cases, almost Herculean struggles to get themselves established. Very often this was done through sheer sweated labour and by competing on price; they aimed to provide a similar service to competitors but at a much cheaper price. They could 'afford' to pursue this business strategy only at the cost of taking extremely low wages (if anything at all) and while being subsidized by the EAS (and after a year this safety net was pulled away). We found that two-thirds of the whole sample of young people in business (i.e. not just those who 'failed') were working for an average, weekly, 'take home' wage of about £50.[7]

In short, youth enterprise was not a lucrative business and new, young businesses were vastly underfunded. They had none of the necessary capital with which to establish themselves properly (to buy stock, obtain decent premises, take on employees, develop products and services, advertise, etc.). In small and risky ways they tried to get a commercial toe into a local economy which even the giants of British industry were leaving. The most fundamental problem faced by 'fallers' like Trevor was that the economy did not need them. In an 'enterprise culture' of new, small firms, some will always make it (e.g. Caroline with her expanding publicity business) while the majority will either fail, like Trevor, or continue to 'plod along', struggling, like Ronnie, to carry their risky businesses on to firmer ground.

This typology of 'runners', 'fallers' and 'plodders' echoes that developed by Roberts (see Chapter 9, this volume) to characterize the trajectories of the whole spectrum of youth, with some, in his model, experiencing academic success through school and college, some in a second route comprised of 'good jobs' and a third less successful group who moved between government schemes, insecure jobs and unemployment. Of course, here I am dealing with a very specific set of people, the majority of whom had entered 'enterprising careers' from Roberts' third 'career trajectory' and who hoped that self-employment might finally bring them a decent working life in their twenties. Most of the people in my sample were like Ronnie and Trevor – ordinary, working-class young people who were hoping to get their feet on the bottom rung of the business ladder.

Some of the 'runners', however, possessed attributes and characteristics which helped them in business. For instance, Caroline's middle-class background underpinned her comparative material wealth and advance education and training. She used this advantage to promote her business successfully. The handful of middle-class, university graduates in the sample were able to cash in 'cultural capital' for bank investment capital, and used the social skills and educational advantages of the young middle-class (confidence, 'professional' articulacy, business studies courses) to their advantage. They could call upon the help of financially secure and supportive parents and, if businesses failed, a comfortable family background was there to cushion the fall.

Gender and 'race' also played their parts in the successes and failures of 'young entrepreneurs'. To give brief examples: two 21-year-olds, Mary and Jane, described how they had been treated in a sexist manner as 'silly little girlies' by a male bank manager when they requested a loan of £1000 in order to participate in the EAS. They were denied the loan and had to work illicitly doing 'fiddly jobs', while claiming unemployment benefit, for a year in order to raise this sum and so become officially self-employed. They cite this slow start to their business as one of the reasons for its eventual collapse. Nasim, a 19-year-old British Pakistani woman, described graphically how racism was affecting the success of her market stall business. Apart from the low level of custom she was getting (in comparison to similar stalls nearby), she became frightened of the racist taunts and abuse she suffered from white shoppers.

In short, structural aspects of social inequality played their part in business success and failure. However, while I have pointed to some of the class cultural factors which helped to distinguish Caroline from 'fallers' and 'plodders' like Trevor and Ronnie, *overall* what was most striking were the similarities between these three categories of experience. It proved very difficult to identify any critical background factors (e.g. educational quali-fications, class, gender, apparent commitment, hours worked, income earned, etc.) which could be used comfortably to *predict* success and failure. This three-part typology of youth enterprise was developed in order to illustrate how a handful became very successful, how a sizeable minority of the sample failed dismally but how the majority experience of youth enter-prise was one of dogged determinism – neither success nor failure in easily understandable forms.

I must also stress that these three broad types of experience of enterprise shared much in common and the labels I have given them apply to the experience and not to the individuals involved. The boundaries between 'running', 'falling' and 'plodding' were thin, shifting and permeable. Runners became fallers and plodders could become runners. For example, I inter-viewed a young woman called Dawn who had run a designer shirt business for three years, had won numerous small business awards, had represented her country in international conferences for 'young entrepreneurs' and, had she been interviewed a month earlier, would have been classified unproblematically as a 'runner'. However, when I talked to her she had closed down her apparently successful business because of the severe emotional pressures, hard work and minimal income it brought. She had fallen from the upper reaches of 'success' into the group of people who no longer traded but now, instead, were again looking for employment in a depressed labour market.

Working the Tory Way? Political Interpretations of Enterprise

One of the most interesting sociological questions for this study concerns the political *responses* of young people to the *rhetoric* of the enterprise culture and to the contrasting *reality* of their own experiences. I was particularly keen to explore political consciousness given the assumptions often made about the politics of 'young entrepreneurs'. It might be expected that if the politics of the Thatcher decade were to find support among any sections of youth, it would be among a group like this. To what extent were young people inculcated into the values of the 'enterprise culture'? If enterprise had become a 'dominant ideology', had this group become dominated? Can these young women and men, apparently prime beneficiaries of enterprise policies, be seen as the archetypal 'Thatcher's Children'?

It should go without saying that politics is a broader field than can be explicated by voting intentions alone; however, I still thought it interesting to ask the sample, following the usual format, 'if there was a general election tomorrow would you vote and, if so, for whom?' I was able to ascertain voting intention from all but ten of the ninety-four people in the sample. Opinion polling is also a tricky business and I would not wish too much to be read into the details of party support. Two points only will be made. First, support for the Conservative Party was very low given the working 'hypothesis' that this group may be prone to support the government of the day and its enterprise policies. Approximately 11 per cent of the sample said they would vote for the Tories (29 per cent said they would vote Labour, 6 per cent said they would vote Green, 4 per cent supported the SDP/Liberals). Secondly, and this point will be developed more fully, half of the sample claimed that they would not vote or that they did not know for whom they would vote. The use of ethnographic interviewing (as opposed to questionnaire surveying) had considerable advantages in pursuing this topic. While many said that they did not know who they would vote for, when pressed, and as the discussion developed further, it became apparent that what they meant was that they had serious reservations about voting at all. In addition, a large proportion said that they would *definitely* not vote.

These sorts of answers were interesting because of their frequency and because they are often discounted from published opinion poll results (which favour discussion of the prevailing balance of partisan support). They also tend to be read by more academic investigators as evidence for their thesis that young people are apathetic, bored and uninterested when political questions arise (e.g. Stradling, 1977). Coffield *et al.* (1986, p. 191) found that '. . . men and women slumped deeper in their chairs, rolled their eyes to convey utter boredom, groaned and muttered at the very mention of the word politics'.

This is not, however, the argument that I would like to advance here. On the contrary, by examining the ethnographic accounts gathered in discussion with young people, it will be suggested that these informants were politically conscious and their views of enterprise and unemployment were highly politically charged. In a similar vein, George Riseborough (see Chapter 8, this volume) vividly captures how YTS lads are constantly engaged in 'political' battle to redefine their local, social reality.

It was extremely difficult to isolate unequivocal support for the Conservative government, enterprise policies or Mrs Thatcher, the then Prime Minister. Even those who said that they would vote Tory hedged their comments with disclaimers:

> Well, I've always voted Conservative. Don't know why – just have. It's just one of those things. I'm not interested in politics. Very, very little. I don't care. I just let everybody get on with their own lives. As long as I am happy I don't care [Adrian, Middlesbrough, classed as one of the 'runners'].

Far more common were broadly anti-enterprise views. These tended to cluster around two main themes. First, there was an extremely common view expressed that enterprise schemes designed to encourage the unemployed into business (e.g. the EAS) were part of a cynical attempt to lower unemployment *figures*. As one young woman described it: they try to juggle the unemployed from scheme to scheme 'keeping a million or so in the air at one time'. EAS and other enterprise initiatives were seen as being no different from a host of other government schemes encountered on Teesside. Their main purpose was to reduce the political visibility and embarrassment of unemployment. Lynne, who had failed in her business with severe emotional and financial repercussions, talked as follows:

R.M.: What is your view of the government's enterprise policies?
Lynne: The way I see it is that they think something's got to be done about all these people who are unemployed: 'We've got these massive figures – we'll have to get them down. We don't want a true figure of how many people are out of work. So we dream up these schemes and one of them is called enterprise and one of them is called ET'.
R.M.: You have had fairly extreme experiences of the things that the Tories are promoting and yet you say that you are not interested in politics?
Lynne: I am not interested in it because it is above my level of understanding. I don't understand how it works. If I don't understand it, I avoid it. I can talk about the issues that affect me, like being a single mother.
R.M.: I would say that the way you have talked about it is very political.
Lynne: I would say practically.

Secondly, self-employment and one-person businesses were thought to be ill-considered and ineffective solutions to the economic problems of the area. Enterprise culture initiatives directed towards the establishment of myriad new, small firms would eventually lead to saturation of the market, an unhealthy level of competition and, inevitably, further redundancies (echoing the worries of the National Audit Office). While they as individuals had pursued an individual solution to the collective problem of local unemployment, some informants realized that it was illogical to suggest that all should follow this path into self-employment. I quote Bob, a freelance forestry worker:

R.M.: One of the things behind this idea of the enterprise culture is that people have become too dependent upon the dole . . .

Bob: That's the government policy – to get people off their backsides, to make people get on with it themselves, to be dependent upon themselves. It's not something I go along with . . .

R.M.: Why not? People might look at you as a perfect example of a very enterprising young man, a young Thatcherite?

Bob: I don't agree. I think the government should put more money into this area and put more factories up and get people back into work. I think it's more the government's responsibility to create work, not individual people.

R.M.: But you said earlier that anybody could do it?

Bob: Yes, if they *wanted* to and if they had some skill, fair enough. Why not? But it shouldn't be left down to them, should it?

R.M.: Why not? People might say if *you* can do it, why can't everybody?

Bob: Everybody can't be self-employed can they? It's ridiculous. There's 50,000 unemployed people in Cleveland. You couldn't expect all of them to become self-employed all of a sudden. Some people have families and mortgages to consider. I'm different. I live with my parents. I don't need a lot of money to live on. I don't have the worries. Other people have. It should be more the government's responsibility.

In short, informants had a critical view of the government's enterprise policies. A minority of informants, like Bob above, spoke more fully, developing more sophisticated objections to 'the enterprise culture' and associated policies. These tended to focus on, for instance, and to paraphrase: its trendiness and vacuity as a fashionable political catchphrase; the enormity of the economic decline addressed by (what they described as) an inadequate political and economic response; the over-emphasis upon individual effort and responsibility for job creation at the expense of more macro-level, industrial development; and the unfair way in which the responsibility for local economic rejuvenation is passed to young people who really only want a decent job.

Yet, when asked directly, most of these young women and men claimed not to be interested in politics. Even Bob, above, claimed to be only marginally interested in it. It was true that young people professed a profound lack of interest in politics, and emulated those in the study by

Coffield *et al.* quoted above. It was '... the most boringest subject out'. Yet very many talked emotionally, cogently and at length in ways which I would call political (as I have shown above). How can we reconcile these apparent inconsistencies?

I would suggest that when these people said that they were not interested in politics, what they meant was that they were not interested in the official world of Politics with a capital P (a point also noted by Roberts and Parsell, 1990). Young people avoid Politics because they see it as uninteresting in the extreme and because it is a subject upon which they feel they *should* be able to pass comment. Unlike the sixth-formers in John Quicke's study (see Chapter 5, this volume), they felt themselves to be uninformed, uneducated and unsure about Politics, and some obviously felt embarrassed in their silence. Most young people receive no direct education in politics, be it in school, in employment or in training (Harber, 1987). The most some can hope for is a brief session on trade union rights or 'citizenship'; often rather staid contributions which help fill the induction weeks of training schemes. As Phil Cohen (1983) and Bob Hollands (1990) have both argued, young working-class people are no longer apprenticed into the politics historically associated with their class. As traditional apprenticeships into the manual trades have diminished, so has the informal schooling of the work place in trade unionism, collectivism, welfarism and the Labour Party.

Politics for most young people means something quite particular (grey men in grey suits, the World of Westminster and party political broadcasts, etc.). They feel alienated from Politics. For them, it refers to a world of which they know little, which is far away and over which they have no control. To paraphrase C. Wright Mills, they often do not feel their individual, private troubles (of unemployment, poverty, business hardship) to be connected to the public issues of society, government and Politics. Unemployment is still often experienced as a personal failing (and often treated by societal agencies as such) rather than as a collective, social problem created by failings of the demand side of the economy and experienced by millions of people. In this same way, Politics belongs to this 'other' public world, not to the immediate world of personal experiences.

Interestingly, there often seemed to be a geographical element to people's disavowal of Politics; the 'real life' of personal concerns was centred on home, friends, the concrete, their neighbourhood, Teesside. Localism was an important part of political consciousness and 'solutions' to the problems of the North-East, when they were forthcoming, were framed in terms of a vague 'us' and 'them': 'they should set up factories and give us a decent bit of support for the North-East' (Danny, Middlesbrough).[8] I would argue, though, that this sort of individualism and localism only partially limited the development of a more collective youth perspective. Many of this group *shared* aspects of a political consciousness which, as we have seen, clustered around anti-enterprise views and a distrust of formal political structures and parties.

In short, by 'Politics' I mean something much broader than the narrow interpretation usually used by academics (and by this group); something which permeates people's lives more deeply. Hollands (1990) argues that if we define politics as party and institutional politics, then the conventional wisdom, that young people are not interested, holds true, but:

> ... if, however, we take politics to mean an awareness of what is happening in society, a concern over the forces and events shaping everyday lives and anxieties about the future, then surely young people must be viewed as political beings.

Hollands goes on to question:

> ... the limitations of a politics based around purely party or even traditional labour movement concerns. The whole issue of youth politics must be turned on its head and we need to ask how relevant existing parties are to young people's everyday concerns (pp. 180–81).

I would argue that no party, of left, right or centre, should feel happy with the level of support they receive from young people. Even when people had begun to glimpse the structural, social relationships between the political world and their own personal world, they were not convinced by the promises and programmes of the politicians. Certainly the anti-enterprise, anti-Thatcher and anti-Conservativism of this group should not give too much hope to the Left. Young people were disenchanted with the whole political spectrum. They claimed to be anti-Politics – meaning that they did not believe the promises of politicians and that they could see little real difference between the various parties. As Trevor, the failed businessman, put it, when asked if he was interested in politics at all:

> Mixed. I am of the view that I have been poor under this lot and I will under the rest. No matter who gets in I will be poor. It's as simple as that.

So informants talked politically but did not all call their comments Political. We can understand their views as 'common sense'; practical, ordinary ways of making sense of common, shared experiences (in this case of enterprise). Antonio Gramsci's notes on philosophy and 'common sense' are relevant. He argued that '... philosophy is not just the abstract cogitation of a few professional intellectuals but a concrete social activity in which, implicitly, all men [sic] are engaged' (Gramsci, 1971, p. 321). In this sense, philosophy is not confined to the classrooms of the academic ivory towers but can be understood as an everyday, common activity undertaken by all social actors. Within the historical life of the working class, Gramsci continues, people will develop their interpretations of collective experience and their own political views of living under capitalism. In other words, individuals, as a matter of course in their everyday lives, develop their own philosophies or folk-theories of the world. These may be totally at odds with and *resist* the dominant ideologies of the ruling class, they may be fully *incorporated* by and reflect dominant, hegemonic ideas, or, as is perhaps more likely, these working-class political views of the world will both accept *and* resist aspects of the dominant, ruling class interpretation of social reality (see Anyon, 1983).

And so while 'young entrepreneurs' would seem, judging by appearances, to be conformist and conservative, in fact their political responses were quite oppositional and highlighted the ideological contradictions of their experience. In this way, they are what Gramsci might have called 'good sense': practical, critical ways of understanding the economic conditions under and through which people live. These anti-enterprise and anti-Politics views are not what *they* would class as Political; rather, they are good sense, working theories which emerge 'organically' (to borrow another of Gramsci's terms) from the daily practices of trying to survive economically through youth enterprise in Cleveland. To repeat Lynne's phrase, they talk *practically*.

This point lies at the heart of our exploration of informants' political understandings of enterprise. While young men and women in business carry out all the activities of youth enterprise, they nevertheless develop political responses which are quite at odds with the official ideologies and rhetorics of the enterprise culture. Despite the millions of pounds spent on the host of agencies and schemes to graft an enterprise culture on to a locality of declining industrial significance, young people have not been bound up in this ideological project. There has not been a cultural transformation among young people as hoped and planned for by some. Rather, young people in business stoically and doggedly plod on drawing not upon the enterprise skills of business school texts but upon unemployment skills (skills in surviving, getting by and making do); skills learnt in their locality and in their class over many years. The explicit ideological project of the Thatcher years seems to have left this group largely untouched. They have 'resisted' the gospel of enterprise but find in the *practice* of enterprise alternative, positive experiences (e.g. feelings of pride and self-achievement) which they value and celebrate.

Summary and Final Comments

Most of these young men and women did not embark upon the road to business and enterprise with high hopes. They were not, in the main, attracted by the glamour and riches popularly imagined to befall the successful entrepreneur. They did not see themselves as anything special or as living examples of the Thatcherite faith – far from it. The cultural worlds that these young men and women occupied shared far more in common with that of their friends and families on Teesside than with the imagined, rhetorical world of enterprise espoused by politicians and policy-influencers. They were closer materially to the unemployed than to any of the entrepreneurial role models. Their lives and careers were embedded within a local class culture which relied heavily upon welfare benefits of one sort or another. Informants conjured up an image of 'Scheme Land': sometimes brothers, sisters, mothers, fathers all existed on schemes (Employment Training being, at the time, the centrepiece of many working lives). Enterprise had not lifted them out of this culture, though many *had* hoped that it would be an escape from the treadmill of dead-end job, unemployment, government scheme, unemployment.

Lynne, for instance, described her life as a succession of failures from school, through casual jobs, the dole, schemes, failed relationships, a collapsed business, bankruptcy, to the point, in her mid-twenties, from where she now looked back on her 'career'. Ken Roberts' comments (see Chapter 9, this volume) about how working-class young people can interpret a series of disappointments and 'major setbacks' as normal, goes some way to explain the doggedness of this group as they faced quite desperate situations. Lynne, when I last talked to her, was considering setting up in business again. And, at the time of writing, Trevor, who was made unemployed in the first recession of the early 1980s, is now unemployed again in the early 1990s. In the intervening years, he followed all the government's advice: he participated in training (on numerous schemes), he got on his bike and moved to a low-paid, temporary and part-time job in another part of the country and he started his own (failed) enterprise. He is still looking for his first proper job.

With the economic restructuring of Britain radically reshaping the organization and culture of work, perhaps we should be acknowledging that the reality of many people's working lives in many parts of Britain (not just the young of Teesside) is becoming more flexible, fragmented and casualized. Of course, some traditional class-based paths of transition into the labour market remain, as Ken Roberts points out. Prime among these is the academic ladder of A-levels/higher education generally afforded to middle-class youth. While others – for example, the male, skilled, manual apprenticeship route into core employment – have virtually disappeared in localities like Cleveland.

In the place of these time-honoured routes, new ways of making the transition to adulthood are emerging (see Hollands, 1990). The enterprise policies of the Thatcher years certainly helped to develop and promote self-employment and small business as new options for young adults.[9] People like Caroline, one of the few informants in our sample from a non-manual, middle-class background, will continue to draw upon their social, material and cultural advantages to get new firms up and running, with or without the encouragement of politicians and the aid of the government's enterprise schemes.

What I have argued, though, is that enterprise policies have been directed largely at the young and working-class in areas of marginal prosperity – at the unemployed of the so-called 'dependency cultures' of economic decline. I would suggest that it seems a particularly cruel form of economic policy which places the task of individual prosperity and of local economic rejuvenation squarely upon the shoulders of some of those least able and qualified to take the burden. I have hoped to show that some of these young, working-class adults *will* make it, against the odds, to become successful business people. The 'runners' in this group were by no means all middle-class and people like Ronnie may very well plod their way to business security in the long term. Most, though, will return, with Trevor, to the ranks of the unemployed.

In conclusion, what we find in the everyday reality of youth enterprise, behind the jubilant rhetoric of the 'enterprise culture', is simply a new and politically fashionable way for some young, working-class men and women to fail (often drastically), for some, if they are lucky, to become prosperous, successful business people, but for the majority to join a growing number of workers who struggle to make a living in an increasingly casualized, insecure and marginal economy.

Notes

1. I would like to thank the ESRC and Durham University for providing the financial support for this research. The project was carried out with Frank Coffield and his comments on earlier versions of the manuscript are gratefully acknowledged. I would also like to thank Inge Bates for her help in editing this chapter. My main vote of thanks must, however, go to the people who became informants to this study.
2. The numbers of self-employed grew by more than one million during the 1980s (to over three million), and Hakim (1989) has noted a growing involvement with self-employment among young people.
3. The informants were planning to start up, were running firms or had now closed down their businesses. The first group were selected through local enterprise agencies and these were supplemented with later informants contacted in a 'snowballing' strategy. Interviews were audio-taped in people's homes, shops and offices. They were broadly ethnographic in nature, allowing issues not necessarily prefigured in my starting paradigm, to paraphrase Willis (1980, p. 90), the opportunity to arise. Unfortunately, only a handful of informants were met more than once. All the informants have had their names changed to preserve anonymity.
4. I have discussed the problems of classing youth elsewhere (MacDonald, 1991). The sample were working class overall and I will suggest later that the most of the clients of the enterprise industry in Cleveland are working class.

5. Patterns of work in youth enterprise were not surprisingly structured by gender, at least at the initial stages of start up. Some women who had children and associated domestic commitments developed a 'flexible' way of working, which combined this work with part-time jobs and self-employment. Having established businesses, however, the experiences of success and failure that were reported were very similar for men and women and I have not attempted to dissaggregate the analysis by gender.
6. None of these terms should be read as criticism of the personalities of people categorized in this way. I tried unsuccessfully to think of alternative terms, especially to 'plodding', but given that this was a phrase they often used to describe their own experiences, I have decided to retain it.
7. This amount *includes* any Enterprise Allowance (i.e. £40 per week) that informants still received (and most did). Most worked over 50 hours per week to earn this income and, finally, this amount was in many instances used to support informants' own families. The sample we are dealing with here were older than most in studies of youth and some were married with children.
8. This polarity has been observed in earlier studies of working-class culture (e.g. Dennis *et al.*, 1956; Hoggart, 1957).
9. The growth of self-employment during the 1980s can, however, only be partially explained with reference to the enterprise policies of the Thatcher government. Fundamental changes in industrial production, it is argued, have given rise to new patterns for working lives (for a discussion see Piore and Sabel, 1984; Pollert, 1988; Burrows, 1991).

References

Anyon, J. (1983) Intersections of gender and class: accommodation and resistance by working class and affluent females to contradictory sex role ideologies. In S. Walker and L. Barton (eds) *Gender, Class and Education*. Lewes, Falmer Press.

Banks, M. *et al.* (ed.) (1992) *Careers and Identities*. Milton Keynes, Open University Press.

Burrows, R. (ed.) (1991) *Deciphering the Enterprise Culture*. London, Routledge.

Coffield, F. (1990) Hunting a heffalump in the world of the enterprise culture. *The Independent*, 29 August.

Coffield, F., Borrill, C. and Marshall, S. (1986) *Growing Up at the Margins*. Milton Keynes, Open University Press.

Cohen, P. (1983) Losing the generation game. *New Socialist*, 14, 28–36.

Coles, B. and MacDonald, R.F. (1990) From new vocationalism to the culture of enterprise. In C. Wallace and M. Cross (eds) *Youth in Transition*. Lewes, Falmer Press.

Dennis, N., Henriques, F. and Slaughter, C. (1956) *Coal is Our Life*. London, Eyre and Spottiswoode.

Department of Employment (1990) *North-East Labour Market Review*, Summer.

Department of Employment (1991) *Employment Gazette*, June.

Finn, D. (1986) Free Enterprise? *Unemployment Bulletin*, 22, 5–10.

Gramsci, A. (1971) *Selections from Prison Notebooks* (edited and translated by Q. Hoare and G. Nowell Smith). London, Lawrence and Wishart.

Hakim, C. (1988) Self-employment in Britain: recent trends and current issues. *Work, Employment and Society*, 2(4), 421–50.

Hakim, C. (1989) New recruits to self-employment in the 1980s. *Employment Gazette*, June, 286–97.

Harber, C. (ed.) (1987) *Political Education in Britain*. Lewes, Falmer Press.

Hoggart, R. (1957) *The Uses of Literacy*. Harmondsworth, Pelican.

Hollands, R. (1990) *The Long Transition: Class, Culture and Youth Training*. Basingstoke, Macmillan.

MacDonald, R.F. (1991) Youth, class and locality in rural England. *Youth and Policy*, 33, 17–27.

MacDonald, R.F. and Coffield, F. (1991) *Risky Business? Youth and the Enterprise Culture*. Lewes, Falmer Press.

National Audit Office (1988) *Department of Employment/Training Commission: Assistance to Small Firms*, Report 655. London, HMSO.

Piore, M. and Sabel, C. (1984) *The Second Industrial Divide: Possibilities for Prosperity*. New York, Basic Books.

Pollert, A. (1988) Dismantling flexibility. *Capital and Class*, 34, 42–75.

Roberts, K. and Parsell, G. (1988) Opportunity structures and career structures from age 16 to 19. ESRC 16–19 Initiative Occasional Paper Series, No. 1. London, City University.

Roberts, K. and Parsell, G. (1990) The political orientations, interests and activities of Britain's 16–18 year olds in the late 1980s. ESRC Occasional Paper Series, No. 26. London, City University.

Robinson, F. (1990) *The Great North?* A special report for BBC North-East. Newcastle.

Shilling, C. (1989) The mini-enterprise in schools project: a new stage in education–industry relations? *Journal of Education Policy*, 4(2), 115–24.

Storey, D. (1982) *Enterpreneurship and the New Firm*. London, Croom Helm.

Storey, D. and Johnson, S. (1987) *Are Small Firms the Answer to Unemployment?* London, Employment Institute.

Stradling, R. (1977) *The Political Awareness of the School Leaver*. London, The Hansard Society.

Teesside Training and Enterprise Council (1990) *Corporate Plan: 1990–1993*. Middlesbrough, Teesside TEC.

Unemployment Unit (1990) *In With Your Eyes Open*. London, Unemployment Unit.

Ward, R. and Jenkins, R. (eds) (1984) *Ethnic Communities in Business*. Cambridge, Cambridge University Press.

Willis, P. (1980) Notes on method. In S. Hall *et al.* (eds) *Culture, Media, Language: Working Papers in Cultural Studies, 1972–1979*. London, Hutchinson.

Chapter 5

A Yuppie Generation?

Political and cultural options for A-level students[1]

John Quicke

Introduction

The link between social class, education and political attitudes and beliefs has been reaffirmed by a recent analysis of the ESRC's 16–19 Initiative survey data (see Banks *et al.*, 1992). In general, pupils who succeed in the education system tend to identify with the middle class and vote Conservative. For pupils from middle-class backgrounds, educational success reinforces a conservative political orientation. For working-class pupils, the social class for which they are headed, as indicated by educational attainments, exerts more influence on their political views than their class of origin. The authors conclude that although there may be 'a long term trend in Britain towards a weaker relationship between politics and social class ... according to our evidence, the links are being transmitted to incoming generations of voters in the 1980s'.

In this chapter, the aim is to examine some of the social–psychological processes involved in the production and development of these links. The analysis draws on data from an ethnographic study of sixth-formers in Sheffield in the late 1980s. The students in question were all taking A-levels. With one or two exceptions, they came from families who were socially mobile and had experienced considerable 'improvement' in their material situation and social status in the previous ten years. Most might be described as upper working class or lower middle class, who perceived themselves as still in the process of 'rising' by their own efforts into the middle class. Given their parents' success and their own educational success in a period of right-wing political leadership, we might expect of such students that they would favour conservatism and even be among Thatcherism's most ardent supporters.

On the other hand, one might also speculate about possible countervailing tendencies to these powerful determinants. The political culture of the neighbourhoods in which many of them had been brought up, and to which many now lived adjacent, was strongly pro-Labour. Sheffield was a city where traditional working-class politics was still a dominant if declining force. The families had remained near enough geographically to relatives and old friends to make regular contact a possibility. Moreover, these particular students were all taking A-level sociology as one of their subjects and were therefore perhaps more aware than the average student of alternative views of society. The fact they had chosen this particular subject may in itself have suggested a predisposition to a 'left' rather than 'right' orientation.

Method

The study involved interviewing twenty-one students (ten males and eleven females) from the upper and lower sixth in groups and individually in a sixth-form centre. The interviews were semi-structured and wide-ranging, covering matters to do with family background and leisure activities as well as 'politics'. An interview guide was used that consisted of items partly derived from an overview of the relevant literature and partly from informal conversation carried out with students during the course of an ethnographic study. The researcher had previously negotiated a teaching role in the school and had spent many hours over several weeks talking to students informally in the centre. At the time of the interviews, he was a familiar figure and on friendly terms with most of the interviewees. Some aspects of the interview responses were readily checked in conversation outside the formal interview structure and by observation of interactions in the classroom and the centre. Rapport was established, the students were forthcoming and seemed to welcome the opportunity to put their views on tape. Since they were taking A-level sociology, far from being perceived as a waste of time, participation in a research project was considered useful as well as interesting.

The set-up had possible advantages and disadvantages. The obvious disadvantage was that, although the researcher had been invited into the school initially by one of the students, the study had eventually been officially sanctioned by the school. The students might therefore have regarded the researcher as part of the authority structure and as someone whose opinion might contribute to the teachers' assessment of them in some way. One of the obvious advantages was that the students might turn out to be sociologically astute observers of themselves and their peers, making access to relevant material easier for the researcher. Clearly, there were many arguments for and against this approach, but it was decided that on balance there was more to be gained than lost by using this opportunity sample.

The Study

Interest in and knowledge of politics varied among the group, but most were not as politically apathetic as their initial diffidence on interview seemed to suggest. Some who denied an interest in politics, as conventionally defined, at the present time were adamant that this was a temporary state. In the future, they anticipated taking more of an interest. In fact, most of the group showed themselves to be capable of articulating reasonably informed views on a wide range of political and social issues. Some issues were more up front than others because they were perceived as more 'relevant' to the concerns of young people.

At an early point in most of the interviews, the interviewees were asked point blank about their views on three political characters – Margaret Thatcher, Tony Benn and Arthur Scargill. The aim was to obtain their immediate responses to three familiar and controversial figures with a view to establishing a starting point for the exploration of political consciousness. Previous research has shown that young people are reasonably well informed about national political leaders and about local politics (Furnham and Gunter, 1983). These three therefore seemed appropriate choices: Thatcher for obvious reasons; Benn because he was MP for a nearby constituency; and Scargill because of the proximity of the coalfields.

Interestingly, Benn was not as well known as anticipated. At least half the interviewees said that they did not know he was MP for a nearby constituency. The other half had nothing positive to say about him. They felt he was a 'loony lefty', someone who had done a great deal of harm to the Labour Party by destroying its electoral appeal. Scargill was also in general viewed negatively as someone who had 'benefited the Conservatives by his antics', who fomented trouble for personal gain, who used the miners as a political tool, who was too confrontational, who was 'utterly left-wing', who 'over-reacted', who was an 'idiot', 'a complete waste of time' and who was always contradicting himself. However, unlike Benn he was known to all the interviewees and attracted at least two critical but supportive comments – 'His heart is in the right place but he went about it [i.e. the miners' strike] in the wrong way' and 'He was trying to save the community but he should have had a ballot.' Thatcher was also unpopular with nearly all the group. She was 'pigheaded', 'ruthless', 'cold', 'heartless', 'helped the Tories line their own pockets', 'was too biased towards the rich'. However, there was one crucial difference compared with comments on Benn and Scargill. Over half the interviewees, even though they did not agree with most of her politics, felt she was a 'strong leader'; they admired her for that and thought she had done 'some good things'.

These comments on the three figures suggested further lines of enquiry. Perhaps the negative comments reflected a rejection of what were perceived as the politics of extremism and an embrace of the politics of the centre?

However, perhaps there was a difference in attitudes towards left and right extremism – with the former being treated as 'treacherous' or, alternatively, as 'a joke', and the latter more as a necessary evil; the implication being that the only serious political debate was between centre and right rather than centre and left or right and left.

In relation to the first point, voting intentions were revealing. Of the twenty-one students, four were don't knows – two of whom seemed to be moving towards the Conservative Party ('I think I'm more Conservative than Labour, but I'm not sure') – five were Labour supporters, six Conservative supporters, three SDP (as it was then called) and three were wavering between Labour and SDP. Both Labour and Conservative supporters said they were 'middle of the road' or words to that effect. When asked to say more about why they would vote for a particular party, most said they would vote Conservative because they were 'good' for the economy and Labour because of their 'caring' policies and support for the Welfare State. But neither Conservative nor Labour supporters were in favour of all the policies of their chosen party. Most of the Conservatives, for example, were particularly scathing about the poll tax and wholesale privatization.

Support for centre politics was also evident in their definitions of right- and left-wing and their attitudes to trade unions, gender, race and education. The majority felt that right-wing was about 'personal achievement' and left-wing about the redistribution of wealth and support for the weak (e.g. 'standing up for people who can't stand up for themselves'). The dominant view was that a balance should be struck between individualistic and collectivist policies, although as we shall see later some students leaned more towards the left end of the spectrum, others towards the right.

There was no support for radical or militant feminism. Most felt strongly that women should have equal opportunities in education and the job market and that for the most part this had been achieved. With some exceptions, both the male and female students felt that boys and girls had been treated equally in their schools. Whatever their political allegiances, most of the girls agreed they had never experienced gross discrimination at any stage of their school careers and they felt that they personally had had an equal opportunity to succeed in the system. This was not to say that further reforms were not needed. Sexual discrimination still occurred, but they felt society was improving in this respect and that feminists took it too far, anyway. As for racism, they were all opposed to it, but felt that some people made too much of it, usually for political reasons. Racist attitudes existed but it was only because the people who held them lacked education. 'Education' in fact was perceived as a cure for most social evils. All these youngsters were great supporters of it. Of course, they believed in education for all, but education as a ladder of opportunity was emphasized even more. Most had a favourable view of their own education, said they believed in state rather than private education, were grateful for the opportunity to succeed and felt that those pupils who failed to seize their opportunities did so either because they did not have the ability or because they had received no support from home. They contrasted this with their own experience. If they had to pick out one factor which explained their own educational success, it was the encouragement given to them by their parents.

As for trade unions, the general thrust of their responses suggested support for the existence of trade unions and industrial action that was within the law. When asked for their views on the current seamen's strike, most said the seamen had a right to strike even though in this case it was somewhat futile: 'The employees are bound to win. The workers haven't a hope!' Attitudes to trade unions also reflected attitudes to left and right extremism. Politically motivated trade union activity of the Scargill variety was definitely beyond the pale. It was immoral, undemocratic and counter-productive. The abolition of trade unions – perceived as the Thatcher line on unions – was also thought to be an extremist policy, but it was taken more seriously and rather than dismiss it out of hand, the argument needed to be engaged with.

> The unions do have too much power and they used to practically run the country before Mrs Thatcher . . . but now it's gone too far in the other direction. She doesn't like the unions – doesn't really want them to exist. You'll always need trade unions. You've got to have free collective bargaining – that's the fairest way.

A typical view, but underpinning this was a general belief in the need for a well-run, efficient and competitive economy and it was one of the 'good things' of Thatcherism that this was on the way to being achieved. Even among Labour supporters, the rejection of Thatcher was not as uncompromising as some previous studies have shown (see Billig and Cochrane, 1982).

Processes: An Analysis

In analysing social–psychological processes, we need to keep in mind our starting point of the likely connection between the sixth-formers' emergent political consciousness and their social backgrounds. Two things need to be established: first, that this political consciousness *is* linked to key aspects of students' social identities and interests and, secondly, that such aspects are ones which it is reasonable to assume are grounded in primary socialization processes. We cannot be satisfied with an explanation which merely links students' political views to the social class position of their parents. It has to be shown that such a link is subjectively meaningful in terms of 'moral career' development, i.e. the changing sense of self-in-the-world and the changing framework of imagery for understanding the self in relation to others.

To take the second point first – the relationship between current identity and primary socialization. It is perfectly possible, of course, for these two phenomena to be dissociated, and a 'new' identity created as a result of a complete break with the identity established by primary socialization. Youth have in the past created alternative life-styles and counter-cultures involving 'total transformations' of consciousness and the deconstruction of the social world of their parents. When there is such discontinuity between generations, we often speak of a generation gap. Was that the case here? Given that these students were probaly going to be as socially mobile as their parents, did that mean they were in any sense anticipating transformations of identity as they 'rose'? Or was it more likely their emerging self concepts were continuous with earlier forms, a case of secondary socialization rather than re-socialization (see Berger and Luckmann, 1971).

On interview it was clear that, for nearly all these students, parents still constituted significant others in their lives. Whether relations with parents were perceived as harmonious or conflictual, they were principal agents in maintaining the students' sense of self and identity in the world. When they spoke about their family backgrounds, they did so in a way which suggested that they themselves felt at least partly if not totally immersed in their parents' world. This world was one in which, in the majority of cases, social mobility was a critical and relatively recent experience.

Sixteen of the twenty-one students had fathers who were on a similar rung on the social ladder – self-employed craftsmen, owners of small businesses, foremen or white-collar workers in the commercial sector. Most of the fathers, and in some cases mothers, had begun their working careers in skilled manual or other working-class jobs and had moved on to 'better things', usually, although not always, because they had been made redundant when a steelworks had closed down. Jobs descriptions now included self-employed electrician, small builder, window cleaner, insurance salesman, training officer, foreman, school registrar, college of further education lecturer, merchandizer, Gas Board 'engineer'. Of the remaining five, one still worked in a steelworks, one was unemployed and three had always been in middle-class occupations. Nearly all of the parents were perceived as aspiring and very concerned that their offspring should receive the 'good education' which they themselves had missed out on. Most of them had left school early, but this was not perceived as having 'failed' at school. In those days, presumably the mid- to late 1960s, there was no point in staying on because 'you didn't need a good education to get a good job'. At the same time, there was also a suggestion that parents wanted their offspring to have a better working life than they themselves had had – one that was more secure because of a 'good education' and a 'good set of qualifications'.

All of the students regarded themselves as coming from families which were comfortably off but it was clear that some families were better off than others and the students were aware of this. At one end of the scale were those parents who were buying their own council houses and still lived on a council estate, while at the other there were parents who owned detached houses in one of the more expensive parts of the city. The students accepted their parents' interpretations about the status of the area in which they now lived and which neighbourhoods were a move up or a move down status-wise. All this was quite finely tuned, had several gradations and reflected a working knowledge of the 'worth' of an area which they no doubt shared with estate agents! Thus one female student said:

> Once you're off the council estate . . . well, you might have a private house in Ridgebrook and then you might move to Horton, but then again Big Horton is better than Little Horton and Bagley Street is better than Upper Stavey Lane in Little Horton. Of course, everyone wants to live in Broadhurst!

For the most part, both parents and offspring anticipated success in moving upwards and the 'ladder of opportunity' was an idea they appreciated and accepted as part and parcel of how things were. Thus their sense of self included the notion that they were part of a social grouping which was in a relatively good position on the ladder and had a stake in society. Some families lived in 'nicer' areas, perhaps because their fathers had been established in their new occupations or new businesses for several years longer than other fathers (in some cases, it depended on when they had been made redundant – they were better off if this occurred in the early rather than mid- or late 1980s) or because their mothers were in full-time work or occupationally mobile themselves. But most perceived their families as being in the same social class – upper working to lower middle – and aspiring to be middle class. Even the minority who felt their parents were more entrenched in middle-class occupations and neighbourhoods, apart from two, were only one generation away from the council estate and the manual working class.

As well as perceiving themselves as young persons from socially mobile backgrounds who were themselves socially mobile, the students also recognized that for their parents the process of embourgeoisement or becoming full-fledged middle-class people was far from complete, and that many were still culturally and emotionally attached to the working class. 'Our relatives and a lot of our friends are still from where we used to live' was a typical comment. Many still lived and perhaps purposely chose to live in private housing not far from their 'roots'. Others, however, by accident or design had created considerable geographical and in some cases social and cultural space between themselves and their backgrounds. The process of acculturation was incomplete but relentlessly ongoing – 'My dad doesn't go back there much now. He's even joined the golf club. I'm afraid he's bending with age!'

The point to note here is that being socially mobile and coming from families with 'roots' in the working class was a significant part of the 'framework of imagery' (see Goffman, 1961, p. 19) for judging themselves and interpreting their 'moral careers', in contrast to the findings of some previous studies of working and 'upper working', and lower middle-class girls (McRobbie, 1978; Frazer, 1988), for whom social class was not a relevant organizing category. The salience of social class imagery for the current identities of the present sample was one of the most important starting points for their thinking about politics, because it was readily relatable to politics. If their dominant self-perceptions had featured other continuities with primary socialization (for instance, they may have given more emphasis to personality traits or characteristics – e.g. 'I'm lazy, I inherited that from my mother'), then they would arguably have been less easy to link with emergent political consciousness. As it was, a self-imagery rooted in a culture of social mobility and class consciousness was resonant with political possibilities and may even have made some political orientations more likely than others.

But what political orientations? What political agenda was thereby constructed? To understand this we need to take account of the political culture of a locality where historically 'labourism' and to some extent socialism had been, and up to a point were still, significant if declining ideological forces. Labourism describes that special but loose relationship between the industrial and political aims of the labour movement which gave rise to the Labour Party as a major political force. It was predicated on the split between political and economic institutions and encouraged the notion that trade unions could help working-class people achieve their aspirations within the framework of the existing system. The Labour Party was not supported for its ideals but because it was perceived as the party that represented the interests of labour. Though a collectivist movement as John MacInnes (1987, p. 162) points out, certainly in its early years, labourism may even be construed as having helped to preserve 'enterprise culture' (a culture which has a long history in Britain and is not a Thatcherite innovation) by playing its part in the maintenance of social order and regulation of the economy. The link with socialism was loose. Hobsbawm (1984) refers to how identifying with the working class increased the chances of identifying with the party of the workers, which could mean being in conflict with capitalism and then *for* socialism. In places like Sheffield, it was undoubtedly true that labourism helped to shape what Kiernan (1979) describes as a 'sober municipal socialist mentality'.

Continuing attachment to this declining political culture, though probably varying in strength from one family to another, could well have acted as something of a counterweight to the embrace of the rampant bourgeois individualism of the 1980s. In terms of these sixth-formers' political consciousness, it meant support for those institutions historically ameliorative of the working-class condition – the trade unions and the institutions of the Welfare State, particularly education. Many of the students regarded their own educational careers as a realization of traditional aspirations: 'I'm the first person in our family who is likely to go to university. My parents are really proud of me. I can't let them down.'

It is scarcely surprising, then, that these youngsters, even those describing themselves as 'socialists', were totally opposed to what they perceived as extremism of the left. They could not support a movement which sought, as they saw it, to tear down those 'democratic' institutions which had given them success and which had been constructed by their forefathers in the interests mainly of working-class people. The egalitarian values inherent in labourism would also of course entail opposition to racism and sexism. They themselves were 'educated' and therefore could see how racism and sexism contradicted the principle of equality of opportunity and perhaps felt they could see this better than working-class or ex-working-class people, like their parents, who were not educated:

> It's still a problem. Because I'm a girl, my parents ask me to do more domestic chores than my brother.
>
> Metal work teachers in our school are chauvinistic, because many of them were workers in industry.
>
> My parents are racist but they don't understand.

However, the Thatcherite version of conservatism did not have much appeal either. This was also perceived as in the business of dismantling state institutions. In addition, it was bent on destroying the trade union movement. As indicated above, the general view of the students was that trade unions had a right to exist and a right to represent their members' interests. At the same time, perhaps, because they were more aware of 'new times' (see Hall, 1988), of changing economic, political and social structures, of the decline of the traditional working class, of a new political agenda (including 'green' issues, for example) and of the 'you can't buck the market' philosophy, their own critical consciousness was being formed in a world that was becoming significantly different from the one in which their parents had been brought up. Collectivism may have played its part in creating beneficent structures and institutions, but it was now possibly out of date. In the new world, there seemed to be a greater emphasis on initiative, enterprise, flexibility, self-help, choice, etc., and this was why Thatcherism had to be taken seriously – it was the movement most closely identified with these 'new' imperatives.

Thus the students' subjective reality, while continuous with their parents' social world, was being modified in subtle but significant ways. This was not unexpected because to be part of society inevitably entails involvement in ongoing processes of identity change (Berger and Luckmann, 1971, p. 176), processes which in the students' view would be supported if not fully understood by parents:

> They want me to go my own way. It depends on what job I get and where I live. I might be whizzing off everywhere and not have much time to see them.

> They've no idea what university life is like. It's not all work! . . . but they'd accept it because they want me to get qualified.

Further socialization was anticipated but evidently it was secondary rather than re-socialization, and transformations of subjective reality would be partial and connected with moving up a notch or two on the social ladder to become full-fledged middle-class persons. However, although modifications to identity and political consciousness would be circumscribed, this did not mean variations within these parameters would be socially or psychologically trivial or insignificant. The changes which in fact did occur were not all of a piece. All were 'rising' into the middle class, but their interpretations of this differed and it was here that differences in emergent political identity could be detected. There were clearly some students who identified strongly with one aspect of their parents' world, namely the petit bourgeois, individualist tendency. If anything, they actively rejected what they perceived as working-class influence and consciously made an effort to remove whatever traces of it were left in their own personalities and friendship groups, as they proceeded to cultivate middle-class friends and middle-class life-styles. Their reference group was made up of students whose parents could unambiguously be described as middle class; who were, as one student put it, at the 'top of the spectrum' in terms of social background; who were not a large group but one which was over-represented in the sixth-form; who tended to be cliquey, belong to squash and tennis clubs, went to certain up-market night clubs regularly and had cars 'bought by daddy' or, if not, could always borrow daddy's car; who were the 'jet set' or pacesetters', the ones with 'money behind them'.

Those students who positively identified with the 'pacesetters' I shall call *élitists*. Élitists were aware they were not equal to 'pacesetters' in terms of background and material resources but aspired to a cultural affinity with them. The hierarchical nature of the social order and social classes was accepted as part of how things were, and was not perceived as a disintegrative force (see Robins, 1988). Some tended to talk disparagingly about the working class. One female student recalled having lived in a cheap private house near a council estate, but saw herself as having moved away 'from all that'; it had more to do with her parents than her, as far as she was concerned. She felt that working-class people were unsuitable for many of the jobs which were currently available.

... the steel industry is closing down, and it's going more into the sort of tertiary, you know, private sector jobs and to be honest, a large proportion of the population won't be suited to that sort of job. I mean that rules out a lot of the working class to be honest.

A male student, originally from a school in a working-class area, described how 'if you were not careful your mates would drag you down'. He was referring to the working-class mates that he used to have; that is, 'if you could call them mates – they were always calling me "swot", you know, just because they weren't clever themselves'. Sexism was viewed as a working-class phenomenon:

At some parties, they just treated the girls as 'objects', like a can of lager! I don't go to those sort of parties – well there is a bit of that, but in the sixth-form we tend to talk to girls more.

Like several of his contemporaries, he had made a conscious effort to cultivate middle-class friends. The only thing he now did with his old friends was to go to football matches, and that did not happen very often. Like other élitists, he expressed a negative attitude towards a group of Youth Training Scheme (YTS) students who also used the sixth-form centre. It was evident that relations between these 'lads' and the sixth-formers were not good. Recently, there had been complaints that the 'lads' were rowdy, smoked illegally and made a mess in parts of the centre where they were not supposed to be. Another male student referred to the YTS group as 'looking like slobs, dressing like slobs and behaving like slobs'. All they did was 'riot around school'. A female student felt that, 'to put it frankly, they haven't got a brain between them'. They got paid £28 a week for virtually doing nothing. All they did was knock a few pieces of wood together and they called that training. Another female student from the upper-sixth said:

They [i.e. the YTS group] are terrible ... they run round, I mean, we're here all the time, they're not, and we have to put up with it. They come in a couple of days a week and run riot, leave crisp packets all over the place, smoke where they like and just abuse it ... they're just yobs! It's just a labouring YTS ...

When asked to explain educational failure, the élitists were more likely to emphasize a lack of ability than a lack of family support. Their view of human nature tended to be that people were basically selfish and that the 'right' were more realistic in this respect than the 'left':

Left-wing is more helping less well off people in society, more taking more money from the richer people and giving it out to the poor ... Sounds pretty good, but I don't think it works like that. Right-wing tends to give a more selfish impression, more go for what you can get and doesn't matter about everybody else but I think that's what everybody is after anyway . . . lower-class people say that more money should be taken off other people and given to them, but if *they* had the money they wouldn't be thinking that.

'Going for it' was a typical phrase of an élitist. They didn't particularly like Mrs Thatcher but she did at least 'go for it'. They perceived themselves as 'going for it', not only in terms of educational qualifications, but also in terms of earning money by doing part-time jobs – money which they spent on such things as driving lessons, skiing holidays and keep-fit classes. Their parents were comfortably off but not so well off that they could keep on financing their offsprings' expensive leisure pursuits. In any case, going out to work and earning your own money was 'virtuous' behaviour – it meant you were doing something for yourself and not being a burden on other people. Provided it did not interfere with homework, it was all right to work in a shop on Saturdays, to serve behind a bar or work as a waitress in the evenings. For some, money seemed to be a 'good thing' in itself. When asked about the best things in life, one said 'my family and my money'; another said 'my girlfriend who I love and my money'.

Jobs to which they aspired tended to be in the private sector – trainee managers, hotel and catering, tourism, quantity surveying. They were aiming to go to university or polytechnic, but they did not value higher education for its own sake. If a really good job opportunity came their way in the near future, they would 'grab' it and forget about going on to higher education: 'If I got a trainee manager's job with Marks and Spencer, I'd go for it.'

Politically, although within the parameters discussed previously, this group tended to be conservative or moving towards conservatism. A few said they were not interested in politics. One described himself as 'right-wing' and some liked to think of themselves as 'new' conservatives, but in fact they were not as right-wing as they thought they were. They supported state intervention on most things and did not believe in wholesale privatization or the poll tax. The élitists themselves were a minority but they represented a cultural option for the rest of the group, some of whom were becoming more aspirant; others were oscillating in typical adolescent fashion between different perspectives and some were opposed to the élitist group who they described as 'yuppies'. Although a minority, however, one had the impression that élitists felt they were swimming with the tide and other sixth-formers knew this. It was only a matter of time before most of the others moved in the same direction. This was certainly the view of those subscribing to another clearly definable perspective who for want of a better term we shall call the *nostalgics*. This group saw themselves as a minority group of 'socialists' who, in contrast to the élitists, were swimming *against* the tide. They felt that most of their colleagues, including even some of their closest friends, were becoming part of the 'yuppie generation' and were gradually becoming conservative:

> I would say that there would be about 30 per cent that would definitely vote Conservative. I think there's about 50 per cent that are don't knows, that are certainly on the brink of voting Conservative in my opinion and the rest would vote Labour. It's a yuppie generation.

> The majority of them are Conservative. I get called Karl Marx and commie and things like that; it's only banter, but they're definitely right-wing.

If the élitists emphasized the upwardly mobile, self-help aspects of the parent culture, the nostalgics tended to identify with parents' affiliation to working-class origins. they tended not to see themselves as moving unproblematically into the middle class. The clearest expression of this perspective was provided by a female student, Julia, whose relationship with her father was conflictual precisely because she felt he was 'confused' about his class position and voted Conservative, whereas she identified with working-class attitudes. She felt her mother was still working class, and so was the area in which they lived. Most of her friends were from working-class backgrounds. For her, the jet set or 'pacesetters' were a group whose perspective and life-style were in marked contrast to her own. She felt the majority of them came from middle-class backgrounds and 'set the tone' in the sixth-form because they were the dominant group. She perceived her own reference group as coming from less well-off backgrounds. The main difference between herself and an élitist was that she was not preoccupied with attempts to distance herself from working-class friends and acquaintances.

In general, the nostalgics adopted a more tolerant and less rejecting attitude towards the YTS 'lads'. They thought that some of the views of the other students were 'snobbish'. One admitted that the 'lads' had caused one or two problems, but thought they should not be 'blamed' for their behaviour and another felt they were 'all right once you got to know them'. Other differences with élitists were reflected in attitudes to careers. For most nostalgics, the aim was to go to university or polytechnic and they did not anticipate leaving higher education even for a 'job with prospects' before they obtained their degrees. If they had a career in mind at all, it was to work in the public sector as a qualified professional – teacher, nurse, social worker, psychologist.

Politically, this group supported Labour and tended to be more aware of political issues than the élitists. They described themselves as 'socialist' but their views were well within the parameters described above. There was no sense in which their views were counter-hegemonic (see Prewitt, 1978). They were not opposed to private property, and viewed state institutions like education as unproblematically facilitative of working-class aspirations. They are described as nostalgics because their attachment to working-class culture was retrospective and somewhat romantic. There was clearly a gap between their egalitarian rhetoric and the reality of their day-to-day social relationships. Although their friends used to be working class, they were increasingly less so, despite the fact some of them still lived in areas which they described as 'poor'. They tended to spend their leisure time more quietly and less expensively (!) than the élitists – doing homework, visiting friends who were also sixth-formers, watching TV or reading or other home-based activities, with occasional forays to pubs and clubs.

Summary and Concluding Discussion

To re-cap, an analysis of interview responses of a group of sixth-formers suggests that:

1. Parents were still principal agents in maintaining the students' sense of self and identity in the world.
2. Emerging self-concepts were continuous with earlier forms.
3. Self-perceptions derived from immersion in a social world where the family experience of social mobility and class identity was a significant theme.
4. These identities and the social interests to which they gave rise were readily relatable to an emergent political consciousness oriented towards the politics of the centre and opposed to extremism.
5. Although left and right extremism were opposed, the latter was taken more seriously and the key debate was thought to be between the centre and the right.
6. Abrupt discontinuities within the subjective biographies of individuals had been avoided but modifications and partial transformations of subjective reality between generations were evident.
7. There was scope for choice in terms of moral career.
8. Two moral career options seemed to be available – the 'élitist' and the 'nostalgic'.

It is not being suggested that all students could be fitted into one or other of these ideal types. A number oscillated between options – in one interview veering towards élitists and in a follow-up interview towards nostalgics. Some seemed happy to combine elements from both options in a contradictory way. At least two students denied the continuing social reality of classes, a reality which was a significant feature of both the élitist and nostalgic perspectives. One thought social classes were 'fading out' and another thought that it was 'bad social science' to look at the world in class terms. But whatever their perspectives, for most students these two types were meaningful categories, ones which were adequate (see Schutz, 1972) in the sense that they could be 'translated' into their own terminology, e.g. 'snobs', 'yuppies', 'self-centred', 'socialists', 'hippies', 'old-fashioned'; and ones which acted as cultural markers and reference points for self-definition.

The above analysis has generated categories and hypotheses which, though empirically grounded, clearly require further 'saturation' (see Glaser and Strauss, 1967) and testing. Future research might usefully focus on an elaboration and further illumination of the social processes tentatively sketched here, particularly those relating to the influence of peer reference groups and the role of significant others like parents. But in concluding it is important briefly to acknowledge two other contributory factors, under-investigated in the present study but deserving of more consideration in the future, namely the media and the school curriculum. Phrases like 'loony left' and 'yuppie' are media terms. A number of students said they regularly watched documentaries and current affairs programmes, but since these were often used as discussion material in subjects like sociology, the influence of the media was difficult to disentangle from other influences.

In the present study, in so far as it was possible to discern a curriculum effect, it was evident that the salience of class noted above was reinforced but not produced by studying sociology. The latter also probably contributed to the formation of political consciousness by reaffirming the significance of the 'social dimension' in identity.

In a previous study, Robins (1976) found that social science students were more politicized than other students in the sense that they were more prepared to identify with the left or the right. However, *on average*, students on a British Government course appeared to have similar views to those of a representative sample of sixth-formers. This contrasted with those studying economics, who tended to be more right-wing than the sample. Robins concludes that 'students who assessed themselves as working class were most vulnerable to the curriculum effect and particularly that of Economics'.

With no comparison group of a representative sample of sixth-formers, it was impossible to say whether the students in the present investigation were more politicized than other students. One's general impression was that they were probably more capable of articulating their political views but were no more polarized between right and left than any of their contemporaries. As for school subjects, there was no obvious relationship between different subjects or combinations of subjects taken and political orientation. However, overall, the students themselves felt their studies had contributed to the formation of the political views. Several said they used knowledge gained from their studies in discussions with parents.

There was no evidence that sociology was responsible for inculcating a left-wing orientation, as is often supposed. The students in general felt that it encouraged them 'to look at both sides of an argument'. In educational terms, it seemed to have a liberalizing effect. Nevertheless, there were a few students who felt that sociology did have a left-wing bias and they perceived even the mere inclusion of a Marxist or conflict perspective in the curriculum, as evidence of this. Interestingly, no student complained of right-wing bias.

Note

This study was one of five ethnographic studies conducted in the Division of Education, University of Sheffield. The chapter has been published in *Cambridge Journal of Education*, 21(1), 5–18, 1991, 'Social background, identity and political consciousness in the sixth form'.

References

Banks, M. *et al.* (1992) *Careers and Identities*. Milton Keynes, Open University Press.

Berger, P.L. and Luckmann, T. (1971) *The Social Construction of Reality*. Harmondsworth, Penguin.

Billig, M. and Cochrane, R. (1982) Lost generation. *New Socialist*, November/December, 38–41.

Frazer, E. (1988) Teenage girls talking about class. *Sociology*, 22(3), 343–58.

Furnham, A. and Gunter, B. (1983) Political knowledge and awareness in adolescents. *Journal of Adolescence*, 6, 373–85.

Glaser, B.G. and Strauss, A.L. (1967) *The Discovery of Grounded Theory*. London, Weidenfeld and Nicolson.

Goffman, E. (1961) *Asylums*. Harmondsworth, Penguin.

Hall, S. (1988) Brave new world. *Marxism Today*, October, 24–9.

Hobsbawm, E.J. (1984) Labour: rump or rebirth. *Marxism Today*, March, 8–13.

Kiernan, V. (1979) Labour and the literate in nineteenth-century Britain. In D. Martin and D. Rubinstein (eds) *Ideology and the Labour Movement*. London, Croom Helm.

MacInnes, J. (1987) *Thatcherism at Work*. Milton Keynes, Open University Press.

McRobbie, A. (1978) Working class girls and the culture of femininity. In CCCS Women's Studies Group, *Women Take Issue*. London, Hutchinson.

Prewitt, K. (1978) Political socialization research in the United States: can we get to where we should be going from where we have been? *International Journal of Political Education*, 1, 111–26.

Robins, L. (1976) Social sciences and political socialization in the sixth form: a case study. *Teaching Politics*, 5, 41–53.

Robins, L. (1988) Political socialization in British schools: some political and sociological approaches. *Teaching Politics*, 17(1), 19–41.

Schutz, A. (1972) *The Phenomenology of the Social World*. London, Heinemann.

Chapter 6

Gaining the Edge
Girls at a private school

— Debra Roker —

Introduction

... everything has changed for me since I started here really. Going
to a private school just gives you so much more, in every way.

This chapter explores how private education helps some young people gain
the 'edge' over young people educated in the state sector of education. It
details the ways in which parents and pupils perceived the benefits of
paying for education, and suggests the ways in which the school enabled
its pupils to succeed in education and gain entry into university and high-
status professional careers. It will be argued that privately educated girls
develop an edge over other young people generally and, moreover, other
young women from the same social class. Processes are described through
which these girls acquire an edge over other groups of young people aiming for high-status careers. The link between private education and the
production of an élite in society is also discussed.

The private sector of education has tended to grow steadily, most
noticeably during the time of Thatcher's government. When the Conservatives came to power in 1979, 5.8 per cent of all school-age pupils were
being educated privately. By 1990, this figure had risen to 7.4 per cent,
private schools currently educating over half a million children and young
people (DES, 1991). This increase in the number of pupils in the private
sector was matched by an increased level of support by the Thatcher
government for the private sector. Private education was supported because
it was seen as providing increased parental choice, with the early introduction of the Assisted Places Scheme (APS) designed to extend this choice
to all parents of academically able children regardless of their financial
situation. Private education was also supported because of the association
of private schools with high academic standards, traditional values and
competition (see Johnson, 1990; Senker, 1990; Walford, 1990). Walford
(1987) identifies three main areas of support by the Thatcher government

for the private sector of education. First, the introduction of the APS, which by 1985–86 had enabled over 21,000 children and young people to receive a private education at public expense (see Edwards *et al.*, 1989). Secondly, ideological support, in terms of the introduction of the APS (which implies that private schools are more able to provide a good academic education than state schools) and general criticisms of the state sector. A good example of such criticism was a comment by the then Secretary of State for Education Kenneth Clarke, who said that he did not know anyone who would not send their children to a private school if they could afford to (*Times Education Supplement*, 21 June 1991). Thirdly, financial support has been evident, in the form of funding from the APS (with many schools only able to remain open with the income the APS provides), and various tax and VAT advantages (see Robson and Walford, 1989).

Despite the recent growth of the private sector, and the increased level of support given to it by the current government, the experiences of young people in private schools have been largely neglected by researchers. Research and debate on the private sector has generally been focused either on particular types of schools (e.g. Walford's, 1986, study of life in a prestigious boys school), or on issues of the policy and politics of private education (e.g. Edwards *et al.*, 1984). Most noticeably, the experiences of girls in the private sector have been largely ignored, with the notable exception of Delamont's study of peer groups and social interaction in a Scottish private school (Delamont, 1973, 1984). The paucity of research on females in private education has led Fox (1985, p. 334) to claim that '... there are virtually no details about girls in the private sector'. Most of the research that has been conducted, however, has demonstrated considerable differences in the academic achievement, aspirations and career paths of young people who are educated in private and state sector schools (Eglin, 1984; Halsey *et al.*, 1984). The outcomes of a private education are described by the majority of researchers in terms of high levels of academic achievement, and entry into further education and high-status professional careers (see Walford, 1990).

Some researchers, generally psychologists, have shifted the emphasis of research away from tangible, quantifiable research foci such as the academic achievement and career paths of those educated in the private and state sectors, to exploring possible differences in the attitudes and orientations of the young people in these schools. These researchers have frequently identified the privately educated as having a distinctive right-wing political and socio-economic orientation, demonstrated for example in studies revealing their more individualistic person-based explanations for unemployment and poverty (Furnham, 1982; Feather, 1983), and in their greater acceptance of, and justification for, social inequalities and income differences (Emler and Dickinson, 1985; Emler *et al.*, 1990). Few researchers, however, have explored the actual processes by which the experience of a private education may affect the opportunities, careers and identities of its pupils. Thus the role of the private school experience as an influence on youth socialization has largely been neglected.

The aim of the research described in this chapter was to investigate the ways in which private education affects the opportunities and identities of young people educated in private schools, focusing on the processes by which these young people gain the 'edge' in the areas of education, training and careers. The research was part of a doctoral study, linked to the main 16–19 Initiative, which compared the political and socio-economic socialization of young people educated in private and state schools (Roker, 1991). The study was based on individual interviews held with 67 girls aged 15–18 years, attending a selective and prestigious private girls' school in the North of England. The interviews were designed to explore the attitudes, values and experiences relating to education and careers, as well as a broad range of political and socio-economic issues. In addition, a number of interviews were held with the parents of some of these pupils, members of the careers staff at the school, and eight boys who were also attending the school for a short period. A sample of 60 girls from a nearby state school were also individually interviewed as part of this study. Both schools were located in affluent areas of a large northern city, with good academic reputations and active sixth-forms. Those pupils interviewed from both schools were generally from middle-class backgrounds with parents in professional and managerial occupations. Although the focus of this chapter is on the experiences of girls at the private schools, some comparisons are also made with the results of the interviews with state school pupils. The chapter first details the backgrounds and educational experiences of the privately educated, and their career aspirations and planning. In both these areas, various processes are identified by which these girls gain the edge over both other young women and young people from the same social class, enabling this group to take up positions at the top of the social, economic and career hierarchy. Finally, there is a discussion of the findings in relation to the experiences of different groups of young people under the Conservatives, and to issues of élitism and class in British society.

Going Private: The Backgrounds and Motivations of Pupils and Parents

This section demonstrates that the majority of girls and their parents believed that paying for a private education would provide them with an edge over other young people in the competitive world of academic success and high-status careers. Almost all of the privately educated girls believed that they received a better education at their school than they would have done if they had attended a school in the state sector. Certain characteristics of the school were repeatedly identified by the pupils as providing them with a better education, with these characteristics all closely interrelated. First, pupils described the better standards of teaching at the school, with teachers who were well paid, experienced and demanding of pupils, and whose contractual arrangements prevented them from going on strike. Better teaching was linked to the second frequently named characteristic, smaller classes. Many classes, particularly at A-level, had only four or five pupils in them, allowing a focus on individuals and individual abilities and understanding. Finally, there was the considerable motivation of the girls at the school: many pupils described how they were encouraged to be highly ambitious and future-oriented, in terms of both examination success and career planning. It is of note also that the school staff who were interviewed viewed this as essential for the school to continue to attract parents who were prepared to pay for their children's education. One teacher commented that:

> You can advertise the school's sporting facilities, range of subjects offered, friendly family atmosphere and all that as much as you like, but that's just icing so to speak. Ultimately, parents are looking for exam certificates and a guarantee of a place on a really good degree course.

This combination of smaller classes, better teaching, more academic and better motivated pupils was viewed as a circular process which led (among other things) to higher levels of academic achievement by the pupils. As one pupil described it:

> . . . it's a bit circular I think. I mean people here are all pretty clever. You have to be to get in in the first place, so standards are very high and everyone works really hard to keep up. We all know what we're here for, and at the beginning of each lesson we get stuck in . . . [laughs] . . . you don't get any stupid behaviour or mucking about in any classes. And then because of that and because everyone is clever there's really high standards.

The belief that private schools have higher academic standards was seen by the girls as the primary advantage of paying for education, and was the reason most often named by pupils as to why their parents had sent them to a private school. The interviews undertaken with some parents of the pupils confirmed these findings: the parents believed that they could secure a better quality education for their children by paying for it. One parent, who had no experience of private education herself, articulated this very clearly:

> I'm not totally happy with the idea of having to effectively buy a better education for my daughter . . . but you have to give them the best, and it really is so obviously better at [the private school], the discipline, the teaching, everything. They really are pushed into success.

Indeed, the views of this parent are those traditionally associated with why parents choose to pay for a private education for their children. Additionally, however, some of the parents named reasons relating to their dissatisfaction with particular aspects of state education, such as lack of discipline, low academic standards and large class sizes. In particular, dissatisfaction with a poor state school that their child would have attended was described as a reason for choosing private education. Many of the parents claimed that they would not have chosen a private education for their child if they felt that their local state school could have provided a good academic education. Few of these parents appeared to be the traditional users of the private sector for whom state education was never even an option.

In general, both parents and pupils viewed the state sector of education as offering only average and often poor-quality education, with only a few state schools considered to be exceptions to this. Several of the private school girls had had experience of education in the state sector, with some attending state schools up until the age of 11 or 13 before transferring to the private sector. The majority of this group made very critical comparisons between the two types of school, in particular in relation to what one girl described as the 'leisurely and undisciplined' attitude to school work. She described her experiences of the two schools as follows:

> The differences were just enormous. At [the state] school, no-one knew who you were or kept a check on where you should be or even on how your work was going. Most of the people in my biology class spent their time trying to avoid doing any work or mucking about and being disruptive . . .

She continued, saying that

> . . . it probably sounds naive but I was really shocked when I went there. I'd been at a private school all my life, and you learn how to work so hard and you just become really motivated. Most of the people in my classes at [the state] school just didn't seem to want to be there or do any work. You just couldn't get away with that at a private school.

Even the private school pupils who had never attended a state school were critical of the education in the state sector, naming again the problems of discipline, low standards and teacher strikes. In contrast, the private sector was viewed as superior in every way. Many of the girls identified private schools as having a different (and preferable) attitude to school work and academic achievement, an attitude which was rooted in the private primary school they attended. These girls described the demands made on them as primary school children, in terms of an early focus on large amounts of homework and frequent testing, as well as on individual excellence, effort and achievement. One pupil described her private primary school as an '. . . academic training ground rather than an introduction to the joys of education'. Although many pupils believed that their early years had been 'tough' as a result of this early educational emphasis, most believed it was worth it as a means of guaranteeing later opportunities and success in life. Many of the private school pupils identified the achievement-oriented aspects of their own school as inherent at all levels of the private sector of education, even those schools that had a less academic reputation than their school.

A large number of the private school pupils felt that the strengths of the private system of education were underpinned by 'parent power'. They viewed the state sector as lacking any mechanisms for change and improvement, in contrast to the private sector where parents were central to maintaining high standards as a consequence of their paying fees. Parents could make demands and pressurize the school to change. A good example of parent power was an event recounted by a number of pupils:

> . . . it was about three months ago . . . I think . . . you see several pupils felt that physics at GCSE and A-level wasn't being taught at all well and that they were going to do badly in exams. So they told their parents and their parents told the Head and suddenly there was action. The Head sat in on lessons herself and monitored homework and test results and eventually the teaching improved. You see the Head knew that the parents . . . well, they have clout [laughs] . . . because they're paying for it.

In relation to parent power, it was common for pupils to use shopping analogies to describe the relationship between their parents and the school. Their parents were paying for a product (good-quality education) and they wanted to get their 'money's worth' from it (in terms of a high number of good academic qualifications at both GCSE and A-level). Similarly, many parents in the interviews described paying for a private education as a form of investment, where paying now would result in later benefits in terms of children who went on to higher education and pursued successful professional careers. Notions of 'money's worth', 'investment' and 'consumer choice' came up frequently in the interviews with both parents and pupils, all aspects strongly endorsed by the current Conservative government.

Career Orientations

Achieving the 'edge' in careers and employment was a well worked-out strategy, which centred on early and detailed career planning. A central feature of career planning at the private school was a focus on the 14–18 age period as one distinct phase. GCSEs and A-levels were planned together to maximize future options and to increase the likelihood of gaining entry into higher education; it was pointed out by a member of the careers staff that this is less often the case at state schools where attention has also to be given to those likely to leave school at the minimum leaving age. Career planning at the private school generally began in the third year (when the pupils were 13-years-old), in the knowledge that pupils would follow a relatively fixed route of GCSEs and A-levels followed by a university (or less likely a polytechnic) degree. The only real area of variability in the career paths of these pupils was whether they took a year off after A-levels, or whether they did their A-levels at a different school in order to take a subject not offered by the current school. The vast majority of the private sample interviewed did indeed aim to go on to university and then pursue a professional career, a path which was generally described as the only option available to pupils:

> Oh well yes, everyone follows the same route. Even the youngest children here are told they'll do their O-levels, then their As, and then they'll go to university. That's what everyone does. It's considered really weird to want to go to work or even to go to a college.

The majority of the girls in the study did intend to follow this route, and interviews with careers staff revealed that there were rarely any deviations from this. One pupil interviewed was found to be planning to leave the school at sixteen and look for work, and she was consequently described by other pupils as the 'weirdie leftie'. A small number of other pupils planned to leave the school after A-levels to attend local colleges, though again this was rare. Those planning to leave school at sixteen (or even eighteen) were generally described by those following the majority route as 'weird' or a 'drop-out'; YTS was described as something which no-one would even consider. The large numbers of pupils staying on at age sixteen reflects a trend in the private sector as a whole. Recent figures from the Department of Education and Science (1991) show that, in 1990, 77.8 per cent of private school pupils stayed on in education at sixteen, compared with only 31.2 per cent of state-educated young people. These figures also show that in the same year almost one-fifth of all those in education post-sixteen were in private schools.

There was also a high degree of uniformity in the higher education courses and careers that pupils wanted to pursue after A-levels. The most frequently named courses were those most difficult to get into at university, and those requiring the highest grades. Medicine, law, accountancy and veterinary science were popular, as were foreign languages, architecture and business management. Both pupils and careers staff believed that if a pupil expressed an interest in a particular subject area, then they would be encouraged to aim for the most prestigious career in that area. One pupil explained it as follows:

I've only ever been to a private school, so I don't know what happens there [in state schools]. I doubt if it's like here though. You see you go for the top in everything you do. So like, if someone likes sciences and wants to continue in that, they have to be a doctor, or a vet. No one here wants to be a nurse or anything like that.

The school revealed a high degree of success in getting pupils on to the most prestigious university courses; a large number of pupils also gained places at Oxford and Cambridge Universities. Most pupils achieved such high grades at both GCSE and at A-level that one sixth-former described the school as a highly successful exam factory, with children 'wheeled in' to get good GCSEs and A-levels and then 'wheeled on' to university courses and careers in the professions.

Not only was career planning undertaken at a very detailed level, but it was also started at a very early age. All but a few of the pupils interviewed were able to name what career they planned to pursue, and most also had extensive knowledge of what they would need to do to achieve that plan. The school's careers staff and teachers were described by pupils as emphasizing the importance of an early and firm career decision; this consequently resulted in pupils with a high degree of knowledge of the job types within a particular career. Thus pupils would say that they planned to enter criminal or corporate law instead of 'just' law, and surgery or paediatrics instead of 'just' medicine. It was generally agreed that this early commitment to a career plan and extensive knowledge of the career, in addition to the extensive periods of work experience organized by the school, was very effective in impressing interviewers for university courses and later in securing a good job.

Linked to the private sample's distinctive career plans, were their attitudes to training. 'Training' for this group was used with two quite different meanings. Training was in one sense what all of them would have to do in order to pursue a professional career – training while at a medical school or training while doing articles in a law firm. The majority of pupils distinguished this *professional* level training from general training undertaken by school-leavers and those in manual occupations. Both these types of training were, however, viewed favourably. In particular, the Youth Training Scheme (YTS) was viewed very positively. Most YT schemes were considered to be of good quality, although most of the private school pupils (in contrast to the majority of the state sample) did not actually know anyone who had been on a YTS. A common attitude to YTS was represented by one 17-year-old, who was '. . . all in favour of YTS . . . as long as I don't have to do it'. Making YTS compulsory was also widely supported, as it was generally felt that 16- and 17-year-olds who were not in education or work should undertake training or work experience in order to make them more employable. Some pupils added that they also objected to young people '. . . spending all week in bed and only ever getting up to sign on . . .', and YTS was viewed as a good alternative to this.

Most clearly revealed in the interviews with the private school girls was their relative freedom from the constraints of gender experienced by many other groups of young girls (see, Bates, Chapter 1, this volume), at least at this stage of their careers. The fact that their school was a girls' school was a key advantage named by many of the pupils, and one which gave them significant advantages over girls in co-educational schools. Having boys in school was described as a distraction, with many of the girls describing the greater attention they received at their school in comparison to a mixed school. Some pupils were even able to quote research studies demonstrating that girls in single-sex schools were more likely, for example, to pursue science subjects and to receive greater attention from teachers during lessons. Many girls claimed that this resulted in a greater degree of freedom over the career they pursued, with less of an influence of gender stereotypes on their decisions. There was certainly very little evidence of a gender influence on pupils' career choices, with large numbers of pupils applying for university courses in, for example, engineering, medicine, pure sciences and management.

This is not to imply that these girls had rejected plans for marriage and children. Many of the girls had detailed plans for their futures which aimed to integrate having both a career and a family. The following two extracts from an interview with an 18-year-old demonstrates this clearly, the extract taken from a part of the interview which focused on the role of women in society:

Pupil: Well, as I said I've got a place [at university] to do civil and design engineering, and then eventually I intend to set up and manage my own company. So well . . . In society as a whole that sort of career for a girl well . . . it's not usual is it? Women usually become nurses and typists don't they? And even clever girls do . . . maybe advertising or a career in banking. It's definitely more unusual to do something like I'm doing . . . like engineering.

D.R.: So why do you think that is, what is it . . .

Pupil: Well it's just the way this school is. It's partly because it's a girls-only school and partly because it's private. There's nothing barred to girls here, nothing at all. If you're able to do it and you want to then you do.

        . . .

D.R.: And so does marriage and children come into the plans of people here [at the school]?

Pupil: Oh yes for almost everyone. It's just assumed you will get married and have children if you want to. I mean I don't want to be alone in my life, and I do want children. Most people are like me I would say. You know, you want a good degree, and spend some time getting into a profession for a few years. Then maybe marry say late 20s, have children, spend some time with them, and then pick up the career again. After all this work and effort you don't give it all up just to spend your life as a housewife do you? That's all old hat now for a lot of women [laughs].

In this respect in particular (i.e. the balance between a career and a family) the private school girls were distinct from those girls in the state sample who were interviewed. Some state school girls were often less certain about their commitment to pursuing a career long-term, and a number of this group only expected to work for a short time after leaving school before getting married and having children, and returning to work for some of this group was often only anticipated if it was really necessary for financial reasons.

In many ways, therefore, the influence of gender stereotypes on the future career and marriage plans of girls appeared to be greater among the state sample, suggesting that the private sample were freer from the constraints of gender on their life prospects. Securing this freedom for their daughters was, indeed, one reason why some of the parents had chosen a single-sex private school in the first place. The father of one girl, himself an engineer, felt that attending a single-sex school had greatly increased the likelihood of his daughter pursuing a non-stereotypical career. Indeed, his daughter had just been offered a place on a prestigious physics course. Her father believed that the school was somewhere where '. . . girls chose careers, not where certain careers are chosen for girls'. Despite the optimistic views of both pupils and parents, however, the majority of girls were still aiming to follow a gender-specific route, i.e. a two-stage career of work, children, work. A number of girls also seemed to have dismissed (or at least overlooked) the potential difficulties and obstacles they could face in 'picking up' their careers after taking time out to have children. Few seemed to acknowledge the existence of any difficulties in doing this, and most did not appear to have really thought through the availability of such things as child-care.

The prestigious careers aimed for by the private school girls also resulted in an almost total detachment from the constraints of the local labour market, in contrast to the results from the main 16–19 Initiative. As demonstrated by Ken Roberts (Chapter 9, this volume), in the main 16–19 study the local labour market situation was found to be a key influence on whether young people entered the labour market, stayed on in education or joined a YTS. The local labour market situation was, however, largely unimportant for the privately educated. This group aimed to attend university courses in all parts of the country, and then pursue occupations in national and countrywide organizations. Additionally, many hoped to work abroad eventually. The majority of the state sample who were interviewed were much less certain as to their career paths, with a significant number planning to leave school either at age sixteen or eighteen; many were attracted by career opportunities available within the local labour market, primarily opportunities in banking and management. Overall, in fact, the state sample were much more diverse in their career planning than the private sample, with a combination of YTS, vocational courses, A-levels and employment undertaken at both age sixteen and eighteen. Notable also was the lesser knowledge this group had of their future career choices, with few pupils demonstrating the detailed knowledge shown by many private school pupils. It is important to remember at this point that the private and state samples were from the same, generally middle-class professional, social class backgrounds. Thus the differences between the two samples are likely to be accounted for not by the influence of the home and the family, but by the influence of the different priorities and values of the two school environments and how these affect pupils' aspirations, plans and developing identities.

This chapter has so far demonstrated a number of ways by which private school girls gain the edge over other young people. In addition to the advantages of academic success and career planning, however, pupils also described more subtle factors. These factors provided them with an advantage even over those with equally high levels of academic qualifications, and were of use both in getting on to prestigious university courses and in achieving success in later careers. One 18-year-old had been offered a place on a prestigious law course shortly before the interviews. She described one aspect of the private school edge as simply having a private school background, and the assumptions made by people as a result:

> I think private education does make a difference, even if some people here won't admit it. I've had two interviews at university and you can see it makes a difference. They know you're going to get good exam results and . . . well they're just influenced by it.

Some pupils added that universities in particular believed private school pupils were a 'safer bet', being more likely to get the required grades at A-level, to work hard, and successfully complete their courses. Many pupils believed that having a private school background was particularly important in gaining access to prestigious graduate occupations such as the diplomatic service and high-level positions in the civil service. In addition, it was suggested by many that most private school pupils develop a strong sense of personal confidence that gives them an advantage in all areas of their lives.

... [private schools are] more friendly, certainly more competitive, the exam results are better, the teachers work harder. But it's more than that ... private schools give you confidence. You really feel you can do anything ... you're made to believe it. Seriously [laughing] how many unopinionated, shy people have you met who've been to private schools?

The pupils believed that it was this added confidence and forwardness in particular that gave them the edge over state-educated young people. This edge, they suggested, gave them a long-term advantage in later careers, with one pupil suggesting that 'It's a very subtle difference' but adding that '... it's also very real'.

The Assisted Place Scheme: A Case of Developing Identities?

There was one group of pupils at the private school who very clearly demonstrated the distinctive nature of a private education, and the ways in which certain experiences in education can influence the development of a young person's identity. These were the pupils who were at the school via the financial support of the Assisted Places Scheme (APS). The APS, one of the first educational changes made by the Conservative government, provides free and partially funded places at private schools for academically able young people. In the current research, 21 of the 67 girls who were interviewed were in receipt of an assisted place. These pupils generally came from backgrounds vastly different to the affluent, middle-class backgrounds of the majority of pupils. Most of the APS pupils were from single-parent families, with parents generally in skilled or managerial occupations. The majority of this group had been at local state schools before being awarded an assisted place. In many cases, their parents had been dissatisfied with their child's state school, either because of bullying or what they saw as their child's lack of progress. These parents, some of whom were interviewed, had often not heard of the APS and were only made aware of it through friends or private school literature. For other parents of APS pupils, a teacher at their child's school had suggested to them that their daughter was of above average ability and likely to benefit from a more academically based education. For a number of these parents, the decision to apply for an assisted place for their child was particularly difficult, as they were politically opposed to the existence of a private sector of education. Some of this group were even involved with the Labour Party.

The interviews with APS pupils (and a number of their parents) consequently proved particularly revealing about the effects of a private education on the values, aspirations and identity development of young girls. The majority of this group perceived what one 16-year-old described as 'vast' differences between private and state schools. The most obvious difference (and the one most frequently described) was the overtly academic emphasis of the school and the high level of academic ability of the pupils there. More importantly, many of this group described an entirely different way of thinking and behaving at the private school. They described how private school pupils were encouraged to be opinionated and articulate, with a much greater emphasis in lessons on the abilities and understanding of individual pupils. Of particular interest, however, were those of the APS pupils who felt that the private and state school environments were two completely different 'worlds'. Some believed that they no longer belonged to their home/state school world, but did also not yet belong to the private school world. This was clearly reflected in the following interview extract with a 17-year-old who had been in the private sector for four years:

Pupil: Well it's difficult to explain . . . but it's like being in limbo. I don't belong here any more, like here in my home. I've moved on. But I don't belong with them [the school] either.

D.R.: Do you think you ever will?

Pupil: Oh yes, I'm moving towards that now. It just takes time. I want everything that people at the school have . . . good qualifications, university, a good job, success. You come to see that's everything that everyone wants. At my old school people like me didn't really want those things, or rather you accepted less. So no, I'm in limbo at the moment because I haven't been there that long . . . but I'm more of them now than here. It's just so different you can't stay in both. My mum says I've changed . . . [laughs] . . . that since I've been there different things are important to me . . . She's probably right.

The experiences of a majority of the APS pupils reflected the comments above. Most of the APS pupils described the private school as a 'totally different world', where every aspect of life – people's behaviours, aspirations, relationships and attitudes – was different from what they had previously experienced. For many of the APS pupils, their early experiences at the private school had led to a significant development in their sense of personal identity. Faced with two quite different sets of behaviours, values and expectations, most were forced to incorporate elements of these worlds into their own identity. The last line of the previous interview extract demonstrates how many pupils effectively chose to incorporate the new aspirations and values of the school into their existing values. Indeed, some girls described the enormous pressure to do so, as not moving into the new 'world' of the school would most likely result in exclusion from social and friendship groups at the school, and possibly result in being labelled a 'weirdo', someone who did not fit in. This re-working of an individual's identity through their educational experience was also similarly demonstrated by the 'care girls' described by Inge Bates (Chapter 1, this volume).

The majority of the APS students thus integrated the values and behaviours of the private school into their own identity. This accommodation to a new experience was not, however, demonstrated by all the private school pupils. A small number of girls described an unresolved tension between their school world and their home world. Unable to integrate their previously held values and ideas with those they were now being exposed to at school, some described feelings of confusion and contradiction. The school also proved to be not at all accommodating to those who deviated from the accepted private school girl mould. Pupils mentioned several individuals who had left the school in the fourth or the fifth year, either because they could not maintain the high academic standards demanded, or because they became increasingly alienated from the school. Four pupils were found to have left the school and joined schools in the state sector. One of these pupils, who was also interviewed as part of the research, explained that not only could she not keep up academically, but that she had become increasingly disillusioned by the intensely academic and competitive nature of the school environment. She had left after a series of arguments and conflicts with teachers and the Headteacher, and described herself as leaving with the 'mutual agreement' of both the school and her parents. The private school environment was, she believed, one of 'individualism and selfishness gone mad', with individual success and individual achievement put above everything else in life. It was later found that between ten and fifteen pupils had left the school in this way during the previous few years, suggesting that the school may have an in-built filtration system which encourages those not fitting into the accepted private school pupil mould to leave and continue their education elsewhere.

Conclusions: Educating the Élite

It was frequently proposed by many of the private school girls that society under Mrs Thatcher was one that was based on individual opportunity, where everyone could succeed in their lives if they worked hard enough. The level that an individual reached in the occupational hierarchy was dependent primarily on such factors as individual ability and effort. In this, their views reflected those of Mrs Thatcher and of her successor John Major, that individuals are responsible for determining and improving their own life chances. The views of the private school girls in relation to education and careers were just one aspect of a general commitment to, and belief in, a right-wing political, social and economic philosophy among a majority of the private sample. A belief in the importance of individualism was closely related to an acceptance of social and economic inequality as both inevitable and natural. Related to this, private education itself was viewed as fair, first because it gave parents increased choice and secondly because people would always be able to afford different things in life. In educational and ideological terms, therefore, the private school girls reflected many of the views of the Thatcher government.

In contrast to this view, however, private education has often been described as a crucial component of the establishment and maintenance of an élite in society (Griggs, 1985; Cookson and Persell, 1985). An élite is generally conceptualized in terms of those who are in high-status occupations, those with power, those with a high degree of political and economic efficacy, and those who are materially well off. Both the privately and state-educated samples in the research might legitimately be described as an élite. The privately educated, however, could also be described as the 'élite's élite'. This is because (as demonstrated throughout this chapter) they have the 'edge' over other groups of advantaged young people. The nature of this élitism can be seen as functioning at two main levels: personal and structural. Personal élitism is the development by private school pupils of high occupational aims and aspirations, and the acquisition of personal skills (confidence, articulation) of advantage in the labour market. Structural élitism concerns those privileges and advantages inherent in the structure of private schools themselves; these aspects include better quality facilities and teaching, smaller classes, individual attention and detailed career preparation. In combination, these two aspects provide private school girls with the edge over young people from the same social class and also over other young girls. It is possible that the benefits of being the élite's élite are reflected in the large proportions of the privately educated in high-status positions, comprising for example 25 per cent of university students and 50 per cent of Oxford and Cambridge undergraduates (Walford, 1990). Most interestingly, the privately educated comprise nineteen of the twenty-one members of the main policy-making arm of government, the current Conservative cabinet.

It has been proposed throughout this chapter that the private school girls interviewed revealed quite distinctive orientations in the areas of education, training, employment and careers. These orientations were essentially compatible with those of the current Conservative government, the girls demonstrating a high degree of accommodation to, and acceptance of, the current structure of economic and political relations. Indeed, it was demonstrated that the Thatcher government had given high levels of support to the private sector, and in comparison to other groups of young people during the same period, the freedom of choice of the privately educated was maintained and extended. For less academic groups of young people, their degree of choice was significantly reduced during this period, most notably through the enforcement of YTS and the tightening of benefit rules for the unemployed. Thus the divisions between the most advantaged and disadvantaged groups of young people have been increased throughout the 1980s (see Roker and Mean, 1991, for detailed evidence of this). The privately educated in the current study can therefore certainly be described as being at one end (the most advantaged) of the social spectrum.

The experiences of young people, therefore, cannot be conceptualized solely in terms of the relative advantages and disadvantages of different class or gender groups. It is necessary to explore not only the degree to which young people in different social classes may have moved further apart in the 1980s, but also the degree to which young people within the *same* social class or gender group may have experienced different opportunities in this period. The research described here demonstrates the considerable differences in aspirations and prospects between two groups of young people who are of the same gender, live in the same geographical area and who are from the same social class background. This suggests that educational experience may, in fact, be important not only in increasing divisions between individuals and sub-groups in different social classes, but also within the same social class.

References

Cookson, P.W. and Persell, C.H. (1985) *Preparing for Power: America's Élite Boarding Schools*. New York, Basic Books.

Delamont, S. (1973) Academic conformity observed. Unpublished PhD thesis. University of Edinburgh.

Delamont, S. (1984). Debs, dollies, swots and weeds: classroom styles at St Lukes. In G. Walford (ed.) *British Public Schools: Policy and Practice*. London, Falmer Press.

Department of Education and Science (1991) *Statistical Bulletin* No. 6/91. London, HMSO.

Edwards, T., Fulbrook, M. and Whitty, G. (1984). The state and the independent sector. In L. Barton and S. Walker (eds) *Social Crisis and Educational Research*. London, Croom Helm.

Edwards, T., Fitz, J. and Whitty, G. (1989) *The State and Private Education: An Evaluation of the Assisted Places Scheme*. London, Falmer Press.

Eglin, G. (1984) Public schools and the choice at 18+. In G. Walford (ed.) *British Public Schools: Policy and Practice*. London, Falmer Press.

Emler, N. and Dickinson, J. (1985) Children's representation of economic inequalities: the effects of social class. *British Journal of Developmental Psychology*, 3, 191–8.

Emler, N., Ohana, J. and Dickinson, J. (1990) Children's representations of social relations. In G. Duveen and B. Lloyd (eds) *Social Representations and the Development of Knowledge*. Cambridge, Cambridge University Press.

Feather, N.T. (1983) Causal attributions and beliefs about work and unemployment among adolescents in state and independent secondary schools. *Australian Journal of Psychology*, 35(20), 211–32.

Fox, I. (1985) *Private Schools and Public Issues: The Parents' Views*. London, Macmillan.

Furnham, A. (1982) The perception of poverty amongst adolescents. *Journal of Adolescence*, 5, 135–47.

Griggs, C (1985). *Private Education in Britain*. Lewes, Falmer Press.

Halsey, A.H., Heath, A.F., and Ridge, J.M. (1984) The political arithmetic of public schools. In G. Walford (ed.) *British Public Schools: Policy and Practice*. London, Falmer Press.

Johnson, D. (1990) *Parental Choice in Education*. London, Unwin Hyman.

Robson, M.H. and Walford, G. (1989) Independent schools and tax policy under Mrs Thatcher. *Journal of Education Policy*, 4(2), 149–62.

Roker, D. (1991) The political socialisation of youth: A comparison of private and state educated girls. Unpublished PhD thesis. University of Sheffield.

Roker, D. and Mean, L. (1991) Youth policies in the 1980s and 1990s: one for the rich, one for the poor? *Youth and Policy*, 33, 31–7.

Senker, P. (1990). Some economic and ideological aspects of the reform of education and training in England and Wales in the last ten years. *Journal of Education Policy*, 5(2), 113–25.

Walford, G. (1986) *Life In Public Schools*. London, Methuen.

Walford, G. (1987) How dependent is the independent sector? *Oxford Review of Education*, 13(3) 275–96.

Walford, G. (1990) *Privatization and Privilege in Education*. London, Routledge.

Chapter 7

Becoming Privileged
The role of family processes[1]

Patricia Allatt

This chapter looks in detail at family processes involved in the transmission of privilege. It focuses on how three middle-class families use their resources to increase the life chances of their young, and how the effectiveness of these resources is enhanced when mediated by family processes. These processes are embedded in routines and practices and are underpinned by norms of obligation, fairness and solidarity. It is about how privileged groups pass on their power and advantage to the next generation.

The Young People and their Families

The data are from three middle-class families. They were selected because all of the children in these families had been educated in the private sector, in private day schools. The data comprise interviews with four members of each family: mother, father and a child in the fifth year and one in the upper sixth year of secondary schooling. The young people were at key turning points in their educational careers, witnessed in their involvement in public examinations.

The Jacksons were successful farmers with income from other sources. Mr Jackson was privately educated. He felt he had virtually left home at the age of seven when sent to boarding school and this had influenced his and his wife's decision to send their children to a local private day school. It was a decision of which his father disapproved. There was a tradition of university education in the family; Mr Jackson had an Oxbridge degree, as had his father and grandfather. He was active on local and national committees and had a wide network of colleagues in both farming and other professional groups. Mrs Jackson, from a family of local professionals, was also privately educated but at the same school as her children. She was a qualified music teacher and had taught at local schools before the birth of her first child. She had then devoted herself to her children but had offered her teaching services, in a voluntary capacity, to her youngest child's primary school. At the time of the interviews, she was teaching music part-time in this voluntary capacity (amounting to two and a half days per week) in the primary and the secondary school which the two younger children now attended. She had also just started giving private music tuition for payment. There were three children. Sarah, the eldest, was twenty and away from home on a year's agricultural work experience course prior to entering college. She had intended going to university but had not performed well enough in her A-level examinations. Mr and Mrs Jackson felt that this was partly their fault through misjudging her apparent capacity to cope with the stress of the work. It raised the issue of the fine line between freedom and surveillance (albeit benign) and coloured their approach to their younger children's schoolwork. Charles was eighteen and working towards three A-levels. Like his father he hoped to study engineering at university but was not thinking of Oxbridge. Charles was seen as the heir to the family assets and was being schooled to assume this responsibility. He was active in the Young Farmers', had capably organized a major fund-raising barbecue on the farm, and joined in the farming activities of the family. Deborah was seen as the dreamer of the family. She was fifteen and working for seven GCSE subjects. She intended staying on to take A-levels and was 'thinking' about junior school teaching as a career. Like her mother she was musical, proficient with the cello, flute and piano. The children in this family had money in trust or private incomes of their own and there was no imperative that they work for economic reasons. None the less, there was a strong emphasis on hard work and contributing to 'society'.

The Phillips family also came from a strong educational tradition. Mrs Phillips' mother and father had doctorates and both had held university posts. Mrs Phillips was privately educated, moving schools as her father's career advancement took him to different parts of the country. Mr Phillips' father had had a managerial post in a small industrial community and, although his childhood felt parochial in terms of the wider experiences available to young people today, Mr Phillips was conscious of the social position his parents had held. Although in comfortable circumstances, the Phillips family were not as materially well off as their parents had been. Consequently, educational achievement and occupational success was essential to their children if they were to maintain a similar life-style. Mr Phillips had been to grammar school and university. He had a doctorate and was teaching in a local college. Mrs Phillips had been a health service professional (having been dissuaded from taking a secretarial course by an aunt), had recently re-trained and was now working in the special schools sector and was active in the union. Both Mr and Mrs Phillips had interests in voluntary work, activities supporting the school, and outdoor activities. There were two children. Simon was eighteen and intent on following a medical career, had done well in his GCSE examinations, was preparing for six A-levels (causing some parental concern that he might jeopardize his grades) and was hoping to go to Cambridge. He was involved in school clubs and sports teams and undertook voluntary work as part of the Duke of Edinburgh Award Scheme. Mike, aged fifteen, was preparing for his GCSEs. He was interested in sport – he played for the local rugby club – and was musically inclined. Like his brother, he was involved in voluntary work. He saw public examinations as affecting the rest of his life. His parents were aware that his brother's academic performance was 'a difficult act to follow, Mike could have gone under very easily but he didn't', and conscious of the possibility of a negative influence upon his attitude to his own potential and work. The emphasis placed in this family upon sustained work, effort, getting on with homework and not wasting time indicated the recognition of this stage as critical to the young people's futures.

The Brayshaws had been upwardly mobile. Both Mr and Mrs Brayshaw were from upper working/lower middle-class homes. Mrs Brayshaw's father had been a master craftsman; her mother had died in Mrs Brayshaw's infancy. Brought up by her father and older siblings, Mrs Brayshaw had had a grammar school education and then trained as a teacher, the only one of her family to go to college. She had taught in a local comprehensive school until her first child was born, since when she had been a full-time housewife and mother which she saw as essential to her children's well-being. Mr Brayshaw's father had been a draughtsman and his mother an office worker who had remained in paid employment all her life. Mr Brayshaw had also been to grammar school but had left school at sixteen. He had then worked his way up through a series of jobs, had taken professional examinations at evening class and was now qualified. The firm in which he had been a partner had recently been sold and he was working for the new owners on contract. Both parents were engaged in voluntary work, supporting the school and other organizations. There were two children. Stephen, aged seventeen, was preparing for four A-levels and one AS-level, and hoped to read maths at university. He was a member of several sports clubs as well as school teams. He and his brother had been selected for the County hockey trials and both played for the local cricket team. John was fifteen and preparing for eight GCSEs. As in the Phillips family, there was a special concern for the younger son's attitude, stemming from his more relaxed personality and also the fact that he was following a highly successful academic brother. In some respects, the approach to examinations was conceived as a war campaign, and a good education was seen by Mr Brayshaw as an escape both from the locality and from any danger of unemployment. Again, sustaining the boys' commitment to hard work over the years of schooling was a major concern in this family.

The parents and young people in these three families shared a similar set of values and aspirations. Emphasis was placed on achievement, hard work, productive use of time, involvement in school and other activities, the value of education, self-motivation, individualism and independence. The parents wanted their children to fulfil their potential, to use their talents, to have an interesting job not necessarily with the highest pay, to do something they felt was of value to society, to have a certain standard of material comfort, to have self-confidence, to be liked and to be happy. These interests were shared by the young people themselves. 'To do well at school, get a good job, settle and have a happy family, hopefully. Just do well in life and enjoy it', explained John Brayshaw. However, the high levels of achievement already reached, the clear career orientations of the 18-year-olds and wide options arising from various combinations of ability, social networks and family wealth suggested that high income in the adult labour market was very probable. At the time of the interviews, however, good examination results dominated everything.

The Jackson, Phillips and Brayshaw families, by different routes, were among the more privileged in our society. In this chapter, I examine the common everyday processes they used to advantage their children and how they drew upon their resources. The chapter will show that, in this critical 'domestic transition' (Bourdieu, 1986, p. 244), privilege is not automatically transmitted but depends upon purposeful activity directed towards the maintenance of class position and prevention of downward mobility.

I start by briefly describing the resources employed in these processes and then examine the main contexts in which they were used: education, the family and the social context.

Resources and Privilege: The Various Forms of Capital

Drawing upon the work of Bourdieu (1986), Nowotny (1981) and Wallman (1984), the resources which seemed central to these families were economic, social, cultural and emotional capital. Although it is possible to list resources in this manner, each cannot be considered in isolation. As Wallman (1984) noted in her study of households as resource systems, resources interact with each other. In the transfer of privilege, resources are both interwoven and converted to other uses, and the analysis draws out these inter-connections and transformations. Before turning to this, however, I briefly describe the concepts which informed the analysis.

Economic capital is the money and goods to which family household members have access, although access is not necessarily equal (Pahl, 1983). It is a basic resource which underpins all the others. In this study, it was critical to the education and, in consequence, the future economic assets of the young. These three families were highly conscious of this fact.[2]

Cultural capital refers to personal attributes of two kinds (Bourdieu,

1986):[3] institutional cultural capital denotes formal qualifications, and embodied cultural capital denotes particular styles or modes of presentation, including speech, forms of social etiquette and competence, as well as degree of confidence and self-assurance. The latter also includes identity (Allan, 1982; Wallman, 1984). Here I focus upon a sense of responsibility and individualism, both of which emerged as major values in these households.

Two aspects of social capital were evident in the data. The first was social networks, i.e. those contacts and group memberships which, through the accumulation of exchanges, obligations and shared identities, provide actual or potential support and access to valued resources. The second was the essential asset of sociability, since networks are sustained by both 'the unceasing effort of sociability [comprising] a continuous series of exchanges in which recognition is endlessly affirmed' and the acquired skill and disposition to engage in this (Bourdieu, 1986, p. 250). Ken Roberts (Chapter 9, this volume) refers to the social and cultural supports systems to which the young middle class had access in their educational careers. As will be seen, however, not only did parents possess social capital vested in the social networks they used on behalf of their children, but parents also fostered in the young the skills necessary for the creation of their own social capital – sociability and an understanding of the mechanisms of social networking. This is a critical transfer, since such aspects of social capital have to be recreated with each new generation.

Emotional capital is a term used by Nowotny (1981) to refer to social and cultural capital (e.g. social networks and expertise) whose use, under certain conditions, is largely confined within the bounds of affective relationships of family and friendship. Nowotny (1981) gives the example of a woman's education. For while, in a gendered labour market, a mother's education might not aid her own occupational advancement, it is a valuable and well-recognized maternal resource for investment in her children's educational careers and the promotion of their future success in the outside world. Emotional capital, however, also includes emotionally valued assets and skills, love and affection (Allatt, 1987; Allatt and Yeandle, 1992) and what Bourdieu (1986, p. 253) refers to as the apparently gratuitous expenditure of time, attention, care and concern. It helps to explain the support, patience and commitment that even wayward children can draw upon (Allatt, 1987). Such aspects of emotional capital were evident in all these families, particularly in the way mothers devoted their skills gained from their formal education to the advancement of their children.

These values, aspirations and resources were woven into family practices orientated to young people's futures. The practices were also sustained by particular interpretations of happiness, and familism. Education, for example, was treated as a family project, and certain rituals (rewards and celebrations) maintained the cohesion of the unit by reconciling the contradictory values of individualism and equity within the context of family life. It is the strands in this web which are traced in the rest of the chapter.

The Education Context

The early part of the life course is dominated by the twin domains of home and school; indeed, these remain highly salient in later stages of life if parenting is taken as the focus (Allatt, 1991). During the years of formal education, however, the school becomes the dominant partner, affecting family life in at least three ways. First, schooling influences the timetabling of household schedules, routines and plans, from the time to get up in the morning to use of leisure time and holidays. Secondly, schooling formally determines and timetables the major stages, transitions and turning points in the educational career of young people, e.g. school transfers, examinations and entry into the labour market. Thirdly, it influences the content of certain family practices, e.g. in the talk and help involved in fostering commitment to schoolwork (Allatt, 1991). Within the institutional framework of the education system, however, it is possible for some individuals to weave, to some extent, their own pathways and create additional milestones and openings; for in the passage through the life course, irrespective of social class, individuals and families draw upon what resources they have to ease, shape and enhance their journeys as best they can. Thus when individuals define an educational, or any other, path or juncture as important to their lives, or to the lives of those either entrusted to them or to whom they have a sense of obligation, then their resources (however extensive or limited) are brought into play (Allatt and Yeandle, 1992).

How did these families influence the transfer of advantage within the formal institution of the school? For although central to young people's futures, the school was outside the immediate control of the family. Control over this public domain poses particular problems. Only among the very wealthy or, in our society, by those considered to be eccentric, can education be tailored to suit what key adults consider to be the particular needs of a child. Consequently, for most people, influence over the style and content of education is confined to choosing between educational environments. The juggling between house purchase and school catchment areas, for example, is witness to this and well recognized by estate agents. Moreover, the extent to which even this is possible is dependent upon individual and family resources.

In this section, I look at how parents drew upon their social, cultural and economic resources to select schools which provided an education of a type they felt to be closest to their definition of their children's needs. I look at parents' attempts to ensure the schools served these ends, and at how they supplemented perceived inadequacies. I also examine parental strategies used to ensure that the young people took full advantage of the privileges being offered, one of which was to weave the notion of economic cost into the bonds of reciprocity between the generations.

The heritage of cultural capital endowed these families with a range of assets. It provided parents with a knowledge of the educational system, a recognition of the importance of educational qualifications for future well-being, whether in terms of material comfort, the sense of personal fulfilment in doing something of value, a satisfying job, or what they defined as happiness. Experience within the education system by a parent in each of the families, and an awareness of the changes that had taken place since their own schooldays, underpinned parental views about what children should be learning at school at particular ages and stages of the educational career. It also provided parents with some means of assessing both the style of teaching and the content of the curriculum. 'No, they seem to have pretty firm ideas about the school, what school should be like', replied Mike Phillips when asked if he might have influenced his parents' views on education. Such certainties also led parents to emphasize that goals were achieved by hard work and focusing on the task in hand. In this respect, good grades in public examinations were the immediate goals.

Parental perceptions of the constituents of a good education included the need for order, structure and demands for hard work. This led to dissatisfaction with the academic standards and what was seen as the *laissez faire* atmosphere of the state primary schools their children attended. The comments by Mrs Phillips on the format of religious education in her son's primary school reveals the extent of this demand for order and rigour: 'I thought he ought to have some religious teaching. [They were] lackadaisical. Everybody sings a few sort of so-called hymns round a guitar . . . It wasn't really very structured religious teaching.'

All three families moved their children out of the state sector either earlier than they had anticipated or at the stage of secondary transfer. For financial reasons and because it was thought to be too academically formal for young children, a local prep school had not been considered, but of the state primary school Mrs Phillips commented, 'We didn't realize how awful it was. We got him out as soon as we could.' In the case of the Brayshaws, where there had been no intention of using the private sector, social capital was drawn upon in two ways. Mr Brayshaw learned of a private school from friends whose children were already there, and he and his wife called upon a friend who was a teacher to assess the educational attainment of their son. Shocked by her assessment, that he was at least a year behind his expected attainment level, the decision to use the private sector followed. Mr Brayshaw explained:

Our friend just couldn't believe what he hadn't done, what he knew . . . what he hadn't done. She had children in her school who were further

ahead than him, and that's a school with . . . if you want to be blunt,
a 'D' catchment area against an 'A' catchment area. So we thought,
'Heavens', you know, 'Another year and he's going to be even further
behind.' That's . . . why we took him out, you see.

Like the parents in Jackson and Marsden's (1968) study, Mr and Mrs
Brayshaw had confidence in the abilities of their children irrespective of
performance.

Decisions were explained in terms of the child's best interest: the need
for structure and order to promote hard work, the importance of children
fulfilling their potential and, underpinning this, parental definitions of what
they felt would make the child happy. This concept of happiness was not
just tied to the child's current mental state but also took account of the
future. Thus, based upon their knowledge of each child's personality and
their own social experience, the parents felt that not only did they know
what would make their child happier at the moment – they were also
aware that happiness in adulthood was highly dependent upon economic
security and, in consequence, the importance of educational success. These
two dimensions of happiness met in the emphasis placed upon hard work
and a conducive social setting. Thus, according to Mrs Brayshaw, they
moved Stephen, their eldest son, from the state system 'because he was
unhappy at the primary school. Well, he wasn't unhappy. He was happy
at the primary school, but he likes a working atmosphere.' In contrast, the
younger son, John, had:

> . . . gone for a different reason . . . He'd just [have] sail[ed] through
> and ha[d] a whale of a time, doing nothing . . . whereas we felt that
> [he] needed a bit more pressure . . . because he can do it you see. But
> if he's in with a group who don't work, then he wouldn't work.

On this reasoning, two apparently competing cultural tenets of familism
– individualism and fairness – were accommodated, treating siblings alike
while recognizing their differences (Backett, 1982; Allatt and Yeandle,
1992). This concept of fairness was echoed by Mrs Phillips. 'We have a
policy of doing the same for both children', she said.

Underpinning all this was the fact that the families had the economic
resources (stemming variously from current income, inherited wealth and
aid from kin) to buy the type of education they felt would enhance the
young people's economic opportunities as well as their present and future
happiness. Two families, the Brayshaws and the Phillips', one upwardly
mobile and the other less affluent than the previous generation, were highly
conscious of the economic cost of this type of education and made it clear
to their children.

Economic cost, however, played two roles. As well as a material resource cost was also a symbol emphasizing both the importance of education and, in this case, its specially selected character. Mrs Phillips, for example, discussing how she insisted on her elder son, Simon, 'getting on with' his homework, observed:

Mrs Phillips: So, I mean, I can't force them, but I encourage them, obviously. When you're paying all that money, you know, you've got to get your money's worth.
Interviewer: Do you say that to him?
Mrs Phillips: Yes I do. Yes, he might as well be aware of the fact that he's had a very expensive commodity. Mm . . . don't sort of rub it in all the time, but it's something . . . he's quite aware . . . Yes, I think you have to be aware of it.

The young people were also conscious of the symbolic value of this economic cost. Education was a valuable 'commodity' to which Simon Phillips referred to as 'mostly a bonus'. Implicit to the Phillips boys was the understanding that their education was something over and above that which others received 'at ordinary comps', who, according to the younger son, Mike, were likely to be disadvantaged in the examination stakes. In this case, there was a sense of being set apart.[4] This economic investment in education was woven into family norms and practices in ways which, in these families, furthered the creation of cultural capital in the young in terms of educational success. Thus parental economic investment was parallelled by normative expectations about obligations and reciprocities between the generations. There was a bargain to be kept by young people. This notion of exchange was clearly expressed by Mr Brayshaw when asked what he would do if Stephen did not work hard at school but asked for support in some of his other activities (the young man's commitment was, in fact, high – he was sitting six A-levels):

Sorry, but if you don't keep your side of the bargain, y'know. It's costing us . . . It's costing me a lot of money for you to go to school. If you don't utilize, then you don't expect me to support you the other way.

Thus young people's side of the bargain was to repay in kind, displaying their appreciation through hard work, and, because of their expensive schooling, the achievement of as good examination results as possible.[5] 'I've had the best education [and glowing reports]', observed Simon Phillips:

. . . if I went to an ordinary comp, and just an ordinary sixth-form . . . or if I went to a non-comp and I just left at sixteen, then they'd probably expect rather less of me than they do at the moment.

In sum, the act of selecting a particular type of school and the ensuing obligations created in the young, could, if met, involve young people more deeply in the co-creation of their own cultural capital.

Resources and intervention in education

All the parents had selected these schools as appropriate agents for the transmission of advantage. They spoke enthusiastically of them, gave them their support in terms of time and fund-raising, and some made a point of never criticizing them to their children. As Mrs Phillips observed:

> We're all positive about the school. In fact, I think, if we weren't, we would take him away, because it would be silly to waste money on something we didn't feel . . . was sort of good value.

This, however, did not mean that the schools always lived up to expectations. But when such occasions arose, the parents again could draw upon their store of resources. Their cultural capital of confidence and skill, and their social capital embedded in appropriate social networks, enabled them to take matters into their own hands in order to supplement what they felt to be deficiencies. This had meant, for example, that Mrs Phillips had sought other first-aid classes, part of a Duke of Edinburgh Award Scheme, when Simon was barred from the one provided at school – blamed unjustly, she felt, for bumping into a member of staff when someone had pushed Simon. Although she had not complained, since it was their policy always to support the school, the incident which had taken place three years ago obviously still rankled:

> And what can you do anyway . . . We had to go out and find the Red Cross or first-aid course ourselves. Well we went ahead and did that. I happen to know the lady who runs the Red Cross for the [county].

In the case of the Jackson family, however, this interaction between school and home was more complex, providing an intricate example of the interweaving of economic, social and cultural capital over time and their conversion into emotional capital used to advance their child's skills in the way they wished. As noted earlier, Mrs Jackson, a trained music teacher, had renounced paid employment on the birth of her first child. However, when the primary school asked if anyone knew of a music teacher, coupled with the fact that she wanted her daughter to be taught music at school, she offered her services free of charge. Her reason was her wish to ensure the continuation of her daughter's musical education. It suggests the depth of commitment some parents have to their children's education, sustained by economic resources and available time, that is, substantial household income and domestic help which relieved Mrs Jackson from domestic obligations. Moreover, the accumulation of her social capital as a voluntary teacher at the secondary school also enabled her daughter to join the secondary school choir while still at the primary school.

The last example of parental intervention upon the formal environment of the school is what Debra Roker (Chapter 6, this volume) refers to as 'parent power'. The girls at the independent school Roker studied commented on the power of money; the complaints of fee-paying parents were acted upon by the school. There are, however, other ways of exerting influence. One is in the support parents give to the schools by serving on school committees or associations. Parents in all three families described here had adopted such roles, frequently through fund-raising activities, which was seen as benefiting their children directly. In the Jackson family, however, there was a clear hint of surveillance, the young people reporting back to parents as to whether recommendations had been carried out by the school.

In sum, the parents used their resources to select an educational environment propitious to the reproduction of social advantage in their children (ultimately translatable into economic capital) and drew further upon their resources in their attempts to hone this environment more closely to their requirements. The return on this investment was enhanced by the way in which it was woven into the practices and norms governing their family lives.

The Family Context

Whereas control over educational values was largely achieved indirectly, the shaping of values within the family was more directly controlled through life-style patterns, discipline and the forms of relationships. In the families studied, it was noted that particular emphasis was attached to the development of a sense of responsibility and individualism.

Responsibility

One means of inducing a sense of autonomy is to create in the individual the belief that he or she can affect events. It is about agency. The elements of agency – independence, responsibility, self-motivation and individualism – were highly valued in these families. They are also components of cultural capital important to self-esteem, future careers and a particular world view. The cost of a sense of control over the direction of one's life, however, is the acceptance – indeed, the embracing – of responsibility for oneself. Within these families, this was nourished through the transfer of responsibility from parent to the young person him or herself. This transfer, however, was not an abrupt handing over but a gradual release from stricter parental controls and definitions, reflected in the comment: 'I ask him out of habit [if he should be doing homework].' As noted earlier, it was a handing over which could also go wrong. The assumption by Mr and Mrs Jackson that their elder daughter, Sarah, could cope with sixth-form work had led to poorer A-level results than expected and a more careful watch on the two younger children.

As well as being graduated, this transfer was set within special boundaries, taking place within a framework of shared assumptions, expectations and objectives. There were expectations, for example, underpinned by day-to-day routines and parental models, that you worked hard. 'It must rub off . . . He knows that we haven't got where we have by sitting back', said Mrs Brayshaw. While this relationship between work and material advancement was particularly evident in this upwardly mobile family, all the families were aware of work models. The young people commented on how hard their parents worked and their engagement in a wide range of activities. You did not waste time, and you 'got as much out of things as you could'. The objective was to achieve as much as possible. That such assumptions were strands of a family's history was well described by Mr Phillips when asked about the influence he felt he might have had on his sons' attitude to university:

> [It] probably has . . . But . . . you see, so much of it we take for granted . . . not only in our house but in Ruth's [his wife] parents' house . . . it was always . . . It was just there, the fact that you . . . the expectation that in your immediate family is that you go to university . . . and they [his sons]see some of the benefits and some of the disadvantages from following the undergraduate route.

Such family models and assumptions constituted the boundaries of an area of freedom within which a particular style of transfer was adopted. This was to offer advice and help in a generalized manner rather than in specific detail. As Mr Phillips explained:

> I've tried to provide the experience and the facilities without really saying, 'Well, look, why don't you read', or . . . it's been a question of, 'Do you want to come?' This kind of thing without pushing it at them.

And his younger son, Mike, when asked, 'Do they tell you what to do a lot?', replied: 'They give me suggestions of what I could do, and then they let me choose.'

Probably because of the shared beliefs about the value of education in these families, no parental anxieties were expressed about the outcome of a young person's decision. The following quotation suggests the grounds for this confidence: 'It's been purely my decision . . .', said Mike Phillips, 'My parents wanted me to stay on, but they didn't say you must stay on. It was purely my choice they gave to me . . . I never thought of leaving school at sixteen.'

There were further examples of this contained transfer of responsibility: in the approach to school work and homework, in the use of time, in money management and in the ownership of space. Comments by Mike Phillips also illustrate the nature and effect of the transfer and the changes in the process over time. His comments also reveal the weather eye on the situation kept by vigilant parents and the steps taken, within the same style of transfer, to sustain effort when the demands of school begin to feel oppressive:

Well not so much now they don't force me [to do homework] . . . but they just remind me that . . . they say, 'Well, if you don't do it then it's your problem. It's going to affect you in the long run.' . . . Which is not actually forcing me to do it, it's making me think about it, so in the end I will do it.

And when asked if this kind of parental intervention was constant or just in the background, Mike replied:

I think its just in the background until I don't want to do some work. You know, 'I'm sick of school', and everything . . . and then they'll just remind me, and I'll start thinking again and working.

Reflected in these comments are particular styles of communication (see also Allatt and Benson, 1991). These families attached importance to discussion: 'We don't argue, we discuss', said Mr Brayshaw, 'We discuss what a reasonable time to come in is.' 'We discuss things as they arise', said Mrs Brayshaw. 'They talked things through', said John Brayshaw.

The principle of circumscribed freedom also applied to the use of time and money. Mrs Brayshaw helped with the setting out of revision timetables; Mr Brayshaw saw it as a matter, with homework, of '. . . monitor[ing] starting, what they've got, when has it to be in . . . setting up the timetable framework, rather than, "What are you actually doing?" And showing interest in what they're doing.' As one boy explained, advice about time could take the form of: ' "Try not to waste it". That's really about it. They don't give a counselling session on "How to make the best use of your time".' The progression from spending money to allowances was also perceived as a means of transferring responsibility. 'If they've got money they've got to have responsibilities', said Mr Brayshaw; Mrs Phillips, on giving Simon his first allowance with which to open a bank account, gave him a cheque and 'told him to get on with it'. And there was particular concern that a sense of economic responsibility was achieved prior to leaving home for university.

This is not to ignore the fact that these parents could and did give detailed advice and academic help. The point is that extensive familial support was set within a system which encouraged a sense of responsibility for ones's own actions, transmitting to young people a valuable form of cultural capital.

Individualism

This section looks at the part individualism, increasingly reported in studies of youth, played within these families in the acculturation of the young middle class into a particular type of economic identity, creating in their case a valuable resource for the future. Identity is both a private and public commodity. It provides the individual with a sense of self. It also, as Inge Bates shows (Chapter 1, this volume), identifies the individual as suitable or not to those who select personnel for particular occupations. Moreover, depending upon a person's location within the social structure, individualism can limit as well as expand economic and political horizons. Robert MacDonald (Chapter 4, this volume) discusses this constraining element.

Individualism appeared in these families in several ways: in the emphasis placed on the uniqueness of the individual, in the value seen as residing in the individual, in the view of the labour market as a landscape of opportunities rather than a predetermined track, and in the sense of difference between persons arising from privilege and ability. I look at these in turn as they appeared within these families.

A sense of the uniqueness of the individual emerged in the frequent references, both by parents and the young people, to the differences between siblings – in their personality, their academic performance, their 'excel[ling] at different things' according to Mrs Phillips, in their approach to school work, their interests and leisure time pursuits, and their attitudes to money. Moreover, such differences were actively recognized. Thus within the familistic ideal of fairness, and a policy of providing the same opportunities for each, siblings were treated according to their perceived needs. 'You've got to treat them differently', said Mrs Brayshaw. In the Brayshaw family, a different pocket money/allowance system to that of his brother's was to be devised for the younger son in an attempt to develop a more cautious approach to money.

Parents wanted their children to have the satisfaction of achievement, and the young people recounted their pleasure in achieving. To this end, money was seen as of less importance to a satisfactory career than a choice based on interest. The emphasis on value to society was highlighted by the Jackson family whose members were not dependent upon earned income. 'They could choose, and do something of value', said Mr Jackson; and the elder daughter, Sarah, had refused any payment during her work experience year. The duality of personal fulfilment and social contribution was captured by Mrs Philips, who said of her son: 'I wouldn't want to see him wasted', a metaphor legitimating individualism within economic identity.

This emphasis on the uniqueness and value of the individual, along with an awareness of the need for hard work now in order to keep employment options open, was set within a context of flexible futures, a landscape of possibilities rather than discrete and rigid paths (although Simon Phillips, for example, had a clear idea of the medical career he wanted to pursue). This kind of contextualizing of futures meant that the stages of a young person's life course – choice of subjects for public examinations, decisions about university, possible careers – were taken step by step, great emphasis being placed upon the task in hand; but such immediate goals were set within an environment of knowledge and access to information from formal and informal sources to be drawn upon when the time was right. This was captured by Mr Jackson when he referred to 'anticipating' what his children might need rather than preparing them for specific types of occupation.

A sense of uniqueness, as members of a privileged group, was enhanced by the young people's awareness of an education which set them apart. Their perceived ability as reflected in examination success was itself a differentiating factor; one boy felt that only those with ability could benefit from private education. In his view, this meant that most people in the state system would not be candidates for the private sector. The young people defined themselves as middle class, and Simon Phillips saw qualifications as a major distinguishing feature between social groups, 'professional, non-professional, manuals and completely unskilled'. The fact that they were privileged was highlighted by the nature of the voluntary work they undertook and the fact that some parents felt it important that the young people be made aware of their 'privileged upbringing'. Although these distinctions were made in order to increase young people's social awareness and sense of social responsibility, they also served to emphasize their difference. The high and endemic unemployment of the region was only rarely seen as relevant to themselves, largely serving as a spur to acquire even better qualifications.

Again, however, there were boundaries; individualism was contained while permitting it to flourish. This was not an individualism which allowed any path to be trodden, or one to be followed in any way one liked. Rather, individualism and freedom were underpinned, and thereby controlled, by the pressure and will to work hard, an orientation towards achievement, the productive use of time, and the encouragement to develop interests and talents in as many directions as possible. One dimension of this control, with regard to hard work, lay within the definition of happiness described earlier.

A second controlling mechanism lay in the integration of education and familism, the latter itself a powerful tool in the transfer of advantage. In these families, school and homework influenced the pattern and timetabling of daily routines. But in addition, family resources and those of family members were devoted to the furtherance of young people's academic and other successes and woven into the fabric of family life. Indeed, educational support took the form of a family project, hinted at, for example, by the frequent use of the pronoun 'we' when parents were asked about their children's decisions on examination options and their futures, and in the young people's descriptions of the discussions that had taken place. Thus, in these projects, as well as the investment of money, space was provided and allocated and parental time made available. In the Brayshaw family, there was a clear and explicit division of parental labour, mother providing the academic support and father the responsibility for sport (the provision of free music tuition to the school by Mrs Jackson has already been noted).

An emphasis upon individualism, however, can pose problems, since within the family it competes with two other highly regarded tenets, solidarity and fairness (see Backett, 1982; Allatt and Yeandle, 1986). Paradoxically, however, the transmission of individualism was both sustained and controlled by integrating it with these two familistic parameters. First, family members shared leisure time activities or supported each other in their various interests, for example, in attending concerts or matches. Secondly, individualism was contained within a reward system which, while recognizing and lauding the individual, also celebrated the family as a unit. In this system, emphasis was placed upon the pleasure of achievement for its own sake, and young people said they 'would work hard anyway'. A place at Cambridge would be enough for 'thirteen years hard work', said Simon Phillips; although parents might feel it important to recognize the lesser milestones of achievement – 'with a book or a kiss' said Mike Phillips. Mr Brayshaw observed of an 'A' grade for an O-level taken a year early: 'It's a cause for saying . . . "That's one under your belt. We'll go out, even if it's only a bar of chocolate but we'll get something. We will do something that will recognize you".' Additionally, however, reward was frequently embedded within a family celebration, going out for a meal or 'cracking a bottle'. The ritual both acknowledged a policy of fairness, of 'doing the same for both of them', while publicly affirming the collective nature of the family-household. It comprised a system, incorporating both control and encouragement, which attempted to sustain family solidarity while celebrating individual achievement.

The Social Context

While individuals might be born into a rich store of social and cultural capital embedded in a family's social networks, this inheritance is not necessarily sufficient to maintain the advantages it might offer. Not only must the young learn the skills of exchange (sociability) which sustain these relationships, but also those skills which enable them to create social and cultural capital of their own.

There were two areas where these resources were nurtured. They were lodged, first, in the joining behaviour of young people, rooted in young people's own interests and parental models. Secondly, young people were integrated into the networks and processes of using parental contacts.

In these families, the parents provided vivid models for the young people as active participants in leisure pursuits, organizations and committees – for the schools, the community, professional groups and industry. The parents could identify and describe how they themselves came to be involved – 'Well, you offer don't you?' – how then (in the exchanges which constitute sociablity) they were invited to join special groups, and the processes leading to their election to committees. The young people both shared some of their interests and were also drawn into helping roles, thus contributing themselves and seeing the skills of parents and others in action. This model of parental involvement was complemented by parental encouragement to fill any spare time with activity, the potential foundation of social network formation. As John Brayshaw put it:

> On a weekend, if I'm just lounging around, watching TV, or doing something, they say, 'Ah, come on, you could be doing this, doing that', and things. But sometimes they say, 'Ah, just leave him.' That's mostly if, perhaps, I've been doing stacks of work. They let me have a day of rest or something.

The number of activities in which these young people were engaged, and the standards of performance in them, were remarkable, and this boy was no exception. Moreover, he was aware of the value of such social activity for the development of the cultural capital of social competence, if not, as yet, its role in the formation of social networks which might later be drawn upon.

Thus he felt it to be important that young people joined things because 'it'll help them again later in life when they . . . say, get involved sort of in the Round Table or something . . . mingle, get to know people' (Mr Brayshaw had been heavily involved in the Round Table, and the boys had joined him in some of the activities). And his elder brother, Stephen, observed: 'I've always, like, done all my homework. And any time left I go out and play sports, and do things like that', commenting that his parents were pleased that he was 'in as many things as possible'. The social relationships in which such activities are grounded, especially when located within a privileged social stratum and reinforced by private education which produces its own exclusive networks, are the raw material of social capital.

To be effective, however, social networks have to be coupled with a knowledge of how to use them. While information can circulate within a group, and privileged access or inside information about jobs or other valued positions may be offered merely by being an accepted member of a group, it is also important to know how to to take the initiative in these processes. The nourishing of this skill was embedded in a system whereby parents offered their own social networks as a resource for their children's use. The parents used such networks for a variety of reasons, some of which have been noted. In other instances, however, the young people were drawn into the exploitation of this parental resource in a way which developed social capital as a property of the child. Instances of this were when parental contacts were used to further a school project or for career or university information. A parent would identify and speak to the appropriate contact, but the young people had then to follow this up themselves. For example, as Mrs Brayshaw explained, 'It was through me that he got in touch with the WRVS [Women's Royal Voluntary Service] . . . he goes and helps on the geriatric ward [for the Duke of Edinburgh Award]'. While it was Mrs Phillips who learned from the matron, a personal contact, of the opportunity for her son to work in a children's nursery, it was he who had to make the official contacts and arrangements through the local authority. Mr Jackson had business contacts willing to talk about differences in university courses to his son, emphasizing, however, that it was Charles who went to see them. And although Mrs Jackson had already established that her daughter could join the choir of the school she was to enter a year later, Deborah still was told to go and ask if she could join. In effect, not only were these young people the beneficiaries of parental social networks but they were also inducted into the necessary social competencies for their exploitation. In these instances, the fact that parents had prepared the ground meant that the results of the formal and informal approaches would be positive, but no doubt this was not always so. More importantly, and the case of the school choir is an example where there was no necessity for the daughter to ask if she could join, situations were constructed so as to directly involve young people in the transaction.

Conclusion

We know very little about what goes on in other people's families. Indeed, we sometimes have difficulty understanding what is happening in our own. This chapter has attempted to tease out from qualitative data aspects of the stock of resources which some families have and to show how these inform the processes through which privilege is transmitted across the generations. For while there is a rich literature on the transfer of privilege, there is little on the intricacies and detail of the mechanisms through which this is achieved. This kind of analysis also links the minutiae of daily family life to wider social processes in the world outside the family. It is particularly relevant in a political climate where the rhetoric of 'classless society' is used not only as though historical accumulations of resources were suddenly cancelled out but also where this rhetoric is accompanied by a call to a familism which enjoins all parents to do their utmost to enhance the lives of their children. Indeed, in the current political debates, this latter quality is applauded and encouraged, as well as being one to which many, irrespective of social class, subscribe.

In this study, the focus was on the resources of economic, cultural, social and emotional capital. In themselves, however, resources are not sufficient for the accrual of advantage, and the chapter has shown the complex interplay in the processes directed at reproducing them in the next generation. It has been shown here how privileged families can select and to some extent shape and supplement the formal educational environment of their young. Systems of transference have also been revealed, constructed out of resources, values, norms, controls and freedoms. These elements were woven systematically, over the course of young people's lives, into the fabric of family life. Through these systems, characterized by freedoms within boundaries of control, the families attempted to build young people's social and cultural capital, handing on skills and attributes to the young. The qualities encouraged, developed and sustained through family practices over the long years of schooling – responsibility, individualism, hard work, effort and pleasure in achievement, social competence and access to critical social networks – are those which have long been associated with occupational advancement and economic success among the middle classes. In these families, however, emphasis was not placed on economic reward for its own sake, as might have been expected given the cultural climate of the last twelve years. Emphasis, rather, was on fulfilment, job satisfaction and contribution to society, although, as noted, the high achievement of these young people set them on course for well remunerated careers. Class did not figure largely in the young people's perceptions, although they placed themselves in the same class as their parents. They were, however, conscious of being set apart by a privileged education, upbringing and ability, in fact by their advantages.

In two of the families, the necessity to achieve educationally in order to maintain this advantage, and the increased pressure for examination success generally in our society, should be noted. All the families remarked on the latter. Thus as well as advantage and satisfaction gained from achievement, there was also a cost paid by young people from privileged homes in a decade, and from a social stratum, which has placed so much emphasis upon individual responsibility for one's future. It was poignantly illustrated by the boy who said that the happiest time of his life was when he was about twelve, on holiday:

> I could forget totally about school, anything to do with exams . . . and I just found I could totally relax and forget about everything . . . It just made me feel a lot better . . . so I found I could relax completely and therefore I felt so much happier.

Notes

1. This chapter is based on data from the ESRC 16–19 Initiative: *Family Processes and Transfers in the Transition to Adulthood* (Grant No. XC 05250019). I would like to thank the following for their comments: Barbara Adam, David Morgan, Bernadette Murphy, George Riseborough, Chris Shilling and especially Inge Bates.
2. Wealth is also a resource about which, when there are substantial amounts, steps have to be taken to ensure its proper management by the next generation. In such circumstances, money is a responsibility and a trust which extends beyond the individual concerned. In one instance, not developed in this chapter, a son was introduced to the bank personnel who dealt with the family money in order that he learn the skills involved in its management.
3. For Bourdieu, 'cultural capital can exist in three forms: in the embodied state, i.e., in the form of long lasting dispositions of the mind and body; in the objectified state, in the form of cultural goods (pictures, books, dictionaries, instruments machines, etc.) . . . ; and in the institutionalized state', for example, educational qualifications. Essentially cultural capital 'is linked to the body and presupposes embodiment' (Bourdieu, 1986, pp. 243, 244).
4. One of the families, the wealthiest, were Quakers and farmers and had other business interests. The combination of Quakerism and a feeling of a commonality of interests among farmers produced a sense of classlessness, although there was a recognition of material differences.
5. Although not discussed in the text, there were different nuances of emphasis in each family. In the established and secure middle class, there seemed to be a more relaxed attitude, still orientated towards results and achievement, but one which emphasized the fulfilling of potential. This was accompanied by a recognition that money allowed the individual to choose an occupation of value to society irrespective of monetary rewards. In the other two families, one upwardly mobile and the other materially less well off than either set of grandparents, there was a greater awareness of financial costs.

References

Allan, G.A. (1982) Property and family solidarity. In P.G. Hollowell (ed.) *Property and Social Relations*. London, Heinemann.

Allatt, P. (1987) In trust: young people and transfers within households. Paper presented at the *ESRC Workshop Series, Resources within Households*, Institute of Education, June. University of London.

Allatt, P. (1991) Family forms of work. Paper presented at the ESRC 16–19 Initiative Conference, March. Harrogate.

Allatt P. and Benson, L.D. (1991) Family discourse: political socialization amongst teenagers and their parents. ESRC 16–19 Initiative Occasional Papers, No. 37. London, Social Statisitics Research Unit, City University.

Allatt P. and Yeandle, S.M. (1986) 'It's not fair, is it?' Youth unemployment, family relations and the social contract. In S. Allen, K. Purcell, B. Waton and S. Wood (eds) *The Experience of Unemployment*. London, Macmillan.

Allatt P. and Yeandle, S.M. (1992) *Youth Unemployment and the Family: Voices of Disordered Times*. London, Routledge.

Backett, K. (1982) *Mothers and Fathers*. New York, St Martin's Press.

Bourdieu, P. (1986) The forms of capital. In J.G. Richardson (ed.) *Handbook of Theory and Research for the Sociology of Education*. New York, Greenwood Press. Originally published as Okonomisches Kapital, kuturelles Kapital, soziales Kapital. In R. Kreckel (ed.) *Soziale Ungleichheiten* (Soziale Welt, Sonderheft 2). Goettingen, Otto Schwartz.

Jackson B. and Marsden, D. (1968) *Education and the Working Class*. Harmondsworth, Penguin (first published in 1962 by Routledge and Kegan Paul).

Nowotny, H. (1981) Women in public life in Austria. In C. Fuchs Epstein and R. Laub Coser (eds) *Access to Power: Cross National Studies of Women and Elites*. London, Sage.

Pahl, J. (1983) The allocation of money and the structuring of inequality within marriage. *Sociological Review*, 31, 237–62.

Wallman, S. (1984) *Eight London Households*. London, Tavistock.

Chapter 8

'GBH – The Gobbo Barmy Harmy'
One day in the life of 'the YTS boys'[1]

George Riseborough

Background to the Study

But when the day's hustle and bustle is done,
Then the Gumbie Cat's work is but hardly begun.
She thinks that the cockroaches just need employment
To prevent them from idle and wanton destroyment.
So she's formed, from that lot of disorderly louts,
A troop of well-disciplined helpful boy-scouts,
With a purpose in life and a good deed to do –
And she's even created a Beetle's Tattoo.

So for Old Gumbie Cats let us now give three cheers –
On whom well-ordered households depend, it appears.
(The Old Gumbie Cat, T.S. Eliot)

'Blightown', in the North of England, is still renowned for its single, major heavy industry which, because of economic recession, retrenchment and severe contraction in recent years, now provides a rust belt across the city. The traditional industry was characterized by a largely, but not wholly, male working population employed in subordinate primary-market jobs (see Edwards, 1979).

At the time of the ethnographic research, the city's official rate of unemployment was about 16 per cent (*Employment Gazette*, 1988). In 1988, only five of the city's twenty-nine electoral wards had unemployment below the national average. In the central parliamentary constituency, there was an unemployment rate of 23.1 per cent, while it was as high as 25 per cent in some areas. At the time the ethnographic data were collected, only 9 per cent of 16-year-olds had a full-time job, 47 per cent were on a variety of Youth Training Schemes (YTS), 32 per cent were in other full-time education or training, and a further 13 per cent were not in full-time work or education/training (presumed unemployed).

'Artisan Further Education College' is modern and on a single site. It has well-established building-trade departments which provide its major curricular provision and gives the college a distinctive ethos. This chapter is a product by a 'participant-as-observer' (Gold, 1958), researching over a period of two years (1987–89) with a group of 'lads' – 'The Wolf Pack' (see also Riseborough, forthcoming) – who at the time were in the second year of a Building Operatives Youth Training Scheme in which the local authority was the designated 'managing agency'. It was intended, the economy allowing, that this Scheme would eventually take them into general unskilled and semi-skilled labour in the construction industry. Generally, all the trainees are completely devoid of, or have very poor, educational qualifications from school. In college, they were never observed writing anything other than perfunctory necessities, e.g. name, address, time-keeping, etc.

The college's building workshops are at the rear surrounded by stores of materials – sand, bricks, timber, drains, etc. They are large, modern, insulated, steel-framed, brick structures which contain small classrooms and large work areas, characteristically containing students' 'practicals' – road works, elaborate brick walls, roofs, joinery, etc. There is also a centralized 'mill' – a large mixing machine – where 'gobbo' (mortar) is prepared for a variety of courses. There is normally the hum of the building site – concrete mixer, sawing, hammering, whistling, singing, trowel-on-brick, talk, etc., combined with the incessant hum of ventilation.

College mortar is made only from sand, lime and water, so that it never sets. Consequently, all materials can be cleaned down after use and re-cycled. Even the mortar is recycled. Given the gobbo's inherent weakness and its inability to handle stress, only small half-finished structures can be erected.

Publicly, the Building Operatives Scheme was a model of the new vocationalism of the then Training Commission, having a degree of national recognition for 'the quality' of its provision. It was characterized by glossy literature, premised on contract, systematized 'skills-based object-ives' and 'competences', week-by-week structured curricular modules, con-tinuous monitoring, counselling and assessment, bureaucratized records of achievement, etc. In the material given to trainees, it was stated:

> The aim of YTS is to to give you a good start to your career. Dur-ing your time as a YTS trainee you can get a training and further education to develop your skills. You can also gain work experi-ence . . . YTS will give you well organized training and the chance to study for a worthwhile qualification . . . By the end of your YTS programme you will have had every chance to learn skills necessary in a particular job, and to develop general skills of value in a wide range of jobs – for example, skills in communicating, working with numbers, problem solving and planning. You will also have been shown how to adapt quickly to new working situations, and your effectiveness as a person, for example in dealing with others, will be improved (MSC, 1988).

The researcher remained with the trainees throughout their formal and informal college time. The Scheme had a variety of college-based, timetabled components – Communication Studies (three hours per week), Information Technology (four hours), Building Theory (three hours) and Practical Vocational Projects (twenty-one hours), together with, of course, blocked work experience with employers. The college component over the two-year period represented twenty-three weeks, an average of three to four weeks per term. The rest was work experience. The maximum working week was forty hours and trainees were entitled to eighteen days holiday per annum, plus bank holidays.

The Ethnography

Geniuses don't adjust their interpretations to suit the taste of tyrants!

A man who's warm can't understand a man who's freezing.

Who's the zek's main enemy? Another zek. If only they weren't at loggerheads with one another – ah, what a difference that'd make!
(*One Day in the Life of Ivan Denisovich*, Alexander Solzhenitsyn)

The start of the day

It is 9.05 a.m. Mike Mason, the lecturer, has arrived as the class dawdles into the room and waits for the rest to arrive. Previously, 'the Boys' have been doing workshop-based activities related to a 'Practical Vocational Project' module – the construction of the foundations, floor and lower brick courses of a series of garages. Today, the class is timetabled to continue this practical work in the workshop all day, finishing the module by demolishing it. As they arrive, Mike Mason is progressively collecting the lads' attendance cards which must be signed at the end of the morning and afternoon if the YTS allowance (£35 in the second year) is eventually to be paid. Given lost, mislaid, forgotten and forged cards; lateness, wagging and 'sendings home'; and high rates of absenteeism due to real and imaginary job interviews and illness, they are a major source of negotiation between teachers, the college bureaucracy and 'the Boys'. What will he do with those who arrive at break-time? Will deviating lads eventually forge his signature? Can he be coaxed into signing for absence by a plausible explanation? Can he be persuaded to sign the cards early so they can go? Either way it provides a lot of work for Mike Mason, some of which he undertakes while he waits.

Wolf: Will ya fill in this new card, only I lost mine in tha washer? I were 'ere all last week.

Mr Mason: Listen [Wolf], if you lost your card in the washer, how come I've got it here? Besides you were missing last Wednesday. If

you are going to tell whoppers, you've got to be fool-proof.
[Guppie], you are down 'ere as absent all the week.

Wolf: Well my ma' washed somethin' in tha washer.

Guppie: [Convincingly innocent] . . . I posted it for certain. A doctor's
           note, ma mother did.

Mr Mason: So would you like to check with the office. Tell them you have
           sent a sick note in and ask them if they have received it. Also
           tell them that up to now you have been recorded as absent.
           Where did you send your sick note into? Are you sure, how
           can you be sick when you look so well?

Guppie: Ma money is short as well. I forgot to get Mr Sands to sign
           ma card one afternoon. 'E signed it aftawards. But I've lost a
           day's pay. I've phoned them up. Remember I was tellin' ya?
           They should 'ave stopped 'alf. 'E filled card in and said, 'Wait'.
           And they said they are goin' t' pay it, the other 'alf back
           the week afta. So I've lost 'alf a day's money. They 'ave
           stopped me a full day and it should 'ave been 'alf a day but
           I should 'ave been paid a full day anyway. Remember I were
           tellin' ya?

Mr Mason: [Overwhelmed by the convolutions of the argument] . . . Any-
           way, well get to the office and sort it out. [Guppie disappears
           smiling and is not seen seen for some time. This is a fringe
           benefit of absenteeism.]

While undertaking these routine tasks, the rest chat among themselves
about the previous evening's happenings and future intentions, as others
arrive.

Alice: George, I'm not leavin', George! I'm not! [Just arriving. He had
           an interview the day before] . . . They're a reet set of wankers
           at that steelworks. I've been talkin' to ma uncle abart firm. 'E
           says they're wankers. They sack ya if ya 'ave a day off, 'ours
           are longer, 7.30 t' 5.30 and it would take me an 'our t' get
           there. They lay ya off as soon as . . . My uncle says there's a
           chance 'e'll get me a job, an apprenticeship. So I am stickin'
           on this job meantime. Forty-five quid weren't enough, were it?
           I'd be out of pocket! I fiddle me travellin' 'ere, don't I? That
           makes me five quid more but if I took this job I'd be out of
           pocket travellin', wouldn't I? I'd go f' £80! I'd miss tha lads
           wouldn't I? And tha 'ours are easier. I need a good laff and
           that!

Wolf: You're late boy! [The use of 'boy' is a much favoured 'send up'
           in exaggerated form of a schoolteacher-type usage!] . . . Now
           then, fancy 'avin' next Thursday off and comin' down t'

MacAppenines at Churchgate. Theere's labourin' goin' in Derby and tha lot, £3.20 an hour, Derby. Easy get there and ma mate can take two in tha car. Just labourin', ground work, diggin' 'oles and that. Abart a month, two month, three month, could be owt. We can go down in tha dinner 'our and see if we get set on. Fuckin' 'ell its 3.20 an 'our, comes to £130 a week on top. Can't go wrong f' that. Come out with about £108. We could get some 'oliday from 'ere, put in f' our 'olidays. Then we'd get it on top of our YTS money. That's not bad is it! I might fuck off altogether. Ma mate says there's just a chance of us goin' t' London, five quid an 'our. Fuckin' ell!

Jar: Ma mate when 'e went down, 'e wa' on 12 quid an 'our. Reet fuckin' money that, bricklayin'.

Wolf: Five quid an 'our though, ten 'ours in a day, ya'd get 50 quid a day. Will tha take us down, George?

George: I'll take you down. I'll do you a favour if ya put 50p in the meter! [Laughter]

Jar: What, if tha puts 50p in our meter, ya mean! [Laughter] . . . I were goin' f' an interview. I phoned but 'e 'ad already taken someone on. So 'e took ma address and phone number.

Wolf: What were it?

Jar: 'Eatin' engineers.

George: Oh, all right then, gladly! On Thursday.

Jar: Last day George, we'll take thee f' a piss up! We'll see thee reet! Did tha see tele last neet?

George: I ain't got a tele, have I, so I didn't see it?

Alice: Ay, George ain't got a tele. I don't know how 'e lives, me. 'E ain't got a tele, 'im. Listens to radio and reads fuckin' books 'im. Fuckin' uni'. Reads books about YTS lads, daft cunt. I wouldn't fuckin' be able to live me without a tele.

George: You would. How much tele do you watch?

Alice: Abart four 'ours a day, I'd say. Videos. I'll be 'onest young man, old son, you're fuckin' brain-damaged you, no fuckin' tele. [Laughter]

Jar: Reet good laff last night on video. This woman firin' ping-pong balls out of 'er fanny. [Laughter]

Alice: You're jokin'!

Jar: Ya know those book of matches, you can get, eh? She lit a full book all together and put it there . . . [pointing to crotch] . . . and blew 'em out with 'er fanny. Yeh, she put fag smoke up 'er cunt and she were blowin' smoke rings out of 'er cunt. [Laughter]

Wolf: I don't believe ya!

Jar: I'll show thee. I've still got video at 'ome.

George: How much did you pay for this dubious pleasure, then?

Jar:	Nowt, I got it from ma mates. She were doin' it on 'er 'ead, upside down! [Laughter] . . . It's called *Miss Magnificunt*. It's a reet good laff.
Wolf:	Were tha ma' and dad watchin' it with tha? [Laughter]
Jar:	Come on up and I'll show it tha. We 'ad some stuff while we watched.
George:	I thought you said you've given it up.
Jar:	Butane, glue sniffin' is kids' stuff, use to do it. 'Elium is right good, it doesn't do nowt but it's reet funny. We went shoppin' and that last neet and take it and ya talk reet funny. When ya talkin' to people they look at ya reet daft. It were a real laff. [Laughter]
Wolf:	'E's a dealer 'im? 'E'll get ya owt? [Laughter]
Jar:	I ain't!
Wolf:	Don't believe 'im. 'E's got a D on 'is left ear. 'E's tha one who brought those 'poppers' in last year. [Laughter]
George:	What are they?
Jar:	You know they 'ave tha swimmin' bath smell, it's like that chlorine. When it gets to air it evaporates.
George:	What effect do they have?
Wolf:	It only lasts for minute but it's funny like. Bit of a laff.
George:	How much are they?
Jar:	You can either buy a bottle for six quid or three f' eleven pence. But the effect only lasts a minute.
Wolf:	It's alreet, funny, we 'ad some last neet. Ya can't stop laffin', just laffin'. Ya 'ead starts t' spin. Just fine! It's alreet, it's funny!
Jar:	'Draw' is tha best stuff.
Wolf:	I'll 'ave owt, me!
George:	You wouldn't have the hard stuff though?
Wolf:	I'll try owt, I'd give owt a try. I'd see what it were like. What are you lookin' at you fuckin' alien, ya vandal, ya cunt-duck. [Laughter. He is responding to Wing-nut, why in this manner will become evident later]
Wing-nut:	Nowt!

At about 9.25 a.m., the day's programme is outlined.

Mr Mason:	Listen lads! [Silence descends] . . . I want to have an individual word with you about placements and your college work, holidays, etc., this morning and there's reviews to finish off this afternoon. Whilst that is going on I want that work out there dismantled. Now there is two ways we can go about this. The easy way and the hard way. Which way are you going to do it? That's right the easy way! No silly billies! I'll

be keeping an eye on you but you know how important it is on a building site to work unsupervised. There is no-one more important on the building site than the man who can work unsupervised. When you get down to your concrete, get two skips, fetch those up before the bricklayers get in your way. Get them near to where you are working. Let's do it logically! Not like usual. Are you listening? [All look attentive] ... I don't want you just wandering about and materials all over the place. Block pavements first, on pallets and ask Dean ... [the non-teaching workshop technician] ... where he wants them putting because he will be using the forklift. Do it in consultation with him. Blocks first. Stacked neatly on pallets wherever he wants them. Next the brick walls cleaned off. Put your mortar straight into a barrow. Don't let your mortar drop into the work area because if that happens we won't be able to use that again. So you are cleaning bricks, mortar straight into the barrow and straight up to the mill. Your bricks stacked up neatly on their sides with plenty of air so it can circulate and dry off. And then we get down to the concrete foundation. Excavate it and put that straight into the skip. Everything on pallets and bricks stacked on the side. Alright? Is that clear? Right let's go through that again. Jason, what are you going to do first?

Jar reiterates perfectly the prescribed plan of action. Wing-nut and Wolf tussle over a curricular booklet related to a module which has been pains-takingly prepared by Mike Mason and his colleagues.

Mr Mason: What's happened to that?
Wolf: What? It's got ripped, 'asn't it?
Mr Mason: What, on its own? How did it happen?
Wolf: Yer what? 'E were pullin' it!
Mr Mason: [Agitated] ... You will look after this because I've spent a lot of time getting them together for you. A lot of time and effort has gone into that. And I am not satisfied, alright! If I don't look after this no-one will! Alright!
Wolf: [Surly] ... Yeh!
Mr Mason: This is a worthwhile experience ... in the future, if you are taking a skill test or exam this exercise ought to be filed away in your file and referred to. I'm not satisfied!
Wolf: I've never taken an exam in ma life and I don't intend to start now!
Mr Mason: The opportunity is there for you to take.
Wolf: Stuff that!

It is only now the lads change into their working clothes and go outside.
They have been issued with an overall and boots but these have been lost,
stolen, sold or have otherwise disappeared. 'The Boys' do not like them.
Graffiti puts on his Walkman which he keeps on most of the day! Whenever
he moves he rattles with tapes. 'The Boys' leave the room sniggering at
Wolf and Mike Mason. Then they moan among themselves, as they are
faced with a sea of dog-toothed-laid decorative bricks on the ground, walls
chest height, all resting on a concrete base.

Wolf: 'E's a shit'ead! I like 'is little neck and I'll wring it! I fuckin' 'ate
this! Move out of me way Alice. Doesn't make sense some'ow. Layin'
them all down yesterday and then liftin' them up today. It's fuckin'
work. I'll stand around lookin' intelligent. Spark up, Jar. [Jar lights
a cigarette which the two smokers share. It is transferred as usual
by throwing it between each other] . . . D' ya reckon 'e'll give us the
afta' off? Pull thy weight Wing-nut, pull thy weight, go get some
pallets, ya pillock! Ya know the rules 'round 'ere, pillocks get pallets! [Laughter] . . . So fuck off, duck arse! Ya bleedin' mong!
[Prejorative dimunition of mongol, that is, Down's Syndrome. As
will be seen, this is applied mainly to subordinate group members
and any deemed inferior category of person]

Jar: Wing-nut, get some fuckin' pallets, boy! Or get a boot up tha arse.
'E's like a bag of wank. 'E's a woman, tha big shitter. The trouble
is tha' can see the job right there in front of ya eyes. 'E wants it
done before we go t'night. It's real work i'n't it? It's soul destroyin'.
Ya lays it all down and then it's all to come up.

Wing-nut disappears around the back of the building. In the meantime,
Guppie returns from the College offices, smiling. He admits freely that no
sick note has been sent by his mother. However, he has convinced the
office that there has been an administrative error and he has been assured
he will be paid normally.

Alice: Doooohh! Helloooooha! Gooppeee! [Baby-like]
Guppie: Doooohh! Helloooooha! Alleeece! I've just 'ad a shit on the way
back, it were a right fuckin' corker! I were in shit 'ouse ten
minutes. Pit-pat! Pit-pat! A reet corker!
Wolf: Is that gel in tha 'air or just lard, Guppie? I think I'll call thee
Gossie! [Pun on Bros' surname and Guppie's nickname.
Laughter] . . . Where's tha been?
Guppie: Couldn't be bothered comin' in. Day befor yesterday got up,
right, about twelve o'clock. Took ma mum to work with ma
brother in 'is car. Sat watchin' tele. Then this kid came over to
see me. Then we pick 'is sister up. Went to town. Walked around

a bit. Went out that night and got blasted and I mean blasted. Twenty quid I spent and I didn't buy anyone a drink. I 'ad about twenty shots of gin, 'ad about eight in about two minutes. I took 20 quid with me at 6.30 and when I got 'ome at 1.00, I 'ad 2p left. Yesterday I got up about three o'clock and then I went on tha town. I went to *Cleo's* and this kid 'e works there just kept givin' me another and another. 'E gets it for nowt. 'Ave another and another. Then steak sandwiches. Then I met this bird, she were blasted, kept puttin' her arm around me like and kissin'. Puttin' her tongue down ma gob. We went 'round the back and she raked me off. A right pro. Right laff, I got blasted again but not as bad as the night before and I'll fuckin' get paid for it. [Laughter] . . . Can't be bad but I'm knackered and I've got to work this Saturday, my firm phoned us and ask if I'd come in, 15 quid in the back pocket and I'm workin' in tha club tonight.

Wolf: I 'ad 14 pints at *Casablanca Bill's* last night. Know 'ow much it cost, 7 quid, cheap night, 50p a pint. This bloke eat a fag f' a 50p bet! I'm still pissed now!

George: Give over. You are dizzy after a half! [Laughter]

Wolf: Fuck off, George! [Laughter]

Jar: I know someone who can drink 30 pints, a reet blubber bag! 'E's a ton of drippin'! [Laughter]

Wing-nut arrives back with a broken pallet, lays it down where a fork-lift cannot operate and begins work.

Wolf: Look at tha fuckin' pin'ead, tha dosey cunt. It's broken, ya dosey twat. Don't ya know, ya dimbo? 'Ere put it there where th' fuckin' fork-lift can get it!

Wing-nut: It's tha only one I could find.

George: But its no good, it's broken!

Wolf: Doesn't matter! I don't care, we're not bothered. Put it 'ere shit 'ead. Let's see 'ow fast we can go! Let's set an all time record! We can get all this done by dinna' time.

George: It does matter! Pride in your work! [Laughter]

All: Piss off, George! There 'e goes again! [Laughter]

There follows a frantic effort, bricks are being lobbed between lads faster and faster amidst shouts of 'Come on ya dosey bastard, faster. Catch! 'Ere get ya finga out. Pull thee weight, shit 'ouse! Pull thee weight, George.' Soon the pallet is full, the fork-lift is brought up. It attempts to remove it, whereupon the whole lot predictably collapses in a heap. Loud cheers go up! Everybody claps!

Wolf: Great! It's all thy fault, Wing-nut. [Hitting him playfully about the head] . . . Ya dosey cunt. Ya sheep fucker. 'Ere let's go and get some propa pallets. Let's go f' a walk. What time is it? Give us a light, Guppie.

They go around to the rear of the building. Unable to find unused pallets, the lads kick, push and smash materials off existing ones. It goes without saying that this material will have to be put back on pallets later in order to move them.

George: For God's sake don't let Mason see what you have done. You vandals. That's best Yorkshire sandstone that, it cost a fortune. It's a sedimentary rock, it has to be quarried and cut. It's been like that for millions of years and then some YTS lads come along and vandalize it in seconds. [Laughter]

Wolf: [Imitatively] . . . We'll get to the bottom of this. Who's vandalized this? Sedimentary, my dear Watson, sedimentary! Sedimentary me dear Mason, sedimentary. [Laughter]

Graffiti: Take it 'ome as a souvenir, George. Nice bit of crazy pavin' from tha crazy gang! [Laughter]

Alice: Take George 'ome as a souvenir, 'e's a fuckin' million years old. [Laughter]

Wolf: Come on let's get these back. Wing-nut get 'oggin' [carrying] boy! 'Elp 'im, ya tits.

Alice: Oh, fuckin' 'ell someone 'as 'ad a shit 'ere, big brown skidders, it's all over m' boots! [Impromptu urination and excretion are routine around the college building. Everyone starts laughing] . . . Come 'ere ya dopey cunt and I'll shoe [kick] ya! [He attempts to clean his shoes on Wing-nut but cannot catch him. Instead, he uses a pile of sand] . . . That'll make some nice gobbo f' someone! [Laughter]

Wolf: Did I tell ya this one? We were at this 'ouse sleepin' afta a party and Tommy said, you know Tommy, 'Who wants breakfast in bed, lads?', you know? And Tommy went downstairs and shits on a plate. No bullshit this. And 'e gets two slices of bread and spreads it on and 'e comes upstairs and gives it t' me like that, so I stabs 'im in the back with a fork and I showed tha dirty bastard. I just 'ad this pair of kecks on and I took it outside into tha garage, like and set it on fire and put Tommy's coat on it. [Laughter]

Jar: Set what on fire, tha shit? Did it burn?

Wolf: Yeh, put petrol on it. Then I lobs his burnt coat inta the garden. Tha fucka! Tha weasle 'ead! A reet laff!

Guppie: 'E got nicked. Muggin', sort of thing. Everythin'. 'E got done for

stealin' a car, beatin' kids up, robbery. 'E did robbery. A video.
'E got twenty-one charges in court. They dropped nine. 'E got
done for robbery, a stereo, 'e got six months youth custody.
Shopliftin'. 'E said 'e wanted ta go down. 'E said 'e wanted to go
inside. Everythin' is free and that and 'e'drather do time than 'ave
no job. That's what tha mad fucka said! 'E's an idiot, though,
i'n't 'e? 'E were in Armley. 'E's out now. 'E got's all 'is 'air
shaved all 'round tha side 'ere and on front 'ere 'e's got a big
blond streak. 'E looks like Dickie Davis. [Laughter] . . . A reet
'ard cunt, 'im now!

Wolf: Only fools go t' prison, them's all they catch. They come out reet
'ard. 'E di'n't do six month though. 'E wa' on remand for three
month at Armley. Tommy ses 'e'drather do a month in Wakefield
than a week in Armley. One of m' mates 'ung 'issen there. They
make life fuckin' 'ell. 'E 'ated it. The screws 'ave these flat caps
with the peak flat so you can't see their eyes. Right bastards!

The lads wend their way to the workshop with the pallets. Once again
there is a frantic effort loading bricks. Wing-nut is suddenly loaded down
with bricks by the others which he duly drops under the sheer weight to
a chorus of 'tha dosey cunt'. Wolf shows him how to do it.

Wolf: Come on, ya cunts, see how many I can carry. Load us up! We'll
get this done be dinna. There's no stoppin' me when I start!
Graffiti: There's no startin' ya when ya stop, an' all! [Laughter]
Alice: Nay, once we get t' concrete, it'll tie us down.
Wolf: Come on! Come on! See 'ow many! This 'ill be an all time record!
'Ow many is that now?
Guppie: Thirty-two. 'Ere put 'em over 'ere! 'Ere, guess what I found. Ten
quid down tha seat at tha club I work at. When tha pissed they
are always loosin' money! I always look down back now!
Wolf: Come on, who can beat me? [There are no takers] . . . I've done
my whack, this mornin'. Don't anyone say.

Wolf takes out a newspaper to read, while the others carry on. He is
approached by Mr Harry Hardcore, a lecturer, who is passing through.
Everyone breaks out laughing.

Mr Hardcore: You know the rules in the workshop. Put it away or take
it to the toilet and read it there. You don't know who's
wandering around here. Put it away.

During the reprimand Wolf has his hand behind his back, giving an
invisible 'V' sign to Harry Hardcore which is visible to his mates. They all

laugh. Harry Hardcore's nickname 'Yaphoo', 'Yaphoo' resonates around the workshop. Harry Hardcore has a word with George.

Mr Hardcore: Well then, have you come to any mind-boggling conclusions with this research, yet?
George: No, not really.
Mr Hardcore: There's always a total innocence with them when you catch them, when they get caught. You hope they will grow out of it. They cause havoc, raping and pillaging, making vikings look like social workers. [Laughter] . . . Then when you carpet them and say, 'One peep out of you!', they are totally innocent. They've got a lot of learning to do because the world is a lot tougher and nastier out there! Look what they are doing with those bricks! [To 'the Boys'] . . . Hey! Hey! Make things nice and simple for the bricklayer. He doesn't want to be walking four or five yards for his mortar and the other way for his bricks. Bricklayers are very, very lazy people. Have you ever worked with a bricklayer? Very moody. All he wants to do is lay bricks, nice and easy, one after the other. The more he lays, the more he's paid. And you are there to wait on him hand and foot. He doesn't want to move one inch more than he has to. A little pebble in their mortar and you'll probably get his trowel round the back of your neck. Because that is what bricklayers are like. They think they are the bees knees. They are tradesmen, don't forget. All we are is operatives, labourers. Now when I say that I am not being unkind at all, but you have to service that bricklayer and we are going to keep that bricklayer sweet, so we are going to stack that material around him and easy for him. You'll get the blame if it's not. So you don't do the job like that! Do you?

Harry Hardcore disappears. Wolf and the rest set to work, each having a rest in rotation. After an appropriate time, people are reset to work with a chorus of 'Come on, ya bastard!' and bricks are thrown at them.

George: Why don't you do as you are told! I always do! [Laughter]
Wolf: I'm tha best lad in tha class me! [Laughter] . . . 'E's a wanker, 'Ardcore. A shit'ead. Tha ferret arse! Thinks 'e's a great little boss and that. Thinks 'e owns everybody. A wanker. Never liked 'im ever. Look at the beads of sweat on ma 'ead! Come on, George! Come on, George! Tha dosey cunt! I'll show thee, I'm a reet grafter me.
George: Why don't you graft here then? I'm paid to think not work! I've never worked so hard in all my life. [Laughter]

Alice: Tha's a pansy, George! [Laughter]

Wolf: I'm not bothered, it's shit 'ere. When ya on placement ya 'ave ta work. It's real work, ain't it? Like if ya put somethin' up it stays there.

Jar: It doesn't when tha builds it! [Laughter] . . . Did ya see that super 'od-carrier on tele. Starts at 5 o'clock and finishes at 8 at neet. Just 'loadin' out' [trade term for servicing bricklayers] t' this team of brickies. Just carryin' all week. Makes £2000 a week, average. 'E's built like a brick shit'ouse. I don't mean just big and 'efty but I mean muscles like Popeye. Did ya see 'im? Like two fuckin' blokes welded together. Just about as big as me but 'is body were like rock-solid and 'e 'as done it since 'e were a lad. 'E runs like a fuckin' monkey up that scaffold. 'Ave tha tried it? It's fuckin' 'ard work 'od-carryin', 'ard graft. It's not nice gettin' them bricks up tha scaffold when it's blowin' a gale. Now that is fuckin' 'ard graft!

Alice: I bet you'd like t' be as strong as 'im, George! [Laughter]

George: I am, beneath this refined exterior is a regular little power pack! [Laughter]

Wolf: [To Alice] . . . What's tha lookin' at boy? Carrot juice! Look at 'is 'tache, 'is little bit of red fluff! [Laughter. Alluding to his ginger hair]

Alice: Kiss ma arse, it's got a big tail! [Laughter]

All the paving bricks – about a thousand – are palletized in half an hour to the refrain of 'Give me! Give me a man until midnight! Break of tha day!' and 'Yowsers! Yowsers! Yoh!' Everybody then sits down for a rest. Wing-nut gets out a miniature colour television.

Guppie: 'Ow much were that, ya fuckin' wanka?

Wing-nut: Twenty quid.

Wolf: Someone were desperate, they cost a couple of 'undred. Let's look. [Everybody gathers around]

Jar: I've offered 'im thirty.

Guppie: It's no fuckin' good. Where did tha get it?

Wing-nut: In a pub.

Alice: Does anyone want a colour tele cheap, Toshiba, 23-inch, tele-text, the lot? Ask no questions. Tell no lies. I can get ya one cheap.

Graffiti: Ma mate makes £2000 a month! 'E's sellin' three-piece suits that cost £2000, sells 'em f' £500. 'E won't tell us where 'e gets 'em. They aren't nicked but they're a bit illegal. 'E gets ya anythin' ya wants. 'E's only twenty but in business. 'E can get ya anythin' cheap. 'E goes 'round pubs sellin' videos, tellies, video-cameras, anythin'. They're not knock-offs but they are a bit illegal. What do ya think of ma Walkman, George? Can't get anythin' betta, 90 quid they cost in tha shops, 40 quid it cost me, graphic equalizer, alarm, time, auto-reverse, the lot.

George: I didn't believe the Station Sergeant when he allocated me to the YTS lads to crack organized crime in Blightown. I'm CID, you are all under arrest! [Laughter] . . . What's a graphic equalizer, anyway? [Everybody laughs at him]

Wolf: Listen to tha university dimbo! 'E's not clever enough f' CID. [Laughter]

George: Are you extracting the michael again! [Laughter]

Guppie: A kid I know is sellin' gold rolex watches!

Wolf: Do ya want five sacks of potatoes, George. Only 5 quid! Ma dad'll get thee 20 tons of rock salt, if ya want.

George: It's nearly summer! [Laughter]

Wolf: So what? D' ya want it or not? I know I want a piss! 'Ere Alice go tell Mason what we've done and that we've gone for a break. Go on ya pillock. Quick, let's run for it!

Break time

They go to the toilets and noises emanate (Eeeeeeh, aaaaah, etc.), closet doors bang and every visible tap is left running. Wing-nut comes out wet from thrown water. They go to the students' social area, a separate building, where there is record playing and slot machines. There are already some British 'lads' of Asian origin sat there. A silence descends and 'the Boys' stare hostilely straight at them.

Wolf: They wears a ring on tha arse with cunt 'ooks on it. [Laughter] . . . They're all mouth, those Pakis. Right load of shits. Shit scared, 'course they are. They think they are fuckin' 'ard. That Mohammed, I ain't scared of that cunt, tha one with tha thick jersey an' leather jacket. Who's frightened of tha' fucker? I'll rip 'is fuckin' 'ead off. I've nearly 'ad 'im. They want a good 'idin' those fuckas.

Guppie: I know they do. This Paki wanker once at *Cleo's*, pushed me tha twat. I said, 'Ya what?' 'E'd got a few friends with 'im, that's why 'e were mouthy. I walked off like and 'e pushed me like that. So I said, 'Piss off you! or I'll push ya fuckin' 'ead in now'. And 'e wouldn't, so I grabbed 'old of 'is 'ead and whacked it on me knee. Then they were all at it, so me an' me mates went bang, bang, bang . . . [fist action]! We killed tha bastards. This mate, Mick is a right nutter and 'e were out of tha nick. A reet 'ard fucker. 'E killed this fuckin' fanny. Beat tha shit out of it. 'E got this Paki bastard, whacked 'im, got 'is arm up 'is back and whacked 'is 'ead against tha fuckin' wall. Whack!

George: Come on don't be like that!

Alice: Look at tha big brown skidders! They are always together, all stick together. If tha goin' gets tough, we'll call in tha expert, tha 'eavy back-up, George!

Jar: They'll get sorted out soon. [To the Asian-origin lads] . . . What are ya fuckin' doin'? I've seen ya starin' at me. Admit it! I'm not 'avin' it, ya little Paki shits. [To 'the Boys'] . . . They are cocky as owt when they get together. Ya never see 'em at matches or owt, eh? They're scared. When they fight, they pick a little 'un, or it's ten of them against one of us. Reet, isn't it? And the fuckas carry knives, tha little Paki shits. Did ya 'ear abart that kid that got attacked at tha fair, that were 'im who done it. Jimmy 'as got some scores t' settle after bein' beaten up at tha fairground! Look 'e just looked at tha floor, bottled out and backed off.

Wolf: 'E's threatened me before, I've threatened 'im. 'E said 'e were goin' t' get all 'is mates. I said I'll get tha lads then. 'E shut up after that. 'E's a fuckin' wanka. 'E's shakin'. I'll kick tha fuck out of 'im. 'E shouldn't be in college.

George: Do you know them?

Wolf: Some of tha fuckers went t' our school. I know all these Paki lads. They're fuckin' bastards and they bring their family in, brothers and that. They're all fuckin' knob'eads. Fight one of 'em and ya end up fightin' twenty of 'em. Then they run like fuckin' shits. They always say they'll go and get their big brothers, the shit'ouses. That Mohammed, watch 'im. 'E'll turn 'is back on ya and then bang! I saw 'em once, this lad 'e 'ad 'im and 'e stumbled and they all closed in and shoed 'im. We 'ad a reet battle with 'em once!

George: How did it all start?

Wolf: This black kid called me a fuckin' bastard on tha bus. 'E was a wanker. I couldn't understand wha' 'e were sayin'. 'E said all sorts of things about me. I got attacked once by 40 of the black bastards. 'E's just a wanker who thinks 'e is 'ard. 'E can bring as many wogs as 'e wants. They'll not come 'round me. I'll eat 'im alive. Our lads 'll petrol bomb 'em. Our lads, white boys, we'll bomb anyone black bastard who 'assles us. We've done one of their cars. If they bring all of theirs up, we'll bring all of ours up. I can get two 'undred up 'ere easy. Big Tommy will bring 'is fuckin' shotgun up! We've bombed before and we'll bomb again! I'll kick tha fucker. 'E got me once on tha floor and kicked me.

Jar: If 'e stares at me again, I'll break 'is neck. Some of tha fuckers carry blades and threaten t' cut ya up. They stink tha greasy 'aired fannies. Their mouths smell like shit'oles.

Wolf: I'm not bothered. I've been cut before and I'll get cut again. If I find 'e's carryin' a blade, I'll carry one. I'll knife 'em. I ain't bothered. I don't care if I go t' prison.

Guppie: They're always together. They 'aven't got a knife on 'em. Ya can see 'is pockets go straight down 'is coat. 'E's cocky though. It's bin rough up our end, 'asn't it with them fuckers. A reet rough area.

Alice: Ya know what Sands [lecturer with overall responsibility for YTS] says? Any messin' around and ya are out of a job, 'e's a tosser. If ya start owt, 'e'll 'ave ya out of college. 'Es got a lot of power over ya. 'E thinks 'e 'as. 'E knows 'e 'as. I'm not fuckin' abart 'ere, you can. 'E'll sack ya. Ya best keepin ya face straight. They aint worth it! Go on get fuckin' suspended!

Wolf: I don't give a fuck, me. They can't sack ya!

George: Isn't this much ado about nothing? Why don't you shake hands and settle your differences. Do you want me to be the go-between?

Wolf: There goes George again! Fuck off, boy! Tha does not live with 'em, do tha? I live with 'em. No way would I shake 'ands. Tha wouldn't want them livin' next door t' thee. There's no way I'd ever live in peace. Fuck off! You're supportin' 'em! Tha bastards. I'll kill 'em. Ya can go and tell 'em t' come round tha back of tha college! They'll all be in bandages tomorra then!

Guppie: Ya. There's a lot of bluffin' with this Paki gang. I don't like it when they take up with our lasses or they pick on our lasses. They're wankers. Paki I know a' top of 'ill where I lives. That joiner, Jaffa. Right good kid 'im. 'E can't stand Paki's 'im. 'E were adopted 'im when 'e were like two. 'E was a Paki like but 'es bin brought up as a white and 'e talks exactly like us, perfek-like and 'e's sound and 'e doesn't like 'em and what they do and get up to.

Throughout this confrontation, Wing-nut and Graffiti have been on the slot machine. With amazing skill Graffiti is soon scoring over 50,000 points. He talks to the machine and Wing-nut.

Graffiti: Shit I've lost it! I've lost a life! Through 'ere! Go on! Straight through 'ere! There! I blew it up! I got t' end of it once! Another 10,000, look at that! I get an extra life and me weapons back! In through there!

The 'Asians' attempt to leave the room. They are confronted by Guppie who stands in front of them laughing to his mates, makes a threatening gesture and then gives way, mouthing racist obscenities. These are reinforced by the rest. 'The Boys' move out after them and go to the college refectory.

Alice: [To George] . . . Wolf thinks 'e's a reet 'ard man. But they always
            bottle out! They're all wind! I don't give a shit so long as they
            don't 'arm me. Take no notice of 'em, they're all piss and wind.
            They'll not do nowt.
George: I'm not sure! I got the distinct feeling that if someone had thrown
            a match in, the whole thing would have gone up and I honestly
            don't know what I would have done then. Momentarily, I had
            this heroic vision of me being between both sides and being stabbed
            to death by both of them! [Laughter] . . . To be honest, I think I
            was ready to run for it! I was scared! [Laughter]
Alice: Tha fastest runner always comes out best! It's more courage t'
            run off!
George: For ever the philosopher! [Laughter] . . . You lads are always
            reminding me that 'All is for the worst in the worst of all pos-
            sible worlds!'

The lads join a queue to buy tea, a tin of fizz, toast or a bacon 'butty'.
A girl immediately walks up to Guppie, their eyes meet like romantic
movie stars.

Delia: Hi! Are ya goin' out with anyone, Guppie? Sharon were cryin' in
            the pub the other night.
George: Is he still breaking the girls' hearts? [Laughter]
Delia: I don't know, she were cryin' and I were goin' to ask 'er what
            were up but I didn't but I said, 'I bet Guppie 'as finished with 'er.'
Wolf: Ay, George fancies tha! That dirty old man theere. 'Es afta thee!
            'E says 'e'd like t' take thee 'round back!
George: Take no notice. He's an embarrassment!
Guppie: I finished with 'er two or three week ago but she is always
            phonin'.

Guppie disappears along with Delia. They are seen in hushed intimacies
sharing a cigarette.

George: I'm damned if I know the secret of his success! What's the fatal
            attraction? [Laughter]
Jar: 'Is knob! [Laughter]
Wolf: 'E's a wanka that's why. [Laughter] . . . No, I'll tell ya somethin'
            now. I've never known anyone t' pull a bird like 'im. And that's
            a fact! She's a right dog woman her! [He means she is ugly] . . .
            She's an ugly bastard! Mind you I'd knob 'er. She's got a nice
            fanny 'er. Jar'll knob 'er. A nice pair. I'll throw some money on
            the floor, come on ya fuckin' bitch get on all fours! I wouldn't
            mind suckin' that! [Laughter]

Jar:	Crude, ain't 'e George? [Laughter]
Wolf:	Bet tha would like t' lick it, George. Get ya nose stuck up 'er arse! [Laughter]
George:	You're vile. What's happened to meaningful relationships and romance?
Wolf:	What's that? [Laughter]
Jar:	Doin' 'er backside on the backseat. [Laughter] . . . Does tha know what a back-shaft is? [Laughter]
George:	No I don't! Don't be rude!
Jar:	Tha live a sheltered life! There's men and there's boys! [Laughter]
George:	I can't believe you lads have any pulling power whatsoever. These lasses, I don't know how they fall for you. I bet all the girls fall for you with a line in chat like that? God! Real Prince Charmings! [Laughter]
Jar:	Guppie's a smoothy. 'E's a baby-face! A reet poser!
Wing-nut:	Ya get bored with 'em don't ya? It doesn't go anywhere does it?
Jar:	Listen to fuckin' Wing-nut [Laughter] . . . Pram and two kids!
Wing-nut:	I know, that's it!
George:	Yeh, you'll all be married or living together in a couple of years time with a kid on the way. Someone will fall in love, don't worry, little house and a little family. [Laughter]
Jar:	With ya little willy! Can ya imagine Alice gettin' married! [Laughter]
Alice:	Bashin' around tha 'ouse, fuckin' in every room! [Laughter]
Jar:	The kids'll be football hooligans like you, Alice! [Laughter]
Alice:	I'll knock 'em abart tha 'ead, any messin'! [Laughter]
Wolf:	We're not bothered are we? We tell 'em t' fuck off! Y' know what they say George, the *Three Fs*, George. 'Find 'em, Fuck 'em and Forget 'em'.
Jar:	Don't forget the *Three Ws*, boy! [Extolling Mike Mason's maxim regarding concrete but with sexual allusion] . . . The wetter it is, the more workable it is, the weaker it is! [Laughter]
Wolf:	No chance, I'll never get married me. Tie ya down with a fuckin' rope! I've seen too many fuck off from tha wife. My mate got married, went t' Canary Islands, 'oneymoon. Twenty this kid, nineteen 'is wife. And on 'is fuckin' 'oneymoon, 'e fucked off and come 'ome. Left 'er, couldn't stand tha cunt, didn't stop. Ya can get wha' tha wants without marriage. I'm no sucker. Ya don't ask lasses anythin', ya just do it. Take your fuckin' knickers off, show us ya cunt! Get ya flaps out! [A favoured term, alluding to the undercarriage of aircraft but referring, of course, to the vulva] . . . Get that cock stuck up ya fanny! [Laughter]

George: I bet you say that to the lasses and all! I had you down as the class virgin, Wolf! [Laughter]

Wolf: Buy 'em 'alf a pint and ya do. Buy 'em a few shorts and they do! Come out with us toneet and I'll even get thee some bangers and mash. [Laughter]

George: No thanks.

Wolf: Fuck all that! I'm only interested in a good time. Ya only live once, so I says make tha best of it. Do anythin' tha wants and don't get caught! 'Ave a fuckin' good time, tha's only young once, so enjoy theesen. I don't want a girlfriend, I want a one night shag! [Laughter]

George: So you meet all your needs that way, do you? [Laughter]

Wolf: You don't 'ave t' fight f' it! Y' can have it any night of tha week. They don't save it 'til they get married! [Laughter] . . . I'll be married afta I'm twenty-five and before I'm thirty. By then I'll 'ave 'ad my life and then get tied down. In the meantime, I'm goin' t' 'ave a good time, sure am.

Jar: 'Ave you got any kids then, George?

George: No. Have you? [Laughter]

Jar: I thought I 'ad a bit ago but I 'aven't. M' girlfriend told me she were missin' a period. So I told 'er to fuck off! I left 'er. I weren't fallin' f' that one. Told 'er to fuck off and get rid of it! I told 'er to fuck off. She weren't goin' t' get me tha' way! I only went with 'er about five week. Long enough t' put 'er in tha family way! She kept ringin' me up and I were never in! Couldn't be bothered t' answer. Fuck that! [Laughter]

George: Didn't you use protection?

Jar: Ya don't fuckin' care, d' you! If ya get a chance t' knob a bird, ya don't bother d' ya?

Alice: Ya 'aven't got any kids then, George?

George: No. Some couples don't find it easy, you know! And some decide not to have any. [Everybody laughs]

All: 'E don't know 'ow t' do it! 'E can't 'ave any! 'E ain't got one! 'E can't do it! We'll sort it out f' ya, George! Leave it t' tha experts! 'E's a bit of a fag! We'll show ya 'ow t' do it! Poor old man, it 'appens in old age! [Laughter]

Wing-nut: Are ya married? Tha way tha dresses George, I thought you weren't.

George: What do you mean by that Wing-nut? [Laughter]

Wing-nut: I thought ya were queer, goin' 'round with us. [Everybody falls about laughing at him]

Wolf: Watch out George, Wing-nut wants t' bum ya! 'E's a brown bumsy, George! What's she like? D' ya tell 'er abart us!

Jar: I bet 'er face is like a backdoor!

George: Everything! I don't have any secrets! She is my very best friend, something you lot don't understand. She'll come and sort you out no messing!

Alice: What does she do?

George: University lecturer.

Alice: Uni' scum-bag, eh? Snooty-nose cow!

George: There you go, don't be so prejudiced! She's a coalminer's daughter actually. So she knows what little boys like you are made of? [Laughter]

Wolf: That's why she married thee, George! [Laughter] . . . Coalminers! Now tha's talkin'. Salt of the earth them! Way they took this government on and tha fuckin' police. Now tha's talkin'. Did ya see 'em with them fuckin' chargin' horses, beatin' tha shit out of 'em? And they'd done nowt! Tha cunts!

George: During the strike, my father-in-law told me at one pit the pickets built a 10-foot high snowman dressed as a copper with a little black helmet on top. The police told them to take it down but they said, 'Nay! Nay! It's only a bit of fun!' 'Take it down!' 'Nay! Nay! It's only a bit of fun. Leave it be!' So the police rammed it with their Range Rover to demolish it. The only trouble was, the miners forgot to tell them that it was built around a great concrete bollard. So they smashed themselves up! All the pickets fell about laughing and said, 'Ya daft bastards! We told thee it were only a bit of fun!' [Laughter]

They sit down and are joined by Kamikaze and Pods who have only just arrived.

Kamikaze: [To Jar straight-faced] . . . That car of yours, tha' blue 'un, tha' Allegro. It's not tha one that wagon 'as just bump into just now. I don't know who's it were but there's a right bleedin' dint in it, I know that! Tha wagon neva stopped.

Jar: I ain't got ma car 'ere, ya lyin' cunt. The 'alf shaft is gone. We were goin' around and around on tip at about eighty, muckin' about. I'll 'ave t' fix it mesen, it'll cost me ten pound from a scrap yard. [Laughter]

Wolf: It's a rust bucket that. Rotten underneath. [Laughter]

Jar: It's a good starter. It's got bucket seats, only done sixty-four thousand.

Wolf: Are ya sure it ain't gone 'round the clock sixty-four thousand times. [Laughter]

George: How much did you pay for it?

Jar: Two 'undred quid! If I can't fix it I'll blow it up. I nearly made a mistake. I nearly told 'em I bought it for two 'undred pound.

I've got it insured for three 'undred and fifty. Ya can take it to tha Edge, set it on fire and drop it over. Get the insurance to cough up. Make a packet. That's wha' I'll do if I can't get it goin'.

While Pods is not looking, Kamikaze spits into his cola. Everybody breaks out laughing and then innocently wait for Pods to drink. When he does they break out laughing again.

Wolf: Tha dosey cunt! Don't tha feel sickly, boy? Kamikaze 'as just gobbed in tha'. Tha's got Aids now. Can't ya imagine tha green slime! [Laughter]
Pods: I'll get ma own back one day!
Kamikaze: If I ever get Aids, I'm goin' t' eat coppers! [Laughter]

Pods pushes it away from himself and Kamikaze knocks it over Wingnut. Everybody laughs.

Wolf: Where's tha bin tha dosey cunts? You're late, boy! [To Kamikaze and Pods] . . . 'E'll dock tha pay.
Kamikaze: Nowhere. Just got up. I don't care.
Pods: I've been for ma test?
Graffiti: Did tha pass?
Wolf: I bet the dosey cunt didn't, did ya? Tha's still payin' 'alf fare on buses, ya mong. Ya piss pod. Ya bum drum! [Laughter]
Pods: No. I failed on three-point turn and signs.
Wolf: Come on shit 'ot, 'ow many lessons 'as tha 'ad?
Pods: I've 'ad thirty-five.
Jar: At ten quid a piece, that's 350 quid. 'Ow can tha afford that, ya cunt-twat.
Pods: I don't have ta pay keep. I buy one. Then ma dad buys one.
Wolf: Do ya pay that, ya pea brain. My drivin' lessons only cost £5. Everyone else pays 8 quid but 'es a friend of me dad's. But ya can get reductions for YTS and Unemployed, ya pillock! And that's f' a one and a 'alf 'ours as well! Ya daft cunt! Look at 'im, 'e's like a fuckin' bog brush. [Laughter] . . . Who's ever seen a bog brush drivin' a car! Ya fuckin daft emu! [More laughter] . . . You'll be 'avin' lessons when ya sixty-five. The only dipstick pensioner, I know, on a skateboard! [Laughter]
Kamikaze: Pods 'as 'is lesson drivin' a dumper! Put! Put! Put! Get tha girls in tha front bucket! Put! Put! Put! Goin' out, plonkin' a bird in 'is dumper! Put! Put! Put! [Laughter]
George: How much does a test cost now?
Wolf: Fifteen quid, i'n't it?

Pods: Ya 'ave t' wait two months.

Wolf: Ya 'ave t' wait abart 21 days. Ya can get a cancellation if ya 'phone up!

Kamikaze: Ya don't need t' pass test! [Laughter] . . . Great time last night, swiped this car and we wrecked it. Smashed it. Smashed all the windows, bust the lights, pulled out all the wires, pushed it over, cut up the seats, set it alight.

George: Why?

Kamikaze: It's a fuckin' laff!

George: How do you steal them?

Kamikaze: It's easy!

Pods: I know 'ow to do it. Get a piece of wire down the winda, George and just pull it up.

Jar: Get a brick tie that's better, the plastic 'uns.

George: What about the steering lock and ignition?

Kamikaze: That's easy. Smash it with a 'ammer like and put a srew-driver in and it'll start. I'll show tha, where's thy car? [Laughter]

Jar: I got in trouble once. Took this Bedford van from the garage down the road. We nicked it like. Took it from the garage. Took it t' tha cemetery field and we were messin' about right and we couldn't get it goin' and we're tryin' to bump it. And this copper comes along with a police dog. And there were me, ma brotha and ma mate. We all run for it and the dog went for me mate. So I carried on runnin' and got over the fence and the dog couldn't get me. The copper got them two on floor and said, 'Move any more and I'll get tha dog t' kill ya.' [Laughter] . . . I got away but tha bastards grassed on me. Ma brotha and me mate. Good of 'em! I kicked the fuck out of 'em both when I got 'em. I got probation for that.

Wolf: I've got enough money f' a car but I need a job to run it! I'm packin' it all in when I pass ma drivin' test! I'm goin' f' an 'eavy goods job! That's what I want. I drive ma dad's truck now. The police never bother because it's Corporation. 'Eavy goods. Ma dad is goin' t' pay f' that proper like! That'll be a grand, five 'undred f' that. About twenty-one quid a 'our. It's worth it though, 'cos ya can get a job drivin'. They always want Class One. I'll buy ma own lorry. Look at tha spray boys on that bus, Graffiti! Tha vandals! [He has seen a bus outside]

Graffiti: Yeh! Yeh! It's ours! It's ours! We did it last neet! We did it in garage last neet. Thought they wouldn't be runnin' them today! Went out with me wireclippers last night to the bus depot, cut the fence. We just walked in. It's massive. Still got ma clippers in ma bag. I did the lot, my tag on every one, every bus.

Wolf: What do you get out of it, boy, ya knob'ead?

Graffiti: Nowt! It's somethin' t' do, isn't it?

George: Where do you get your paints?

Graffiti: Nick it, that's called 'rackin'. Top German paint is £6 a tin. I've got a 'wild style'. You don't just do it, ya 'ave t' do it with a bit of style. It's got t' look good like.

George: Oh, so there is different styles then? Were you good at Art in school?

Graffiti: No, it were crap. I can read everybody's work, I know who 'as done it. 'Grammar' was my 'tag' but I've changed it t' 'Faceless'. My mate is 'Fez'. Everybody knows everybody. When I were at school, we did the whole wall.

Jar: Why do you do it, ya cunt?

Graffiti: I don't know. It's a bit of a laff! It gives ya a buzz t' see ya name up!

George: You could go to a football match or something instead?

Graffiti: It's borin', too much violence, too much violence! [Laughter] . . . What ya try t' do is get ya name on every bus line, on most buses. It's called, 'Goin' all city', that.

George: Oh, so you've got your own vocabulary then?

Graffiti: Yeh! We call coppers 'beasties'! People think it is a mess because they don't understand it! You didn't see *Cocaine*, *Revenge* and *Tamba* on that bus, did ya? But I did! I know everybody's tag in Blightown and everybody knows me. I did ma mate's girlfriend's cellar! There is a lot of competition for the best style amongst tha teams. Ya never put ya name inside a bus, that's kids stuff. Ya put it on outside and on difficult places t' get it off like bridges. Ya work out ya designs before ya put 'um up. ACT is best in Blightown but we're gettin' more up on tha buses than them. There is right competition.

George: Oh, so there is different gangs then.

Graffiti: Yeh. We're the CLA, that's that Crazy Live Artists. We 'ang 'round Salendine Nook Station, there's a great big wall there and that's ours. It's full from top 't' bottom. The police are always after us but they never catch us.

George: We'll come and see it sometime.

Graffiti: There's Criminals At Work, that's CAW. There is ACT, that's the Awesome Crime Team. They're reet 'ard men, no-one messes up their work. There's TDA, that's Totally Destructive Artists. The Chrome Angels are the best in London, best in England. Reet good style. But New York is tha best, 'ave ya seen their subway. Reet good. I've got a book at 'ome on them, I'll show ya.

Wolf: And there is the SUW, the Sheffield University Wankers! [Laughter] . . . Why d' tha do it, ya knob'ead?

Graffiti: Makes ya immortal for a minute. It gets ya name 'round. [Laughter]

Wolf: Fuckin' wanka. Ya dong! Ya spray boy! [Laughter]

Graffiti: You do what you wants and I'll do what I wants. It's more excitin' than poxin' 'round at Roxy's and bashin' the shit out of people!

Wolf: Shut ya trap, spray boy! [Laughter]

Guppie rejoins the group, announcing he is meeting Delia at Cleo's tonight.

George: You've got a voracious appetite, you and I am not talking about food. [Laughter]

Guppie: Ay, I didn' tell ya, last week at *Cleo's*, tha birds came in all their lingerie [assumed seductive French voice]. From this shop, these fuckin' *modelles* [French voice], the woman who owned this shop did it! She brought 'er stuff and Miss Blightown United and some other tarts paraded! Fuckin' 'ell, ya ought t' 'ave seen tha cunts! Very nice! Little blondes and nice little stuff like! Nice fuckin' little suspenders! Nice little knickers! All tha lads are like that, their fuckin' eyes 'angin' out! Some nice tits! Fuckin' 'ell!

Wolf: Guess what, I daren't tell thee, Guppie.

Guppie: Go on ya knob'ead!

Wolf: I got in with Tracey on Saturday. It were 'er birthday. She were pissed t' fuck. Anyone could 'ave shagged 'er on tha spot. She were as pissed as a fart. [Laughter]

Guppie: Ya didn't. Oh God! She's a dog! [Laughter]

Wolf: I know but tha don't look at tha mantlepiece when ya pokin' tha fire, does tha? When ya 'ave a few pints, ya'll knob owt! If we see 'er, I'm runnin'! [Laughter] . . . I only 'ad three hours sleep, didn't get 'ome t' 4 o'clock. We went t' 'er 'ouse and she paid m' taxi fare. I wonder what she's goin' t' say when I see 'er.

Guppie: She'll be after ya now, boy! Ya daft cunt. She's a dick 'ead! Are ya goin' out with 'er again?

Wolf: I'll see what she looks like in daylight! [Laughter]

Guppie: Ya will invite me t' tha weddin' wont ya! She's a reet divvy! [Laughter]

George: What's this all about then?

Wolf: There 'e goes again snoopin'!

George: I'm very interested in the ins and outs of your social life, so to speak! [Laughter]

Wolf: She's a reet shag, I promise ya! [Laughter]

Guppie: Tell 'er you'll meet 'er again and we'll send Pods! Go on? [Laughter]

Pods: Yeh! Yeh! [Laughter]

Guppie: Eh, Jar! Wolf 'ad t' go and fuck Tracey! [Laughter]

Jar: Are ya goin' out with 'er then?
Wolf: Am I fuck! I'm not goin' out with 'er! [Laughter]
Jar: What, did ya get any fanny?
George: He's asking if you have had carnel knowledge. [Laughter]
Wolf: I did, yeh! [Laughter]
Guppie: So you've been out with 'er! [Laughter]
Wolf: 'Ave I 'ell! I've never been out with 'er! [Laughter]
Guppie: Ya 'ave Wolf! Tha knobbed 'er all neet! [Laughter]
Wolf: That's different! I got in with 'er, that's all! Knobbin' all neet is
            somethin' different! I've never bin out with 'er. [Laughter]

Tracey's friends appear, all giggling knowingly at Wolf.

Guppie: Tha's goin' red! [Laughter]
Wolf: Bollocks! I'm just 'ot! [Laughter]
George: What are you doing with your chest at floor level? You are
            looking very furtive! It's the first time I've seen a six-foot tall guy
            go down to 5 feet 3 inches! What have you been doing? [Laughter]
            ... They are all laughing at you! They all know! I didn't think
            girls blabbed like that! [Laughter]
Guppie: Watch out they're comin' for you, Wolf! [Laughter]

The girls come up to the group of lads.

Wolf: What does tha want? Where's Tracey?
Zoe: She's not in t'day, 'er mother's comin' back from Spain! But she's
            told me she want's t' see ya, though. What 'ave you bin doin' big
            boy? Tracy 'as told me all about it, 'asn't she girls? [Laughter]
Wolf: Bollocks!
Zoe: You've got 'em, boy! [Laughter]
Wolf: What's she bin tellin' ya? It ain't true! [Laughter] ... What does
            she want? Give us a fag? [She gives him one] ... 'Ere George
            wants t' take ya 'round tha back! Di'n't ya tell me you thought
            'e were a pervert, 'angin' 'round ya?
George: Take no notice, Zoe! He's only trying to deflect us from the
            business in hand! [Laughter]
Joanne: She wants t' go out with ya.
Wolf: Tell 'er t' 'phone me toneet! Come on I want a piss! ['The Boys'
            walk off] ... Did ya see that, she 'ad no bra on? Ask 'er what I
            did t' 'er at Roxy's. Why d' ya think she always gives us fags! I'll
            not answer phone toneet! I'll not be in! Look at that mong theere.
            [To bemused girl unknown to Wolf] ... 'Ello, fish! Get ya flaps
            out! [Laughter]
George: Why did you call her 'Fish'?

Wolf: Look at 'er ugly kisser [face], George! She's got a mouth like a goldfish! Is she any good t' you Pods, that dog? 'As tha knobbed 'er? {Laughter]

Jar: 'Ow d' ya chat up a bird, Pods?

Pods: I don't chat up birds, I let them chat me up! [Laughter]

All: Fuckin' 'ell! Ooh! [Laughter]

As the lads go through a large open-plan area, they see 'special needs' students outside. Jar, Kamikaze, Wolf, Guppie and Alice all clamber up on the window-sill, claw and bang at the large window panes feigning the behaviour of Frankensteinian monsters.

All: Mongs! Mongs! Moooooongs! [Laughter]

Wolf: Which one is thine Wing-nut? That little two-foot one with the iron legs. Will tha get tha cock up with your trousers down over ya rolled-down wellies? [Laughter] . . . Mongs! Mongs! [Laughter]

Jar: That one's Wing-nut's with tha chinky eyes! [i.e. Down's Syndrome] . . . 'E'll poke her front and rear. Sweet and sour porn. [Stereotypical Chinese pronunciation. Laughter] . . . Mongs! Mongs! [Laughter]

Kamikaze: Which one's Pods? Mongs! Mongs!

Alice: That little two-foot 'un. 'E'll manage it if 'e gets down on 'is knees and prays. [Laughter]

Alice: Wing-nut's gettin married, she's on crutches and in a wheel-chair, got a plastic nose and a plastic cunt! [Laughter]

Kamikaze: Look at tha dogs! I am from Mars! I am an alien! [Zombie-like. Laughter]

As 'the Boys' go out down the empty corridors, Kamikaze shouts 'Zzzound! Zzzound!', which he likes to hear echo. He will make this noise randomly throughout the day. It appears to have no meaning but is perhaps derived from 'the Boys' use of the word 'sound' meaning 'very good' or 'brilliant'. Whatever, its resonating sound gives Kamikaze a great deal of pleasure.

As they enter into sunshine at the back of the college, workmen are pruning trees. Wolf, Kamikaze, Guppie and Jar grab branches, corner Pods and Wing-nut and beat them. They cringe, hands about their head.

All: Mongs! Mongs! Mongs! You alien bastards! [Laughter]

Wolf: Quick, get the mad bastards, get 'em, get 'em 'ere! In tha rat pit! Tha rat pit!

They throw the branches down, grab Wing-nut while Pods manages to escape. They drag him around the back where there is a trench six to eight feet deep, shored up with sandbags which is used for simulated sewage drain laying.

Wolf: Quick, throw tha fat twat down theere, tha mong!

Wing-nut: Let go! Let go! [Wing-nut is thrown in, they start to throw sandbags at him and spit over him. He cowers]

George: Why don't you leave him alone for God's sake?

Wolf: 'E's one of them paedophiles. 'E looks like a fuckin' child molester. Tha beast! Tha faggot! 'E'd like ya to ram 'im up the back, 'cept 'e's got as much arse as 'e's got brains. Look at the sly wank, the fuckin' wing-nut. 'E's a queer! Tha snide swine!

Guppie: Look at 'is new trainers, full of shit. Look at them red socks from 'is girlfriend's period when 'e rammed them up 'er fanny when she wa' on rags. 'E thinks a sock is 'a johnny'! [a condom]. Fat twat! 'E's a shit! 'E's a bit of a tart! 'E's a reet divvy!

Kamikaze: Knob'ead! Knob'ead! Knob'ead! Knob'ead! [Stereotypical effeminate pronunciation and body language] . . . EEEEE! Piss all over 'im. Piss over 'im! Mong! I'll cut 'is cobblers off!

Wolf and Kamikaze make to get their penises out. Wing-nut desperately realizing his fate, clambers over the building materials strewn in the bottom and manages to escape at the far end.

George: Why don't you leave him alone for God's sake? [He walks away in disgust to a chorus of Mong! Mong! Mong!]

Wing-nut disappears to safety for half an hour. Kamikaze and Wolf urinate into the trench anyway.

Wolf: OOh! OOh! George is fuckin' angry. Calm down, boy! Simmer down, Uncle George! [Laughter]

George: Why don't you leave him alone for God's sake? Why are you so horrible to one another? I thought you lot said you were socialists?

Wolf: We are 'orrible! Wha' ya mean?

George: You all told me you'll vote Labour next election.

Wolf: Ay and we will. Labour me. I'm 'appy with 'em. If I saw Thatcher I'd kill 'er. Smash 'er. She's a fuckin' shit'ouse, ain't she? Labour are for the workin' man. I 'ate bosses me. I'd shit on Thatcher's 'ead, me. Thatcher's a fuckin' bitch! She don't give a shit abart us up North. All my family is Labour! Look at it, 35 quid for graftin' ya bollocks off!

Kamikaze: On cunts like you, it's wasted money, boy! [Laughter]

Wolf: I 'ate bosses me. When I wa' on placement this old codger retired after workin' f' tha firm a reet long time. They wanted t' invite 'im along f' a drink an' meal. And 'e told 'em t', "Fuck off!" 'E ses, "Not fuckin' likely, fuck off. Tha's bin diddlin' me out of m' money all these years. I don't fuckin' see why I should go for a meal with thee now. Fuck off, ya robbin' bastards!"

Jar: Yeh, d' ya know, I fell over some kerbs when I were on work placement and I wa' sent t' 'ospital and I couldn't b' seen 'cos that cow Thatcher were there after tha Disaster [i.e. Hillsborough]. So I 'ad t' fuck it 'ome!

Kamikaze: I don't give a shit! I won't vote, me, they're all out for theesens. I'm not bothered. I don't give two fucks! They're all a lot of wankers who'll never get tha country reet! No-one can do any good f' this country! Labour are all communists! And them others [the then Alliance] are just a load of bollocks! [Laughter]

George: Well what do you think socialism is? Good socialists don't treat Wing-nut and lasses and the disabled and blacks like you do!

Wolf: Oh, Yes they do! [Laughter] ... We can 'it Wing-nut but you can't. We'd beat tha shit out of anyone else who laid a finger on 'im. Wouldn't we?

Alice: What does tha vote, George? Tha's into Greenpeace, is tha George?

George: I've always voted Conservative! [Laughter]

Alice: Why?

George: Because I am a liar! I've always voted Labour. [Laughter]

Alice: Y' know what Jar, ma mate's mother works at that 'ospital and these scousers [i.e. Liverpudlian casualities of the Hillsborough Disaster] says, 'If Margaret Thatcher comes 'round tell 'er, "To fuck off", and if Kenny Dalglish come 'round wake me up! Wake me up!' 'E's a smasher 'im. Man of few words but a reet bloke. Kenny Dalglish brought a bloke out of his coma, di'n't 'e? She's a cunt 'er, what's she goin' to do at tha hospital? Fuckin' close it! She fuckin' closes everything! I 'ate 'er me. Everybody in Blightown is Labour, aren't they? Tha workin' class is. Most workin' class folk 'ate 'er.

Wolf: It's those yuppie condoms in tha South who vote Thatcher. This bloke at tha club, 'e's socialist, a real socialist, from London and 'e lives up 'ere now. And 'e says we're right good up 'ere. When ya see people on street 'ere, it is 'Ello luv, 'ow are ya?', sort of thing. But they are all scabs down theere.

George: What would get the country right, Kamikaze?

Kamikaze: Fuck knows! We're what's wrong with this country! Everythin'
were free and there were no coppers. Just think if coppers went
on strike, we'd go wild, we'd be in all tha shops, lootin' 'course
I would. Free chips for the YTS boys! I'm goin' t' vote f' George
Party. Carrot Power! Vegetable rights! [Laughter]
George: So you are goin' t' vote something then! [Laughter]
Kamikaze: Yeh! I'm goin' t' Australia! [Laughter]

Up t' dinna time

'The Boys' have entered the workshop and Mike Mason is waiting for
them.

Mr Mason: Come on, now. You're late! Where's [Wing-nut]?
Kamikaze: 'E's run off, 'e's waggin' it!
Wolf: 'E 'asn't 'es 'ad to go to see 'is special teacher f' extra readin'.
'E'll be 'ere in a minute!
Mr Mason: I can see that you have done well so far this morning. It only
goes to prove you can do it when you want to. So keep it up.
We want a good clean job, remember. A good operative, I've
probably said before, is the most important man as far as the
general foreman is concerned. Because the good operative is
usually the man there first thing in the morning and he is there
last thing at night, to lock up, making sure, checking around
all the stockpiles, such as cement. He is important to the
general foreman. He is a reliable man. You don't have to
chase him, he comes and goes, sticks to the rules and regulations. He is very much a versatile man as the general foreman
comes to rely on him. So not only does he see to the day-to-
day running but he is the fellow who looks after the delivery
lorries. In the course of a day he will be expected to get down
to a multitude of things, concreting, tarmacing, bricklaying.
And all that demands responsibility and management. To be
of value to anybody if you anticipate what is going to happen
next and that things are ready, then that is a good point. Now
what are you going to do next? [The lads outline the plan of
action.] [Kamikaze] . . . I'll see you, now. Where have you been,
it's gone eleven, we start at nine! Where have you been?
Kamikaze: [Straight-faced innocence] . . . I found this dog on way, so
I took it t' police station. You ask 'em!
Mr Mason: Make a morning of it. Mr Sands may sign your card but I'm
not signing it. It is as simple as that. You are not starting until
this afternoon, make a morning of it. See Mr Sands, he might

sign your card but I'm not! So you have had a good one and a half hours off, you may as well have the rest of the morning. Alright? Have a nice day! [To George] . . . I've had better ones than that in my time! A lad once came into class. I said, 'Where have you been?' He says he was walking back from the chippie and this lollipop lady ran across the crossing and says to him, 'Would you mind if you just watch the crossing for five minutes for me, whilst I go home.' 'So I did do and I was there an hour and a half and she didn't come back.' I thought, 'Well that is it now. I've heard everything!' [Laughter]

Mike Mason goes into the classroom. He occasionally checks on the lads who are always somehow hard at work when he reappears. Kamikaze does not leave but joins the group muttering. He will attempt in the course of time to find some kind of signature for his card.

Kamikaze: I'll fuckin' 'ammer 'im, Mason. I told 'im 'e could phone up. There's not much else 'e can fuckin' do! I'll lather tha bastard.
Wolf: Come on Kamikaze and Pee Pod. Them that come late get tha shit work! Get to it, Emu-Rambo! Come on ya pin'ead. Tha's done nowt. Tha's not gettin' away with it. Fuckin 'ell lad, tha's done nowt thee! Look at tha wankers, they use their right 'and too much, ya wankers [alluding to masturbation]. I'll make thee so sick ya'll choke on thee vomit. Ya idle cunts! Ya fuckin' knobs! There'll be no skivin' out, boy! [Laughter]

Everybody gets on with demolishing the walls, cleaning up the bricks, stacking them and putting 'the gobbo' into wheelbarrows. There are singings, whistlings and shoutings, added to the sound of trowel on brick.

Kamikaze: Hee! Hee! Hee! [chimpanzee noises]. Come on ya bastards! Yaarrahhahhh! Mongo! You're a reet big knob!
George: You know something I don't know! [Laughter] . . . What are doing? Calculating how many bricks we've got to move?
Kamikaze: Calculatin' 'ow to kill you without anyone knowin'! [Laughter]
George: I know you don't mean it! [Laughter]
Kamikaze: I fuckin' do, boy! Ya fuckin' 'ooligan! [Laughter]
George: I'll come 'round your house and throw a brick at your window sometime! [Laughter]
Wolf: Kamikaze thinks tha's a spy from MSC, George! 'E's got it in 'is 'ead! [Laughter]
George: We'll never get it out now then! I wish I was I'd get paid more than I am now. Actually I am Maggie Thatcher's special

emissary, I'm here on her behalf to double your £35 in recognition of your contribution to the national effort! [Laughter]

Jar: 'Ow much does tha get paid, George?

George: £100 an hour! I'm on danger money! [Laughter]

Wolf: Spark up, Guppie! Crash the ash, boy!

Guppie: Fuck off, tha's always beggin', ya tight cunt. When did ya last give us one? I 'aven't got any.

Wolf: Then get t' tha shops and get some, boy! [Laughter]

Guppie: Let's see 'ow many I've got. One f' in 'ere. One at dinna. One afta. One at break. One afta. One f' 'ome time.

Suddenly, Wolf and Jar have got hold of Guppie, have inverted him and are attempting to put his head in the concrete mixer. Fortunately, it is not working. All are laughing.

Guppie: George! George! They're 'urtin' me! [Laughter] . . . They're fuckin' me up! Cut it out! [Laughter] . . . Stop it! Stop it! Ya mad cunts!

Wolf: I've 'ad enough of thee, boy! Tha's a reet tight arse! Who's sparkin' up? Ya as tight as ya bird's arse! Ya mean swine!

Eventually, they release him and a cigarette is lit. Meanwhile the wheelbarrows are filled with gobbo. Everybody is tired, time out is called.

Wolf: 'Ere 'ave a word with those two! Slow down! Play it clever! Slow down! Give us a light, Jar!

Alice: 'Ow do ya slow down someone who's standin' still anyway? Are ya alright, old son? [To George] . . . It's wicked i'n't it? I'm fucked, George! I'm knackered!

George: My back's shot! My knee is swollen, look! I've never worked so hard in all my life!

Wolf: There goes Alice again! Suckin' up t' George! Tha's doin' too much knobbin', George! Come on, Graffiti. Get them barrows moved.

Graffiti: Bollocks! I'm not, you fuckin' do it! Tha does fuck all! [Hostilely] . . . all tha does is got tha 'and in ya pockets supervisin' as usual!

Wolf: Don't give us no lip, ya used jam rag! [sanitary towel]. [They glare at each other, move towards each other and then back off laughing] . . . Cluuuuuck! Where's Pods? 'E can take it!

George: He's in with Mason having his modules assessed! [Laughter] . . . His work for the last week!

Wolf: 'E's done nowt! 'Ow can ya assess nowt! [Laughter] . . . Come on Kamikaze, I bet ya can't put that cigarette out on the back of Wing-nut's 'and! Leave these tarts, I'll race thee with these barrows! Last one down theere is a fuckin' woman! Get started, go!

They race off with the gobbo, careering into each other as they go. Kamikaze takes the lead. Wolf tries to knock him off his feet by swinging his barrow around. He misses and the barrow falls to its side.

Graffiti: 'E's a prick'ead! 'E'll find out one day because 'e'll be fuckin' killed by someone.

Alice: We'll all cop it one day. Someone will give 'im a good towsin' [tawsing?] one day!

George: Are you alright, Wing-nut? [He has reappeared and talks to George alone]

Wing-nut: Yeh, I'm not bothered. They're babies! They won't do 'alf tha things they do now when they grow up! They treat me as a mong but it don't worry me. There's nowt I can do about it really. I 'ad epilepsy when I were younger. I 'ad tablets all the time, its gone now. Still I've got ta catch up on my readin', that's all. Gets on me nerves tryin' t' catch up. I were off school a lot.

George: I'll not say anything. How many years did you lose?

Wing-nut: I lost seven years, seven or eight, at junior and senior. That were the major years weren't it, learnin'. I 'ad these tablets and that. When ya all drugged up, ya don't know what's 'appenin'. I don't 'ave epilepsy now. It just went. Last 'ad it when I was fifteen, 'ad it all me life. It's just me readin'. I read a bit. But teachers 'ere are rubbish. They deal with nutters and that, mongs. Like they give me sums like two and two and that. They think that I'm an idiot, a mong. I can read a bit but not much. They treat ya like a nutter. 'Now then [Wing-nut], are you alright?' [imitating patronizing tone]

Jar appears. He's been selling raffle tickets for his football club around the workshop.

Alice: Doooohh! Helloooha! Jaaarrhh! [baby-like]

Jar: Doooohh! Helloooha! Alleeece! Come on! Buy some, ya cunts! Ya tight little fart arses!

George: I didn't know you played football.

Jar: Yeh, two times a week now, Tuesday and Sunday. It's ma pub team. Alice is in same league, ain' ya? We've got to raise £80 f' league fees, £40 for Tuesday and £40 for Sunday and the bastards 'ave put 'em up. So we might not play next year unless you bastards cough up! Tha season 'as nearly ended, might be league champions, only eight games left. Semi-final next Sunday! They're only ten pence and first prize is a camera.

Alice: I 'ad a trial f' Blightown City Boys when I wa' at school. I went trainin' with 'em an' were told t' come back. But I didn't bother.

George: [To Alice] . . . Why not? You could have been playing for Manchester United now.

Alice: Travellin' were too much. And I just couldn't be bothered.

George: So you decided to be a star YTS deadleg rather than a star striker! Alice in Mortarland! [Laughter] . . . If only you were as fast with a shovel as you are with a ball, you'd do well, my son! [Laughter]

Alice: I'm interested in football, I'm not interested in shovellin'! I'm not interested in work. [Laughter]

George: You don't take naturally to work do you! [Laughter]

Alice: A lot of people don't, do they? But you 'ave t' do it!

George: What's your position?

Jar: Sixty-nine. [Laughter] . . . I'm mad on football me! I belong t' BBC.

George: What's that?

Alice: Blades Business Crew.

Jar: See ma badge. [He has a Nazi-SS-type skull and cross bone under his lapel with BBC on it. It is a parody of an official club badge] . . . There's all these gangs. There's about a 'undred of us! There's the Intercity Firm, that's West 'Am! There's the 'Eadhunters, Chelsea!

Alice: Zulu Warriors, Birmingham! The Bushwhackers, Millwall! The Service Crew, Leeds and there's the Boot Boys, as well.

Jar: There's the Bradford Bully Boys! The CBS, the Chesterfield Bastard Squad! There's the Suicide Squad!

Alice: There's GBH! The Gobbo Barmy Harmy! [Laughter] . . . The Cathedral Possy! There's the Lunatic Fringe, that's Derby! The Neverley Nutter Boys!

Jar: There's all these gangs, all fightin'.

George: So what is it about a good scrap, then?

Jar: You 'ave a chance of kickin' the fuck and shit out of wankas like you! [Laughter] . . . It were great last time, ten of us and twenty of them. We got off bus. We ran down the Brook and dropped them, steamed into 'em. 'Fuck off! Fuck off, ya mad cunts!' We just came steamin' into 'em, jumpin' on t' them. Reet good scrap! Feetin' I 'ad a baseball bat up ma sleeve. All of us, they just ran off! So I just whacked this kid behind knees. The coppers come, so we just fucked off. Bat straight up sleeve again. Made ma weekend, enjoyed it. [Laughter] . . . I'm skint now because I 'ad a brilliant weekend, last weekend. Guess 'ow much I spent in Bristol? Guess?

Graffiti: 'Ow much?

Jar: Thirty-two quid! Everyone spent about that. Stayed out 'til two drinkin' in a club in Leicestershire somewhere afta the pub from eight 'til eleven. Thirty-two quid ain't a lot for an away game. Brilliant.

George: Where do you get money like that from?

Jar: I pay five pound keep and I keep tha rest and I get things from ma nan and dad. And ma dad took this insurance policy f' me, 'e sells insurance and that's in buildin' society! That's 'ow I bought me car.

Alice: I don't go away now since I wa' up for 'ooliganism. Tha' wa' two year ago and I've bin a good lad ever since. I don't look f' 'assles now! I didn't do nowt. It were tha' fuckin' bobbies! Tha lyin' bastards! Stitched us up! We did nowt, 'cept run away from 'em. Fifty pound fine and a conditional discharge for twelve month. Carryin' an offensive weapon. I just picked it up 'cos of all tha fightin'. It were on Leeds railway station. I dropped it but the bastards saw me. Taxi-drivers were witnesses. I pleaded not guilty at first but tha solicitors were wank, so I pleaded guilty. They were shit. Ma parents went barmy. It were snowin' when I went t' court. I nearly didn't make it and I were shittin' me sen that I'd be sent down. I pleaded guilty and said, 'It were all George's fault!' [Laughter] . . . I've kept a clean sheet since then. Been a good boy!

George: So ya didn't act with Alice Aforethought! [George nearly falls over laughing]

Alice: Very funny, George!

George: I can't imagine you two chasing after balls, some how?

Jar: Some 'ow I can imagine Pods and Wing-nut chasin' afta two balls! [Laughter] . . . I do a lot of fishin' as well me. I've got t' find thirty quid for ma season ticket soon. It's game, fly, I've got all tha gear. Once ya've got it all it's alright, tackle and that.

George: I thought fly fishing was a rich man's sport. Trout and that.

Jar: It's a club and once I've got ma ticket, I can fish f' nowt. It's tha Yorkshire Water Authority Reservoir. It's about £15 for carp, bream, pike and that. They stock it every two weeks in season. You're only allowed t' catch two trout a day. I go Saturday and Sunday, once football season is over, the season is March 25th to September 1st. I had a fifteen pound pike last Christmas, caught it on luncheon meat. I go about thirty or forty times a year.

Guppie: Go fishin' in tha Riva Don, there's plenty of Barnsley trout ya can catch in there! [Laughter. 'Barnsley trout' is excrement suspended in water] . . . Sunday is bed day! I'd like to be lyin' on a river bank in tha sun and I wouldn't b' fishin'! I can't wait f' m' fuckin' 'olidays, Magaluf, Majorca! Six of us are goin', a reet laff! It's six weeks and five and a 'alf days precisely. Ya can 'alf knob tha girls. It's so easy! Fuckin' 'ell! 'Olidays is so fuckin' easy! Isn't it? Ya knobbin' as soon as ya throw ya bags in ya apartment, get pissed and then snatch tha birds. A good laff. It's so easy t' pull a bird on 'oliday! Like that! [click of fingers]. Reet fanny! Not 'ard is it! English girls, Dutch, Danish any cunt! They go mad. They go daft. Last year I spent eighty quid in a week! Went with this bird like an' she 'ad this tattoo right there, a butterfly [points to top inside thigh] and she were a right fuck! I came back a right 'appy man! Ya can 'ave as many fucks as ya likes. Some reet nice fanny. Ya can't keep 'em out of ya apartment! Ya drink all night and sleep and fuck all day! Leave the night clubs at six in mornin' for some breakfast and cunt! Seven weeks to go! I might fuck off t' Spain next summer any way! Get a job out there, easy as shit! Get about a bit. Waitin' in tha bars at night, knobbin' tha girls by day! Ya only live once!

Graffiti: I want tha camera. What kind of camera is it?
Alice: One that take pictures. [Laughter]
Jar: A disc camera.
Alice: It plays 'Top of the Pops'. [Laughter]
Jar: Don't be silly and wipe ya arse! [Laughter]
Alice: It's got an automatic winder but we don't need tha' tha way Wolf winds up Kamikaze! [Laughter] . . . It's for people as thick as thee, George. [Laughter]

Wolf and Kamikaze come back with their barrows playing 'dodgems' as they come. Everybody buys tickets. People set themselves back to work, cleaning and stacking bricks with the usual banter and noise.

George: Where have you two been?
Wolf: There 'e is snoopin' again. Pykin' [spying?] for tha MSC! [Laughter] . . . Tha's got a fuckin' big nose! [Laughter. George feels vunerable given his physiognomy!] . . . Ya a reet nosey bastard, you. [Laughter]
Kamikaze: We've bin 'avin' some fun 'round back. There's this woman, fifty, out there, she's comin' 'round and we've run back. We shouted, 'Get ya fuckin' flaps out!' And she walks up t' fence with 'er Great Dane and we 'id behind bricks, 'Get ya fuckin' flaps out!' And she says, 'I can see you and I'll be coming back this way!' [Imitating an assumed posh voice] . . . And we said, 'Flaps out! Oh, fuck off!' So she says, 'I'm coming around and I'll see the lecturers about this! What are your names?' And we said 'Wing-nut and Pods!' and ran f' it! [Laughter]
Wolf: Now then let's 'ave some work, I don't want to do nowt this afta. So come on tha dosey cunts. Who's pinched ma trowel?

Graffiti has hidden it. Wolf's predicament is instantly solved by grabbing Pod's trowel. They press on with the work in usual fashion.

Kamikaze: Eh! Rambo tha looks like a piece of shit, tha! Oooh! Ooooooh!
Oooh! [Chimpanzee noises. He throws some bricks outside the
door!]

Guppie: [To Pods] . . . Tha ought t' be on a YTS f' coppers with boots
like that! [Laughter]

George: What are you doing?

Kamikaze: I'm actin' daft. It comes natural t' me! Oooh! Ooooooh! Oooh!
Zzzound! Zzzound! [Bricks go flying indiscriminately at people]

Guppie: Go on ya fuckin 'ooligan! Give o'er or I'll start a war! Ya
stupid mad cunt.

Jar: Eh! This bloke I knows. 'E's got this moonshine stuff. Does
tha want any? 'E makes it in 'is garage. Secret recipe, 'undred
percent proof. Fuckin' good stuff! We went to this party at 'is
'ouse and 'e 'ad three bottles for everybody. Smashed out of
our minds. I kept fallin' over. No-one knows 'is recipe. It takes
the varnish off ya teeth. [Laughter. There are no takers]

Alice: It can kill ya that stuff, ya pillock!

Guppie: Ay but its cheap! And it strips paint! [Laughter]

Kamikaze: This is fuckin' borin'! Zzzzound! Zzzzound! Go wash ya feet
and give ya brains a scrape, boy! [Laughter]

Kamikaze alleviates his problem of boredom by throwing boomerang-
fashion the butterfly-shaped wire or plastic brick ties (used in joining two
brick courses together for greater strength) at people. They reciprocate.
Suddenly there is a maelstrom of ties about the workshop!

George: Blood and sand! Be careful! You'll blind me!

Any such protestations are met with additional firepower aimed at the
complainant.

Graffiti: 'ere watch this!

With a flick of the wrist, he implants a tie in the roof which is lined with
insulation-board. There are already dozens there and these are quickly
added too. Eventually, the activity subsides.

Wolf: Come on it'll soon be dinna! Wha' time is it? Let's finish this off.
Let's 'ave the appliance of science. Smash tha fuckas! Smash them
bricks and put 'em straight in skip. Get 'em in and 'ide 'em.

George: Now then, what about ratepayers' money! I'll put the MSC onto
this! [Laughter] . . . Come on do the job properly! It's just as
easy! You vandals! [Laughter]

Wolf: Fuck thee George, we're not bothered. It's all reet f' you, ya

fucka! You're paid t' think not work! We're tha donkeys. We
know what we're doin'. So don't bring ya rule 'ere, George! We'll
not be 'avin' two foremen! Smash tha fuckas, get 'em in 'ere.
Quick before Mason comes. [Laughter]

Guppie: Put it down t' natural wastage! [Laughter]

Soon the skip is removed with the concealed 'natural wastage'. The
remaining bricks are stacked. Wolf and Kamikaze have taken the remaining gobbo away. The concrete 'footings' (foundation) for the walls are
exposed, ready for the next operation. Time out is called again and a
cigarette is shared between Guppie and Jar. Various people go off 'walk-
about'. Soon Kamikaze and Wolf return. As they come, they use their arm
and wrist power to bounce their wheelbarrows higher and higher in competition, against a verbal backdrop of mutually obscene recriminations.
Sweat breaks out under the exertions.

Wolf: Come on, let's 'ave some BMX barrowin'! See if ya can gerrit in tha
skip, Kamikaze, go on!

Kamikaze ferociously bounces the wheelbarrow higher and higher.
People cheer him on and he manages eventually to get the front of the
steel wheel support on the rim of the skip and collapses in exhaustion.
Not to be outdone Wolf steps back fifteen metres and starts his approach
like an olympic athlete. With great exertion the barrow eventually arrives
in the skip, amid claps and cheers. Kamikaze, not to be outdone, uses the
Wolf technique, and eventually succeeds.

Wolf: Come on then, see if ya can gerrit above ya 'ead. Go on, Kamikaze!
George you be judge.

Frantic bouncing is set about again. Ultimately, Wolf is adjudged the
winner and both protagonists collapse. 'The Boys' and George then go into
a regular ritual. The outcome is a foregone conclusion.

Wolf:	Are ya goin' to take us in ya car to tha chippie, George? Go on. [Winningly]
George:	Not you vandals! [Laughter]
Wolf:	Ya, tight cunt! Go on! What does tha think?
George:	Not a lot! [Laughter]
All:	Go on, George. [Pleadingly]
George:	No chance. I'm not desperate for friends!
Wolf:	Tha's got no friends, boy! [Laughter] . . . Tha never will 'ave. No, I'll tell thee what, you're OK you, good f' a laff. You've

passed tha test! We wouldn't want to go with some fuckas, I'll
tell thee that straight!

George: Lies all lies. You'd sell your grandmother you. It's cupboard
love! You are only out for what ya can get! [Laughter] ... Besides the last time we were in the car, Kamikaze put his hands
over my eyes as we were driving along and I could have killed
you all. It wouldn't have been a bad idea except I would have
ended up killing myself as well. [Laughter] ... What was the
test anyway? I've never worked out why you have me around!

Wolf: Tha passed first day when tha became chauffeur to tha firm!
[Laughter]

George: I thought is was because you were desperate to join my gang!
[Laughter]

Kamikaze: We let ya tag along if tha drives us abart! [Laughter] ...
It were tha' ride in tha car!

Wolf: I'll make sure everybody's on their best behaviour or I'll paste
them for ya.

All: Go on, George. [Pleadingly]

George: So the key to your affections was my little Fiat Panda! There
are too many of you.

Traditionally, no-one is ever left behind but given rates of attendance
this is rarely a problem. If it is, the group walks, stays in college or goes
to a nearby pub. Occasionally, Jar's car is also used but often does not
have much petrol in it.

Graffiti: I'm not goin', Pod's not goin', we're goin' f' some stereo ear-
phones. There's a swap price at Cosmic of 5 quid, they should
be 8.

George: All right then but no muckin' about! [George knows on the basis
of previous experience that there will be a lot of 'mucking about'.]
... It's just as well otherwise we'd not go. The car can only carry
7 and we're not going without Wing-nut. He comes.

Guppie: We could do with it bein' a bit bigger! Why don't tha get a better
car, like a Robin Reliant. [Laughter]

Wolf: We'll give ya petrol money.

George: You what? Never!

Wolf: We will, six of us, ten bob each, that's three quid!

George: I couldn't take it. I don't want money! I want a rest!

Wolf: We'll give it tha, anyway! [He conveniently forgets]. Swear t'
God, they'll be no messin'! Come on Guppie crash the ash, ya
twat! Alice go and see if Mason 'as finished. Tell 'im t' come and
see what we've done.

Mike Mason arrives and compliments 'the Boys' on their productivity.
The class is dismissed.

Dinna time

The group shortcuts across waste land, through a well-worn hole in the
wire fence, to where the car is parked. People stop to urinate in the bushes
as they go. There is a frenzied negotiation of which 'chippie' to visit. 'The
Boys' have a vast repertoire of chip shops, hierarchized by such criteria as
the quantitative and qualitative nature of portions, the thickness of fish
cakes, the length of fish, the diameter of the chip 'butties' and the ethnicity
of the owners. Such decisions are not taken lightly in the context of combining it with an eventful joyride. Together George and 'the Boys' have
journeyed all over the city.

When 'the Boys' arrive, Kamikaze lies over the bonnet, writes obscenities in the road film and then pushes the car up and down exercising its
suspension.

Kamikaze: Come on prick'eads let's tip it over! I'll take it t' bits! If we all
    do it, it'll only take 2 minutes! [Laughter]
George: Now that's clever isn't it if we want to go to the chippie! We
    are not going anywhere with the car upside down. Make up
    you're mind, Kamikaze! [Laughter]
All: G' over, boy! Ya pillock! Let's git goin'!

The car is so small George has the back seats permanently removed.
People strategically stand by a door, holding a handle. Bodies eventually
clamber in, the horn is repeatedly beeped. There are shouts. 'Get in, ya
spastics!' 'Get seat up!' 'We'll never do it!' 'Get out of the fuckin' way!'
'Oh, my bleedin' knee!' ''Ere move this fuckin' petrol tin!' 'Three can't get
in there.' 'Get ya foot out of ma back!' 'Now then boy, move ya daft
bastard!' 'Look at the fuckin' seats, they're like deckchairs.' 'The fuckin'
'andbrake is like a dildo, Wing-nut sit on it!'

The final negotiated seating arrangements characterized by such raucous
banter and joustling, is Wolf in the front passenger seat, Guppie, Alice and
Jar seated where the rear seat normally is, with Kamikaze and Wing-nut
lying crossways in what was the boot area. Consequently, there is a high
degree of body contact with plenty of opportunity for interpersonal grop-
ing and thumping. This persists throughout the journey. Eventually, everybody is secured. The radio is put on at maximum output on Radio One.
George fights to move the car off.

All: 'Ere we go! 'Ere we go! 'Ere we go! We're the Gobbo Barmy Harmy!
    We're the Gobbo Barmy Harmy! Go on George! Go on! Can we go
    t' Blackpool! Keep on goin' f' ever, let's leave this shit 'eap, f' ever!

The windows are all wound down! As the car passes female students, they shout and immensely skilful, high-decibel, wolf whistles go up.

All: Flaps out! Flaps out! Get tha fanny out! Go on ya cow, get tha fanny out! [More high-decibel wolf whistles go out] ... Tha's got a nice pair of tits! Come 'ere and I'll knob thee. Get thee flaps open! I'll give thee some 'ammer, cunt! Look at that fanny there! [The carhorn is pressed by Wolf] ... There's one for Wing-nut there, that blubber bag theere! Look at that slag there, ya silly old bastard! [More wolf whistling] ... The's Guppie's bird theere! Jar's knobbed 'er! Guppie 'll knob thee! Look at 'er, 'er 'air's a reet mess. Look at tha size of those legs! Come 'ere thunder thighs! Smart one 'ere, reet smart tart! Now then, take tha clothes off! She's got big tits, watch 'em bounce! Dirty cunt! Look at tha' bit of fanny! Come on ya shit'ouse, you've got a big cunt! Look at that reet smart tart, yonder! Look at those two knobbin'. I know 'er I've been out with 'er sister. She come downstairs in 'er knickers and tee shirt! I wanted to knob 'er everywhere. She's a nice size! Look at tha arse on that 'ne! Look at those two bitches goin' down there! Flaps out! Flaps out! Flaps out!

As the group pass male students, obscenities are also yelled and the second finger 'fuck off' sign is exchanged.

All: Up yours ya fuckin' knob! Move shit 'ouse! Shift ya wanka, out of tha way! Up your arse! [More car horning by Wolf] ... Nice one, George. Go on George, get 'im up tha arse! Look at that shit'ouse theere, who are you boy! Shift ya old shit'ouse council estate yokkers! Get one of tha bastards! Now then cunt, move! Now then, ya fuck 'ouse, move! Go on, ya fuckin' 'ooligans! Make way for the A Team, tit 'eads! Bollocks! Look at 'im with tha orange 'air! 'Ey, ginger nut, has tha got a ginger minge? Now then cunt-flap, move ya fat bastard! Move ya idle fuckas! Calm down, boy!

All this externally directed exercise of oralcy skills runs concurrently with in-car pushing, shovings, banter and wrestlings, together with a running commentary for George.

All: Faster! Faster! Come on, George, lad old son! Fourth gear, down to second! Take tha cunt, George! Go on! Get tha wheels spinnin'! 'And-brake turn 'round this corner! Splash that woman there! Ya in tha wrong gear! Left 'ere! Right! Straight on! Go on George, go on straight up that Escort's arse! Left! Right! Left! We're all over tha shop, go for it George! Rev it! Rev it up! What are we doin'? 'It 'im, go on 'it 'im! If tha 'takes that Celica, two litre, GT, I'll give tha fifty quid! No chance.

Eventually the incidence of shouting at drivers and pedestrians diminishes but never disappears if anybody or anything is of note. The car passes an old woman with a walking frame.

Alice: There's one f' thee, George! [Wolf whistle. Shouts to old woman] . . . George fancies thee! Flaps out!

Guppie: You're a divvy George! Jimmie passes 'is test, right? Got an Escort, nose cone on front, numbers on side, tha lot! At traffic lights, right, eighty miles an 'round a corna on the pavement for a bit of fun like. Screeches 'round with the 'andbrake on. A reet laff. I were in car with 'im like. 'Is dad bought it 'im an' 'e 'ad some money. Number One on the bonnet and on doors. On Friday night, 'e got a full tank of petrol. From the Corporation Depot where they keep all the vans, right. Syphoned it off. Over the fence, climbed in, petrol can full. Sometimes there's security but there warn't any. 'Undred miles an 'our up tha motorway! We can get t' motorway this way, George! Come on let's go, George!

Wolf: This ain't a bad car is it, George? That mini theere is a load of wank! 'Ow big is it?

George: Only about one thousand c.c.

Wolf: Not bad, 'cos theere's seven of us in 'ere, say ten stone a piece, I'm over thirteen stone, Kamikaze is same, 'ow much are thee? Then there's these little bastards! That's er over a quarter of a ton. Not bad! I want a black Capri me, ya can 'alf get tha fanny! That's a nice car theere! Sixteen 'undred Injection Ghia Orion, electric windows, that is bootiful. It's sound that! One 'undred and twenty 'orse power, 'orse shit!

Guppie: Ma brother's got an open Suzuki Jeep!

Jar: GTR 1.9, they're reet bullets them!

Kamikaze: I wouldn't mind a Grenada 2.3 LX with leopard skin seats, or an XL2 with five gears. They've got a brilliant stereo. Zzzound!

Wolf: We'll 'ave t' whip thee a decent radio-cassette, George! This crap is not even stereo FM or tape-deck. We'll get thee a top-class 'ne. I'll get a receipt, somehow! [Laughter]

George: Shut up complaining or I'll put on Radio 4! [Laughter]

Wolf: Slow down 'ere, there's a cop shop. Tha doesn't know where tha blue bottle bastards are lurkin'! Watch out George, that's a blind man!

Kamikaze: Run tha bastard down then! [Laughter]

Alice: Look at that! I've never seen a cow ridin' an 'orse before! [Laughter. He has seen a mounted policewoman] . . . Moo cow, blue cow! [Laughter]

Kamikaze: Moooooo! Bloooooo! Moooooo! Nay! Away! Nay! Away! Nay!

Jar: Who's farted! Fuckin' 'ell! Uh! Wing-nut tha smells! [Laughter]

Wolf:	I've just shit! All the windows are goin' up! [Laughter]
All:	Get tha windas down, George! [Laughter]
George:	Uugh! Blood and sand! They never told me I'd be into this sort of thing when they asked me to do this research! Oh God! The temperature has gone up in here ten degrees! I'm turning off the heater! [Laughter]
Wolf:	They're all laid out dead at the back there! They are all red-faced and chokin'! Wing-nut is enjoyin' it! [Laughter]
Alice:	Stop prattin' abart! Keep ya 'ands to theesen, boy!

The car arrives and 'the Boys' fall out of the car and join the chip shop queue. There is a relatively restrained discussion. ''Ow much is chip butties?' 'Forty-five p.' 'What's tha 'avin'?' 'Don't know!' 'Look at tha' battered prick!' [i.e. sausage]. ''Ave they got any "scraps"?' [bits of separated batter]. 'I'm gettin' mine on a tray.' 'What drinks 'ave they got?'

Alice:	Ay. Come on, put to f' George's. 'E's brought us 'ere. What d' tha' want, George!
George:	No you don't! You can't afford to buy mine! Don't be daft!
Alice:	It's only reet, George. It's our shout! There's too many takers these days! What do tha want?
George:	No! And that is final!
Jar:	I'll 'ave a chip butty, luv! Can I 'ave some scraps! And a fish cake butty?
Wolf:	Lend us nine pence, George. I'll give it ya back in a bit! I'm skint, it's the old queen's birthday next Tuesday and I bought 'er a present!
George:	You know my policy. I'm not into buying your friendship! [Laughter]
Wolf:	What are tha 'avin', Guppie? Pizza! I'll give it ya back in a minute. You'll see. [George happily gives him the money] . . . I'm no scrounger! [He is but so is everyone except Wing-nut. However, in terms of balance of payments, Wolf is probably ahead!] Can I 'ave cake and chips, luv? And a big bottle of tizer!
Wing-nut:	Can we eat 'em in tha car, George!
George:	No! I don't mind the smell. I take exception to you lot treading them into the carpet! [Laughter]

Every one gets served and they sit on the wall outside. There are the usual conversations. Wolf shares his bottle, others have cans.

Guppie:	I'm daft me. I handed over the reet money and then tried to take the change of tha old bird behind me. Right good stunt!
Jar:	That old bird fancied you, boy! Get ya cock out! She's over there swoonin' at thee.

Guppie: Nay, George can 'ave 'er! At 'is age 'e'll go f' owt!
Wing-nut: She's just fallen over tha' chip tray!
Jar: Shut up you stupid mad bastard! Mong!
Kamikaze: I 'ad a chip butty and a fish cake butty for 86p. She charged 'im £1.16 [referring to Jar].
George: And 'e didn't politely say, 'Excuse me.' Oh no, its, 'Tha's robbed me.' [Laughter]
Jar: It's tha good influence! [Laughter]
Wolf: Did tha see the bloke fryin' tha fish with cross-eyes! That mad cunt Kamikaze stands there crossin' 'is eyes back at 'im! [Laughter]
Alice: Look at that daft cunt, Wing-nut, eatin' fuckin' beans with a chip stick. Ya make me fuckin' sick. Look at that, beans, steak and kidney pie and chips with gravy, all mixed up in a tray. Fuckin' 'ell, it's like the shits! Look at 'is gob, its like a full bog bowl! [Laughter]. [Wing-nut burps loudly and deliberately eats with his mouth open]
Guppie: Anyone want this fish skin?
Wolf: I'll 'ave it, pass it 'ere!
George: What do you want that for? Oh I see, you want a skin graft! [Everybody falls about laughing]
All: Nice one, George! Nice one.
Wolf: Now don't get carried away, George! Can ya imagine mushy peas 'ittin' tha windsceen! [Laughter]

As they finish they throw their chip papers down on the ground or pot-shot the wastepaper basket. There is the distinctive noise of the roll of empty tins on tarmac, as they are caught in the wind and traffic.

George: You're a load of litter louts! I've walked around the whole of Blightown with a brush and shovel cleaning up after you lot. You're an embarrassment!

A rapacious puppy is hanging around and everybody throws down chips which it duly devours.

Guppie: Look at the little greedy bastard!
Kamikaze: Does anyone want these chips?
George: I'll have them.
Kamikaze: I said anyone not thee! [He hands them over. He lets out a belch worthy of an elephant seal]
Alice: Georgie Porgie puddin' and pie, Kissed tha girls and made them cry! [Laughter]
George: That's all I did. I was respectable, not like you lot! [Laughter]

Wolf: You couldn't do much else, George! [Laughter] . . . 'Ere, Jar you've finished, take this empty bottle back and get the 10p on it and give it t' tight-fisted, George. Yuppie lend us a quid until toneet. I'll give it ya at Cleo's. Spark up! Crash tha ash! [Guppie lends him the money and shares a cigarette]

Everybody finishes and a decision is made by some to go to the tobacco and confectionary shop next door.

Wolf: Get ready f' a quick getterway. [Laughter. He leaves]
George: Is he thieving, again? Is he?
Alice: Look at tha mad fucka! 'E's puttin' tons and tons in 'is pockets! I can see from 'ere. 'E's a right mong!

Wolf returns again, smiling with the others. His multi-pocketed bomber jacket looks a size larger!

George: Have you been thieving again? Remind me to have a severe word with you about responsible citizenship. [Laughter]
Wolf: A man 'as got t' survive, George! 'as got t' survive! Shy boys don't get pies George! Does anyone want this? [Exposing some of his new acquisitions] . . . Well ya not gettin' any! [Laughter]

'The Boys' load themselves in the usual way into the car. A new route back to the college is selected, one that incorporates a fast stretch of road in which George can be exhorted to go for the impossible 'ton', a hundred miles per hour. This is combined with the usual shouts and whistles to people outside and joustlings between people within. All this is compounded by Kamikaze's elephant seal belches. As the car cruises along, 'the Boys' discuss heritage sites of cultural importance.

Jar: There's Cannerybis Row. Does tha want any black ash? Just drive down there and they come up sayin', 'Does tha' want anythin'?' If ya say, 'Yeh!', then they whistle up the stuff. The police never go in there. Shit-scared. The police try t' grab ya as ya come out! They're yitten! Get stopped, I've got a reet way of doin' it. Pull ashtray out, twenty quids worth, put it in there and shove the ashtray back. They check everythin', everywhere, takes 'alf an 'our. They stopped us on Saturday durin' day. I bought some, got some left. I makes two or three joints out of a fiver's worth. One joint gets two or three of ya nice and 'igh. I make two and 'alf like. King size 'uns, that big, big fat rollo. It's alreet for a laff. There's two white kids in there with rottweilers, any messin' about and they let go. We were in ma mate's Peugeot 205

GTi, C Reg. The coppers searched all our pockets. 'You don't
mind, lads. What are you doin' down 'ere?' 'We're just drivin'
'round like.' They search us and then said, 'On ya way!' Tha
bastards. They daren't go in, they'd get fuckin' pasted.

Alice: Now then, I've got an experience f' thee down theere! Who's bin
t' a gay and lesbian bar then. I 'ave. 'Ave ya ever bin in tha *Little
Red Fox*. Full of fuckin' lesbians, plasters over tha cunts! Listen
t' this, ya 'ave t' put ya name down f' snooker, so m' mate puts
down 'Big Cock!' There's all these homos and lessies touchin'
each other and that. Oh yeh! Fuckin' 'ell. Just went in f' a laff
to cause mayhem! My mate tried pullin' one of these lessies and
she told 'im t' fuck off! Dirty bastards!

Wolf: Now see that, theere! I did me 'Community Service' theere. Forty
'ours and I were fined £85. We worked on that buildin' theere.

George: What did you do?

Wolf: Sat 'round doin' fuck 'all. There were nowt t' it. All day Saturday.

George: No, I meant what did you do to deserve it?

Wolf: I smashed someone in tha face, that's all. I were walkin' down
tha street with tha bird and I told 'im t' 'Fuck off!' Then 'Bam!'
I fractured 'is cheek bone, broken nose, split nose, two black eyes
and a front tooth out. I only 'it 'im once! 'E went t' police and
'e were 21 an' all! They told me if I come in again for GBH, I'll
get prison. 'Is mate came after me aftawards. Said 'e were goin'
t' syringe me with acid. So I leathered 'im an' all. But tha police
didn't know abart that! 'E knew tha bird like and w' afta 'er. I
only went with 'er two weeks. She were buggin' me. She weren't
lettin' me knob 'er! She said I could like but it were never the
right time! [Laughter] . . . So I said, 'Fuck off then!' and tha' were
it!

    Suddenly, as the car goes at a good thirty miles per hour up an hill, the
rear hatch door flies open and upward. Kamikaze has been busy with a
metal object and has unlocked the door from the inside! Cheers go up!
George pulls to the side of the road, gets out and closes the tailgate.

George: You damn fool, Kamikaze! Stop it! Do that again and you are
out walking. The last thing I want is one of you lot hospitalized.
You fool! All I had to do was put my footbrake on right and half
of you would have been straight under that Fiesta behind us. I
can see the head lines now, 'Trendy University Researcher Slays
Six Innocent YTS Trainees! Government To Set Up Independent
Inquiry Into Highly Efficient Use Of Taxpayers' Money!' Do you
want to walk? I don't want to be responsible for your death, even

though a lot of people will pay me to do it! Just pull a stunt like that again and you walk! And we shan't go anywhere again, if that's what you want?

All the rest break into a tirade of support for George against Kamikaze.

All: Go on George make 'im walk. Go on! Tha's too soft with 'im, make 'im walk. Don't give in, George. Make tha bastard walk! Ya soft! Y're a big softie, George!

There is unaniminity that Kamikaze is 'a pillock', yet all agree it were 'a reet good laff!' Others will attempt to emulate Kamikaze at a later date. The tension is soon broken with Alice's observations.

Alice: Look at this little bastard dog 'avin' a fuckin' piss up tha wheel, George. A reet fuckin' go! Look at it! [Laughter]

Wolf: 'Ere Kamikaze tha daft cunt, polish that wheel for George with ya fuckin' tongue. Ya pillock! [Laughter]

Kamikaze: I'm not bothered. I don't give two fucks! Zzzound! Zzzound! [Elephant seal belch]

Jar: See that Dumpit Site there!

George: Oh good, is there one? I'll drop you lot off then! [Laughter]

Jar: See that dump we used t' ride our motorbikes over there, old people are down there scroungin', goin' through tha rubbish. We 'ave a reet laff with them. Shoutin' at 'em, 'What's tha doin' tha pimps' and windin' them up. They fuckin' throw bricks at thee and the lot.

George: It's a sorry world when old people have to scrounge through rubbish.

Wolf: M' uncle does it. 'E's not in our family 'cos 'e does that. No-one talks t' 'im now. 'E worked in tha steelworks. My fatha battered 'im last month. 'E got a tele right on HP and when ya on dole ya have t' put someone's name down. 'E puts ma dad's down without tellin' 'im and didn't pay it. 'E didn't ask and they came 'round our 'ouse f' money. And ma fatha went afta 'im and beat tha shit out of 'im f' that!

The journey continues up the hill, passing through a local community of British Asians.

Wolf: Come on, guns out. ['The Boys' make pretend that they have machine guns in their hands and simulate their noise] . . . Jhee, jhee, jhee, jhee, jhee, jhee, jhee, jhee, jhee, jhee. Rambo the black bastards!

George: Don't be so racist! Everybody is looking at us!
All: Guns out. Jhee, jhee, jhee, jhee, jhee, jhee, jhee, jhee, jhee, jhee.
Wolf: It's all reet f' you, George, tha doesn't 'ave t' live with the
            black twats! Wanker! Look at tha niggers! What's up George,
            does tha like a bit of tha black! Shut ya black flaps! [Laughter]
All: Blackie! Blackie! Niggers! Paki! Paki! Get on a fuckin' bus, ya
            tight black bastards! [To pedestrians] . . . Up your black cunts!
            Black bollocks! Get that black bastard! Jhee, jhee, jhee, jhee,
            jhee, jhee, jhee, jhee, jhee, jhee. Get out of the way tha fuckin'
            black bastards! I wouldn't fuck a black cunt like thine! Get tha
            guns out! Now then, tha fuckin' black bastards! Jhee, jhee,
            jhee, jhee, jhee, jhee, jhee, jhee. Look at tha' fuckin' big black
            mamma! Tha nig-nogs! The niggers! The nig-nogs! The big
            brown skidders! Black flaps shut! I'll batter thee!
George: Come on! Don't be so racist! Thank God I can see the college!
Wolf: Go on run the black cunt over. Guns out. Jhee, jhee, jhee, jhee,
            jhee, jhee, jhee, jhee. Nigger! Nigger! I'll shit down thee throat!
            I'll slit thee throat!
All: Run tha black bastard down! Jhee, jhee, jhee, jhee, jhee, jhee,
            jhee, jhee. Ya right Paki black bastards! Tha looks like a piece
            of shit! Yo brotha! Yo man! [attempted West Indian patois].
            Look at tha black bastards! Shut ya black flaps!

The car passes a funeral parlour. 'The Boys' are distracted.

Kamikaze: Let's go in theere and knob owt dead! [Laughter]
Wolf: Fuck off, Weirdo! Ya fat git! Wing-nut can 'ave 'em. 'As tha
            got a rubber doll, Wing-nut? I bet it's a black 'ne! Tha dirty
            bastard! [Laughter]
Wing-nut: Yeh! [Laughter]

The car arrives in the college car park. George observes Kamikaze
headbutting the rear window.

George: You lot have given me a headache! I need a rest! Bloody hell! I
            feel as though I've gone through a hedge forward, never mind
            backward. I see Kamikaze is attempting to give himself one as
            well! [Laughter] . . . Just let anyone in that damn university ask
            what I have been doing today and if I've earned my money! I'll
            tell them! A big softie locked in a little Panda with a pack of
            wolves! It's cruelty to animals! [Laughter] . . . I am not cut out
            for this work, I must be mad! I've been smitten by you lot! I'm
            a crazed werewolf!

As the car is unloaded, it moves involuntarily forward downhill towards a mobile classroom. Someone has released the handbrake for 'a laff'. Everybody smiles innocently and blames someone else. George manages to grab hold of the brake in time, takes a deep breath but knows he will gladly take them out again.

Wolf: Anyway George, I'd just like t' say thanks. It were alreet this dinna.

George: Now don't be funny, you're embarrassing me with this feint praise.

Wolf: We're not bein' funny. It were a change, weren't it from bein' stuck in fuckin' college all tha time. We just sit abart bored t' shit. We'll see thee reet. You wait and see!

George: Yes, YTS would be really borin' without me! [Laughter] ... You'll look back in 20 years' time and you'll not remember anything and you'll think about YTS and you'll think of me, I know. [Laughter]

Kamikaze: When we're still queuin' up f' dole in 20 years time, we'll think of that knob'ead who took us in 'is car! [Laughter]

Alice: 'E's not a knob'ead, old George. 'E does no 'arm with is fishin' coat and his CND wellies. [George is wearing a wax jacket and red leather boots] ... Look at those boots! Tha looks like Wank 'Angford! [Laughter]

George: You are all the highlight of my dreary life! I don't know what I have been doing all these years without you! [Laughter]

Wolf goes across the hill to urinate in the bushes. As the rest go, conversation shifts to films.

George: Look at Wolf, one bottle of Tizer and he has to pee all over Blightown! [Laughter]

Alice: 'Ave ya seen that one where 'e blows that Chinkies 'ead off with a machine gun. It just splatters! *Hamburger Grill* or wa' it *Platoon*. Tha Chinky kept on runnin' and 'e says, 'Fuckin' 'ell, I've not seen brains like that before!'

Jar: See that one where 'e put a shotgun down 'is mouth and blew down it t' get dope!

Alice: I've bin to Vietnam me! Ma dad were there! [Laughter]

Jar: It were good when 'e stabbed 'imself! Shoved those Chinkies into tha pit. Tha bloke got 'is arm blown off and 'e's just talkin' t' 'imself and 'e doesn't know!

Alice: Did tha see that nigger, 'e were a right racist. 'E 'as glasses on. 'E's always sayin', 'These white 'onky bastards are shit! We niggers never get nowt!' Pickin' fights with whites all the time.

'E were goin' on, 'You white 'onky guys, the brothers 'll get you.'

Jar: That white kid with tha National 'Ealth Service gigs [spectacles] was always in front goin' in t' those Chinkies, then 'e got killed. I felt reet sorry f' 'im!

Alice: I were cryin' when 'e got killed! 'E were barmy. 'E 'ad National 'Ealth Service gigs.

George: What about *The Killing Fields*, that's the only one I've seen?

Alice: Ugh! That's noddy. Knob 'eads watch that. Not violent enough that. I like bollocks bein' chopped off. 'Ave ya seen tha' with dolls, where they go 'round cuttin' everybody up and sawin' ankles off!

Jar: Them Zombie films are wank. Tha best films I've watched are *Ragin' Bull*, *Apocalypse Now* and *Wankin' Dundee*. Did tha see that fifty stone bloke in tha *Sunday Sport*?

Alice: Did ya see tha girl with them burns in that? I've got 'er phone number for Pods!

Guppie: Did ya see that 6 horse race and that horse come in at 100–1 and this bloke put 15 quid on it? Come on we're goin' t' be late.

Kamikaze: Don't matter, 'e's never early! They've stopped learnin' us owt!

Wolf: [Rejoining group] . . . You don't learn owt anyway! [Laughter] . . . I've got a reet picture on my wall at 'ome, Linda Luzardi, tits out, full size! Bootiful!

Afta dinna time

The 'footings' and Mike Mason await 'the Boys'.

Mr Mason: Now let's get down to it this afternoon. If you decide to stop in the construction industry and get a job, then the opportunities are there. Put it this way, when there was a lot of employment, jobs for everybody, there was always room for a good man who could just work on a building site and be told where everything was, what went where and what was expected of him, who stuck to the rules and regulations. And when he had done it, he went to the boss and was told something else to do. Right. But now when there are not so many jobs around, people can still get jobs, people who can do the job responsibly, who are independent workers. Workers who can work on their own, don't need to be given a lot of attention all the time. These are the people who are employed, who have got some basic ideas and don't need attention all the time. These

are the people who get the work. Now you can work because
I've had two or three members of staff this last week come up
and say to me, 'Can I bring up my students to look at your
YTS lads' work?' So a good clean responsible job. So let's
have a chinwag, talk. Let's get a method, a plan of attack.
You know everything needs to be done methodically. There is
a knack to everything, a method to it like everything else.
There is only one thing produced by rushing and not thinking,
you know that, babies. I know you lads know all about that.
Carry on then with the footings, clean down the concrete
mixer, all boards around the back, all these bags in the skip,
very nice and tidy, all tools away in the store and checked.
Then sit and wait in there for your review or until you are
told you can go home. Is that clear? Graffiti, I'll see you with
Mr Aggregate.

Henry Aggregate arrives. He is the liaison officer, responsible for the
work placements and their supervision. George chats to them both.

Mr Aggregate: How's things? Come to any earth-shattering conclusions
yet? What are you doing exactly?

George: No not really, but these lads are very interesting. It's a
research programme sponsored by something called the
Economic and Social Research Council. This is only a very
small part of the research. It involves five universities and
covers the whole country. Its main focus is what is called
'economic and political socialization' and involves a big
questionnaire survey over a long period of time.

Mr Aggregate: Oh, really! You'll not find much of that going on here!
[Very sceptical laughter] . . . I don't know what you will
discover here. To be quite honest, I think that one of the
snags is that I am not convinced the course is what they
actually want to do. I am not sure we are offering what is
relevant to them. At the interview stage, you find that an
awful lot of them do not know what the Scheme consists
of or want to be 'a builder'. But there is no such thing as
'a builder', there's bricklayers, joiners, what have you. 'Ah
well, I want to be a bricklayer?' 'Sorry but you can't do
that! The YTS course is just a general operative course.'
You spell it all out and a third drop out before the course
starts, disappear because for good kids this is very low
down the list. Other Schemes, especially the Town Hall
Scheme where they are guaranteed a job and get £50 a
week, creams them off. They are the good lads, they're

keen, there is a bit of literacy amongst them, whereas these lads come on this course because it's the last thing available to them.

George: So you have recruitment difficulties?

Mr Mason: As you know [Wing-nut] and [Pods] are 'special needs'. Last year at interview, we drew up a list of the best 15, then drew up a reserve list of 15. Of the first 15 hardly any turned up. We went to the reserve list, most of them had been fixed up on other courses and we only managed to get about 10 and now we are down to what, 8. The thing is, the trouble is the lads that have gone tend to be the better ones and the ones that stay are the bottom of the barrel really.

Mr Aggregate: There is a kamikaze section to YTS, you know some have got a death wish. It is as though they want someone to throw them off the course. But these lot, they're a bit loud but not a pain, really. These lads are not employable really and the course is not to their requirements really. That's the problem.

Mr Mason: It is certainly not interesting to them. Whether they learn anything at the end of the day is questionable. They must be learning something I suppose. I don't know whether it is a lack of commitment or what? Or whether they are doing it for the lack of anything else. They disappear as soon as they can find any job. Look at Smith, he left last week, a van driver's mate delivering tea! So something, somewhere is not jelling with them.

Mr Aggregate: They [the college staff] are swamped with paperwork generated by the educationalists, modules, reviews, what have you. A lot of them are not low achievers but certainly haven't revelled in schoolwork, shall we put it that way. Really all they are good for is plenty of work. Plenty of manual stuff! But we swamp them with paperwork which ends up being a complete turn-off for them. So we end up having to abandon that really or doing it badly.

Mr Mason: And remember for a lot of the lecturers here these lads are not the desirable work, the Craft lads are the prestige work. The YTS is only a small part of the college's work. And lots of the ideas of the educationalists as well are unenforceable. And really the discipline procedures are lax because although they are low achievers, they are not unintelligent. So we try to hold on to them. Fortunately, in this job it is not like being a class teacher. When it reaches a certain point you can get away from them in the workshop and that's it. But it is not easy! They don't think ahead. They don't make connections. They have to be led all the way. You have to stand over them all the time. None of them are good enough for an exam.

Mr Aggregate: What it is, is we have not educated our bosses into what this kind of student is all about. Some still think they are like craft apprentices who automatically progress onto City and Guilds Certificate. They assume these lads will do that. But they are way out, aren't they Mike? Our pressure is educating our bosses and the politicians to the kind of kids we've got and that it's an entirely different ball game.

Mr Mason: The attitudes from the top, they are garbage really. Some of the things they come out with. Crack-pot ideas what you should be doing. We manage to keep out of it a bit at the back here. It upsets me, George. It's laughable. It's ridiculous. The idea of a college is to come and learn something but its not like that. You can't expect this type of lad to be entered for City and Guilds and I have to convince them and explain why. But they don't easily understand. For them they are just another class. They don't know what I'm up against to be honest. All they are to them are bodies and income. There is no way they will get down to it. They do not retain the knowledge and understanding at all. They are hard-pressed to carry a pen.

Mr Aggregate: You've got to have a bit of a sense of humour or you'd go around the twist.

Mr Mason: You wonder what logic they are working under. They keep saying, 'This is boring!' but I'm not being uncharitable but with minds like that how can they be bored! [Laughter] . . . With this kind of lad, you can give them some basic knowledge and some basic notes and that's as far as you can go really. It's an uphill battle. They are not particularly bright lads and they can see no prospects. Yet they are intelligent in many ways. You've got to be very firm with them or they will take any advantage. You get some lads who are a different kettle of fish, terrific. I have a class Advanced C. and G. Highways Construction and Maintenence, they are terrific. You are on another planet, miles and miles apart.

Mr Aggregate: It is a strange set-up really. It is a bit of a battle. Really, you deserve a Victoria Cross for YTS. Bravery beyond the call of duty! [Laughter]

George: Anyway, I don't want to get in your way. I know you have
                 got a lot to do. I'll get out of your way. Thanks for having
                 me around.

Mr Aggregate: [To 'the Boys'] . . . Listen. We've got t' finish this Review
                 process off. Those we haven't seen, we've filled in your
                 forms. The reports on your placement are made up. I'll
                 want to know from you if you think they are fair and
                 reasonable. Is that clear! I'll want to know if there is any-
                 thing you want me to add to it. And there is also the
                 'Setting Out and Concreting Module' and we'll question
                 you on that! OK?

They call in Graffiti. In the meantime, 'the Boys' are galvanized into
frantic action.

Alice: Doooohh! Helloooha! Geoooorgge! 'As tha been snitchin',
                 boy? 'As tha bin consortin' with tha enemy?

George: You know I have! They know all about you now, how you
                 smashed up that Yorkshire stone single-handed! [Laughter]

Wolf: There's no gettin' out of it! The sooner we start, the sooner we
                 finish. You 'eard what the big prick said, as soon as we're
                 finished we sit in the tool room. Get the big fuckin' 'ammer!
                 Get diggin'!

Alice: Are you alright old son? 'Ow are you old boy? [To George]

Guppie: Move it! Tha sooner we start, tha soon we'll finish!

Jar: I've found ma second strength! 'Ere pass us tha pick! I'll show
                 'ow its done!

Kamikaze: Izzy whizzy, let's get bizzy! Zzzound! [Laughter]

Jar steps back five metres, raises the pick above his head, charges forward and smashes it down on the concrete base. It splinters. Others line
up with an assortment of tools and repeat the activity, sometimes succeeding, sometimes not. Jackets are removed, trousers tightened and raised.
Sweat appears on foreheads and under armpits. Wing-nut, Pods and George
do not exert themselves! Kamikaze storms in.

Kamikaze: Ahhhhhhhhhh! Ahhhhhhhhhh! Come on ya bastard! [He
                 smashes down a sledgehammer and fractures the concrete] . . .
                 Heeeee, heeeee, heeeee! [like a chimpanzee]. Beat that ya bas-
                 tards! Zzzound! Look at that twit-twat! Tha's got a monkey's
                 fore'ead! I am from Mars! Mong! [to Wing-nut and Pods]

Guppie moves back ten metres and has a go. The rest follow. Soon all
the footings are fragmented. All that is required now is to load the debris
into a skip.

Wolf: Jar, get tha pick under it! Pods and you! Wing-nut we've bin workin'.
Come on ya bastard! Get under it and 'eave!

Soon all the smaller pieces of footings are raised and people manhandle
them into the skip. All that are left are large pieces.

Wolf: Everybody, now then, everyone get 'old of this! Come on, ya
               daft bleeders, get 'old of it.
George: Wouldn't it be sensible to break them up first? Mind your
               backs, you don't want to slip your discs. Be careful!
Wolf: Take no notice! There 'e goes again, Doctor George! Fuck off,
               George. Get tha finga out, ya dosey bastards! 'Eave! Eave!
               Look at Pods, tha right snide. Get 'old of it ya bastard!
George: I'm only concerned about your health.
Kamikaze: Fuck that!
All: 'Old it, boy! 'Old it, there! Ah! Timber! Timber! Rest it on
               that wheelbarrow! Watch out!

A spontaneous clap of exaltation goes up as the six-foot piece is
lowered on the wheelbarrow, taken to the skip and hoisted in. The
operation is repeated.

Wolf: Come on ya bastards! We'll start steamin'! Get ya picks under
               this! Everyone get 'ere again!
All: Come on! Come on! This bastard is double thickness. 'Eave!
               'Eave! Get down to it! Get it on its end! Lower it on t' barrow!
               Come on Wing-nut, tha dosey cunt! Lower it gently!
George: Mind your finger! I'm too old for this game! It would be so much
               more sensible to break it up into smaller pieces!
Wolf: There 'e goes again! Fuck off, George! There's only one foreman!
George: I'm thinking about your back! You'll be burnt out before you're
               40!
Guppie: I hope so but it will be from too much knobbin'! [Laughter]

A ten-foot long piece is edged, everybody holding on to it, towards the
skip and heaved in.

Wolf: Come on ya bastards! Everybody get under it. Come on! Come on!
Wing-nut, Pods 'elp us, ya cunts! What's tha fuckin' doin'? We
want t' lift it up this way! Everybody under! Come on! Straight on,
lovely!

The rest is treated in like fashion. Only relatively small pieces are left on
the ground. Pods slinks off to the toilet. Kamikaze finds a cross-like piece

of wood used on a building site 'to take a level'. He goes into his zombie-like Dracula act.

Kamikaze: Mong! Mong! I've got garlic 'round my breath! I come from Mars! Zzzound! [bearing his fangs]
Alice: Doooohh! Hellooooha! Gooppeee! [baby-like]
Guppie: Doooohh! Hellooooha! Alleeece!
Wolf: Fuckin 'ell, George! This is what 'appens when ya take 'em on a day trip! [Laughter]
Alice: Ya 'ave my permission t' take a breather! [Laughter] . . . Are ya alright old son? This job knackers me, I collapse and sleep when I get 'ome! I do!
Wolf: I call that work. I'm a grafter me. Ya can't stop me in full sweat! See if ya can lift tha' un above tha 'ead! I bet thee can't!

Jar succeeds with a high degree of exertion to lift a piece of concrete above his head. Guppie and Alice fail. The rest, including George, do not even try. Wolf gives everybody an object lesson in how it should be done.

Wolf: Come on, let's get this fuckin' finished, once and f' all! Get tha shovels, get tha rakes, level it off. Clean it up and we can finish f' day tart it up!
Jar: Get them cement bags out, Wing-nut! Clean 'round tha mixer, boy!

Soon the work area is raked and levelled, ready for the commencement of a new project. Everybody rests. Kamikaze busies himself with his cross. With it he draws a giant penis and scrotum in the levelled sand and inscribes 'Mason is a knob head, Signed the YTS Boys + Wing-nut + Pods'.

Wolf: Stop muckin' abart, Kamikaze! Pods 'and out of thee pockets, rake it out. Let's get in tha tool room. We've finished f' day!

A pack of dilapidated playing cards is produced. George goes into a display of his Mississippi-gambler shuffle acquired in his mis-spent youth. He partially fails given the nature of the cards.

Guppie: Ooh! Ooh! Look at the fuckin' big 'ead!
Jar: Get tha spot board behind that wall. I'll be bank. I won £6.70 last week at brag. I 'ad t' borrow 20p from 'im t' get started. Maximum stake 10p, £6.70!
All: George'll be bank. I'll deal! Deal me in! Twist, twist, twist. Beat that cunt! You've missed me! Beat that twat! I've got twenty-one! You've bust! 'Old on cunt! I'm first!

George: You are all so busy attacking one another, he's going through the pack sorting twenty-one out for himself!

All: Burn 'em. Tha wants two! Stick! Stick! You can't stop! Can! Can't! 'E's seen mine! I've got a five card trick! Fuck off, boy. Don't tell 'im ya cunt! That jack were mine! Twist! Twist! Wipe thee eyes! [stick], Wipe ya arse! [bust]. Stop spittin' at 'im! I didn't say twist! What are ya doin' 'idin' cards! I've got 'a prowl' of threes! [Aspects of the game of brag are now included] . . . That's no good t' me, it's garbage! AKQua! I've got a bomber! Beat that ya fuckers! I don't like ya anymore!

George: Eh! Eh! In my gang, we'll have honesty! You took that card off the bottom! Give him the proper card! It's a good job you are not playing for money. When it comes down to it none of you cares who the hell wins! It's such chaos! [Laughter]

All: Tha don't want t' play reet! Stick! Stick! Stick! Stick! Twist! I've got a pontoon! Tha's not got twenty-one tha pillock! That's twenty-seven, boy! Stop shufflin' those cards! I've got a royal 'ne! Yeh, but what abart that 'ne on the floor! Give tha' mong time t' think. Give us a card, then. They're all back t' front! Twist! Twist! Twist! Twist! And again, again! Tha's already got five cards in thee 'and! I'm fuckin' bored! Play reet, ya slag! Swap cards with us! 'E's two cards behind! Now then slag I want tha' 'ne off the bottom now! Thas missed me ya fanny! Wipe tha eyes! Wipe tha arse! Wipe thee arse! Bust! Bust! Now then ballocks! Stop gobbin' boy!

George: Stop thumping one another! Decide whether you are playing cards or playing thumping! [Laughter]

The game ends among the laughing and thumping. The workshop technician comes in. He is built and looks like 'a super hod-carrier' and appears angry. As he talks, the lads go very quiet.

Technician: I've warned you, ya little YTS bastards! If anyone touches that fuckin' 'eater again, they'll not get out of this room alive! Who's put a trowel in that 'eater! I'll kill 'im if I catch tha cunt! Right! Some fucker's 'ad 'is fingers in it again! Right! The person I see, I'll fuckin' 'ave 'is fingers off! I'll personally fuckin' chop 'em off! Alright, ya little bastards, you've 'eard me! I'll personally snap off tha fucker's fingers one by one! I've fuckin' warned ya, ya cunts!

He leaves and 'the Boys' fall about laughing. They are not responsible for this heinous crime. However, given their record in the workshop, it was a fair assumption that they were responsible.

Wolf: That weren't us, tha fucka! 'E always blames us! We didn't
             do it! Fuck 'im, tha dick 'ead! Can we go t' Uni', George,
             tomorrow? It's a reet laff. Tha's still not bin 'as tha Jar? It's
             a reet laff!
Kamikaze: 'E won't be 'ere tomorra!
George: Why won't I?
Kamikaze: Because I'm goin' to smash ya 'ead in. I'll give thee a Rotherham
             kiss [head butt]. [Laughter] . . . I'm not comin' tomorra, I don't
             want t' come!
George: Why's that? Oh, I see, It's because you were going to smash
             your own head in! [Laughter] . . . We could go to some art
             galleries or museums instead. [Laughter] . . . There's nothing
             interesting at the university.
Alice: There is! There's those funny lifts [the paternoster] we seized
             up. And its a reet good view up at tha top.
Guppie: Alice nearly vomited in tha lift! 'E were goin' white! Weren't
             ya boy?
Alice: Were I fuck!
Guppie: You're a divvy! Tha top United fighter 'ooligan daren't admit
             it, were shit-scared! [Laughter]
George: I tried to register them all on a Master Builders degree course
             but for some mysterious reason they wouldn't have them! They
             started t' chat up all tha secretaries. [Laughter]
Alice: Them students are all University Challenge scum-bags, CND
             cunts, reet shit'ouses. Shit bags! Did we embarrass you, George?
George: Not at all! In fact you were very well behaved!
Wolf: Who were that foul bird? That friend of yours, George.
Alice: That CND vegetable rights 'ne with communist's gigs. She
             were foul! [Laughter]
Guppie: Ay and she said we could go down to 'er college and we could
             meet some YTS tarts there but George 'as chickened out! Can't
             we go t' Gastronomic College, George? Now there is some reet
             smart tarts there, not like 'ere. Can we go, George? We'll
             behave! We'll just go t' look at the tarts!
Alice: Ay and there were tha' Professor, what were 'is name George,
             Bill Badger? [His own impromtu construction derived from his
             mode of dress] . . . 'E could 'ardly talk t' us, 'is mouth looked
             like it were full of cake. [Laughter]
Wolf: George gave us this coffee and there was this fuckin' box of
             money lyin' there and no fucker swiped it! George says t' us
             t' keep our thievin' 'ands out! And 'e starts tellin' everybody
             I hadn't paid f' it. [Laughter]
Alice: George threw in 50p and took out £1 change. [Laughter]
George: Oh, you noticed then! I'm always doing that! [Laughter]

Wolf:	We pressed the emergency button on tha lift. And it says that tha not t' go 'round at tha top and we did! Alice were shit-scared, weren't ya? [Laughter]
Alice:	Were I fuck!
Wolf:	Kamikaze started belchin' reet loud! There were like this wire [sensitive safety trip] and we pulled it and all these poor bastards were jumpin' ten fuckin' feet down t' tha floor. A reet laff! [Laughter]
Kamikaze:	I fuckin' jumped six feet up! I fuckin' did! [Laughter]
George:	Serves you right!
Pods:	I got lost me and ran down 15 flight of stairs, reet laff!
Wolf:	I think it were ma 'ead that 'it tha wire!
Alice:	And there's this mad bloke on tha mike, 'Someone is messin' on tha paternoster! We are shuttin' it down! Will tha idiots responsible please leave tha buildin'!' [Holding his nose to simulate use of microphone. Laughter]
Wolf:	When are ya takin' us again George? It's a reet laff! And tha chippie and pub on tha corner are sound! Ya can buy us a beer again, George!
George:	We'll go again sometime. I must say it is incredible what you can do with a seat of learning! It's a bit more creative than some academics do with it! [Laughter]
Wolf:	Come on Pods 'as just gone in f' Review. Let's take a break. I've got an asbestos mouth! [To Graffiti] . . . What did they say, boy?
Graffiti:	They goes through everythin' you've done and that!
George:	Let's 'ave a look at your form. These are your occupational skills. [Reading from form] . . . *Drain laying; flag laying; first aid; concrete; plastering; use of telephone; coping with different site conditions. General Comment: Dean has had quite a variety of experiences of different work whilst at Copperthwaites. He is now ready for skill building and competency development.*
Alice:	It ain't as good as mine, look at this Review, boy. [Taking his form out of his pocket] . . . *Skills acquired: Hod carrying; mixing – progress toward; mixing concrete and mortar; place and transport things; compact flags to line and level; and prepare a sub-base. Can cope with behaviour changes required on placements, has sufficient experience to stack and handle a variety of materials.*
Wolf:	Well done! Couldn't tha do that before tha started 'ere! [Deep irony]
Alice:	[Continuing] . . . *He gets on well with most people and enjoys general labouring.* Lyin' bastards! *He's a punctual and reliable*

trainee. Tha lyin' bastards!

Wolf: I'll love to see wha' 'e puts on mine the old bastard.

Alice: 'E asks ya if ya want a mint first. [Laughter]

George: If it's a load of lies, why don't you say something and have it changed.

Alice: Why bother, it makes no difference, does it? Means nowt, keeps 'em off tha street and out of trouble. [Laughter] ... It's a load of wank!

While this conversation has gone on, Kamikaze has taken a woodsaw and cut a steel tape-measure in six or eight pieces. Everybody sees what he does, condemns him and calls him an idiot. As 'the Boys' leave, he dumps the fragments in a skip outside to the sound of 'Zzzound!'.

Break time

'The Boys' wend their way to the student lounge area and sit down around a table. Guppie takes his battery-operated shaver out and sets to work on his designer stubble. Everyone starts to laugh at Kamikaze.

Kamikaze: What's up? What's up, ya bastards?

All: Nowt! Nowt! [Everyone falls about laughing]

Kamikaze: Come on ya cunts, what's up?

Alice: Nowt! Nowt! [Laughter]

Kamikaze: Come on, ya mongs! What's up, ya cunts?

All: Nowt! Nowt!

George: Well it's a bit embarrassing this but you have a large green thing hanging out of your nose! [Laughter]

Wolf: There goes George again! George 'as let it out agin! Spillin' tha fuckin' beans! Keep thee trap shut! Tha's a reet knob 'ead!

George: I hate to say it but I think I am! [Laughter]

Kamikaze pushes his finger ostentatiously up his nose. He leans back, clears his throat and spits at Wing-nut!

Kamikaze: Dopey! Dopey! Dopey!

Guppie: Don't pull it down ya daft bastard, we'll 'ave ya brains all over tha table! Uugh! Look at the slimy thing, it's all over 'is face. The little creepin' fuckin' pig! [Laughter]

All: Uugh! Uugh! [Laughter]

Kamikaze attempts to gather up the offending mucus, eventually appends it to his finger and attempts to wipe it upon anyone available. Everybody flies away from the table. In the absence of a body, the object is spread on the table and left.

All: Uugh! Look at the dirty bastard! Uugh! [Laughter]
Jar: 'Ere Wing-nut there's a Christmas present f' ya there!

The group finds an alternative table. Guppie is wearing his brother's jacket and begins to explore the contents of the inside pocket. Everybody looks on fascinated and some of the objects are passed around.

Guppie: These are our kid's cards. There's 'is bank card, garage card, Barclaycard, Drivin' Licence, Climax Card, Guggi Card, Insurance, that's a picture of 'is bird in Exeter, that's the receipt f' our 'oliday, 'alf price tickets for *Isobellas*. 'E's got a few addresses and telephone numbers in 'ere of birds. Bank book with £225 quid in 'ere. Anythin' else tha wants t' know?
All: Let's 'ave a look! Show us, boy!
Jar: Look at Wing-nut, 'e's spellbound.
Guppie: Nay! Nay! Don't be nosey bastards!

Wolf makes a grab and obtains the wallet.

Wolf: Look there are 'is johnnies in 'ere! Does tha carry 'em, George? 'Ere 'as anybody got a pin? We'll get tha bastard! Come on! Come on, find a pin. We'll do tha fucker in and then put it back in tha packet.
George: You wouldn't do an irresponsible trick like that, would you? [Laughter]
Wolf: Nay! Nay! 'Course not! Get us a pin, boy! [Laughter]
Jar: Split a match! Split a match!

In the absence of a pin, various people start chewing match sticks in an attempt to obtain a fine point. One is passed to Wolf but he fails to puncture the condom.

Wolf: I think its ripped! It's got an 'ole where the ejaculation point is!
Guppie: Give it 'ere! Give it 'ere, knob 'eads! Put it over your 'ead. They do it at *Cleo's* on Wednesday nights. Competition for who can put it over their 'eads quickest and blow it up fastest and pop it. You get 'old of it like that. [He demonstrates only] . . . Put it over ya 'ead like that and then like that and then ya 'ave t' blow it up! The idea is t' put it over tha 'ead and pop it! No-one can do it but if ya can tha gets a free bottle of champagne.

Wolf puts the condom over his head. It horrendously deforms his face like a bank robber with a nylon.

George: Careful you'll asphyxiate yourself.

All: Great, go on asphyxiate yoursen! Everyone get ya 'ands round 'is neck.

George: Wait until I see Maggie Thatcher and tell her you've got money to burst! [Laughter] . . . God, they are tough, aren't they?

Jar: Fuckin' 'ell ya can tell George never uses 'em! 'Asn't tha tried a Rough Rider! [Laughter]

Wolf takes the condom off and exposes his red, gasping face.

Wolf: Blow it up! Blow it up reet big, ya knob 'eads!

When it is blown up like a large balloon, it is knotted and thrown around. Guppie gets out his shaver and attempts to shave it.

Wolf: It's just the reet size f' me now! Put ya ear t' that, there's an 'ole in it! 'Ave you ever felt one before! It's just like a tit! [Wolf sensuously strokes the condom and sucks the end]

George: Polite company wouldn't know what it is now!

A group of girls pass by and all break out giggling! The inflated condom is kept air borne, tapped from one to another.

George: I tell a lie! They recognize what it is! [Laughter]

All: Flaps out! Flaps out! Tools up! Flaps out!

Guppie: Alice fancies that bird there with tha glasses. She's just reet f' 'im! 'E's afta 'er and won't admit it!

George: Come on, Alice! Have I got to show you how it is done? I'll go over for you, if you want, and say, 'I'm Alice's grandfather and he would like to go out with you?' [Laughter]

Guppie: 'E's never knobbed a bird! Look at tha face on that. [alluding to Alice]

Alice: Tha'll knob owt! [Laughter] . . . Doooohh! Hellooooha! Gooppeee! [baby-like]

Guppie: Dooooohh! Hellooooha! Alleeece!

Wolf: Come on someone spark up, spark up! Someone!

A cigarette is lit and passed to Wolf. Everyone scatters, standing well back!

Wolf: Watch this! Right at tha top! A top shot!

The lighted cigarette is applied to the end of the condom. There is a loud bang! Wolf nearly falls off his chair under the explosive impact! Everybody falls about laughing.

Guppie: At *The Birds Of A Feather Sauna*, if ya want a blow job [oral sex], they use a johnnie! [Laughter] . . . I've bin there.

Wolf: You lyin' bastard! 'As tha fuck! Ya sly twat!

Guppie: I fuckin' 'ave! Eight quid t' get in. Sauna, bar, video room. I'll tell thee 'ow it's laid out when ya go in if ya want! There's a naked bird on tha back of a tiger inside, I'm tellin' you, boy!

Jar: Did tha get owt?

Guppie: No! It's twenty-five quid. Ten of us went in. Some kids did. One 'ad this bird, I knew. She were crap! 'orrible!

Wolf: Did 'e knob 'er?

Guppie: No! There's one bird, a right shag, blonde girl, a right dog. A massage is eight quid, they ask ya if ya want anythin' else and then they throw in the extras. Tha says ya skint or they give ya a long list of what ya can 'ave! This kid 'shot m'lord' [manual relief], that's all! Ya can 'ave wha' ya wants. Ya get wha' ya pay for. They do tha lot.

Jar: Look at Wing-nut, 'e's got an 'ard-on just listenin'.

Guppie: If they give ya 'a blow job', that's £25. Ya can stay as long as ya like in tha sauna, watch tha films on tele. I daren't go on me own. Ya go f' a laff. It's an experience. We were pissed and had 'draw', high as a bastard we were. We fell asleep there.

George: I'm amazed how you lads can conjure up the money!

Wolf: [Momentarily losing attention and the thread of the conversation] . . . What?

Jar: Never you mind, this is men's talk, boy! [Laughter]

All: Ooh! Oooh! [Laughter]

Wolf: I've bin t' one, *Randy Mandy's* and tha' is fuckin' it! That is fuckin' it! It were a fuckin' rip off. I'm not goin' again! I 'ad a sauna and rub off and watched video. Showed the fuckin' knob goin' up and down and a tongue on it and that.

George: Oh, so they show pornography do they? I thought it was 'Match of the Day'. [Laughter, but he is absolutely serious]

Wolf: Ooh, George, where 'as tha been? 'As tha been locked away or somethin'? Are tha still a virgin? [Laughter] . . .

Jar: It's not little boys bummin', Wing-nut. [Laughter] . . . Tha middle name's Pokey!

Guppie: I can get ya a fuck at this girl's flat. She's a prostitute.

Wolf: I don't want flossies! I'm not so desperate that I 'ave t' pay f' it!

Guppie: That's what ya get at saunas, mallock! Let's all go sometime f' a laff!

George: I'll stick to the university and the chippie thanks very much. [Laughter]

Alice: 'E's passed it, poor old chap! Boys were boys in your day weren't they, George? Are tha into bondage then, George. [Laughter]

Wolf: Yuppie is payin'! [Laughter]
George: I'll ask my university bosses if I can go, all in the name of science.
           I'll sit in the armchair and do a spot of scientific observation,
           watch you lads trip in with ya towels! [Laughter]
Wolf: You pervert, George. Ya dirty bastard! [Laughter]
George: Oh God, I didn't mean it like that! [Laughter]
Jar: We'd take Pods and Wing-nut but they're too busy bummin'
           sheep or stayin' at 'ome watchin' a big fuckin' turd! What's a
           good night out for you Wing-nut, this dinna time? [Laughter]
Wolf: Wing-nut goes out with Pods. D' ya know they live next door t'
           one another, so they can bum through tha walls? They go t' tha
           pub and order Malibou and coke! [Laughter] . . . Come on, let's
           get back. I'd rather do without a break and leave early. Let's keep
           Mason sweet.

Before home time

On their arrival back, 'the Boys' meet Pods who has come out of his
Review.

Wolf: What's yours say, Mr McGoo? Stan Laurel? Ferret 'ead?
Pods: *Fixing and dismantling; flat roofing, not felting; fixing up-and-over
       door; ironmongery, levelling. General Comment: Has had a chance
       of working in a variety of jobs in a private housing development.
       Paul is making good progress and has acquired a range of practical
       skills, so increasing his confidence. I will follow up employment
       status as a possibility with Hallamshires especially since Paul finishes
       in September. Would like to concentrate on brickwork.* A right load
       of garbage!
Wolf: They're reet cunts them bastards. They're right see-saws. They write
       anything. They just bores ya to death.

   Wolf goes to his Review.

Jar: [To Wing-nut who has returned from the toilet] . . . I 'ope you
           have wiped tha fanny. When I get 'ome, I'll get some fanny, on
           tha settee. Look at fuckin' Pods throwin' that sand. Stop it, ya
           dick'ead! I shagged me bird last neet and I'll shag 'er again.
George: Lies, all lies! You lads live in a fantasy world! [Laughter]
Jar: Do ya want a bet! I'll put a fiver on it!
Guppie: 'E goes with a schoolgirl, 'im! A right cradle snatcher!
George: How am I going to know? Come around and lie under the
           settee and check? [Laughter]

Jar:	I fucked 'er I'm tellin' thee, boy and then went to Tubbies for a Kebab and then t' ma mates and saw them films. And that's a fact!
Guppie:	Tell us abart them films then, Jar? Are they ya dad's these films, are they? [Laughter]
Jar:	Mine.
Alice:	Where does tha hide 'em?
Jar:	Nowhere, in the fuckin' video cabinet.
Guppie:	What 'appens if ya dad finds 'em?
Alice:	'E fuckin watches 'em! [Laughter]
Jar:	'E never comes in ma bedroom.
Guppie:	I bet 'e does. 'Ow many of these films 'as tha got?
Jar:	I've got four continentals.
Pods:	What are they like?
Jar:	Not bad. They are good these German ones, they're worth it.
Wing-nut:	What are they like? I saw one, two lads and a lass, one up the arse and one up tha fanny and then a dog.
Guppie:	Is that all, ya fanny?
Wing-nut:	And she's rakin' another hard off.
Alice:	George's 'as got one with university freaks in it. 'As tha seen any good 'nes, George? [Laughter]
George:	Never!
Jar:	Wing-nut 'as tha seen Farmyard Frollocks?
Alice:	What's good about a bloke fuckin' a chicken? It's fuckin' 'orrible.
George:	Is that what's in it?
Wing-nut:	This bloke sticks his cock up 'er and then puts all the spunk in a bag and puts it over 'er 'ead. [Laughter]
Alice:	It's sickenin' i'n't it, George?
George:	It's vile. It's disgusting!
Jar:	Watch that German shittin' video and you'll be sick. This film like they're standin' like on glass above ya and shittin' down and ya can see tha arse 'ole. Shittin' and pissin' all over. It's that bad. You see arses openin' as shit drops out and then 'is mouth gets full with it and shit just drops out and so 'e has to start pushin' all of it into 'is gob. This is a German shittin' video and 'e's got it all in 'is gob and in 'is beard and 'tache and 'e's goin' uummm, uummm. [Laughter]
George:	Oh God, are they really like that?
Wing-nut:	In one of my films the spunk is put in a cup and she drinks it.
George:	You're welcome to them.
Alice:	You learn somethin' every day don't ya, George?
George:	You're welcome to it. I don't think I want to learn it, thanks very much.

Guppie:	Wing-nut makes 'em, the sheep shagger, don't tha? 'Eello, mallock! Tha's only got a little round 'ead!
Wing-nut:	I likes them comedy ones, those strip films.
Alice:	They're fearful. You get ya cock up 'er gob, they're alright but when they're stickin' cocks up cows, they're fearful. Shittin' in the face and rubbin' it in, all over. It's fearful!
George:	I can't see what's entertaining about it. It's enough to kill feelings and relationships dead. Come on what about love, respect and affection?
Jar:	[Laughing] . . . Luv, tha's fuckin' nuts, George! I'd do it. Kamikaze would fuck 'is own sister and mother!
Kamikaze:	'E lays a pig down on its back, right and tickles its balls and its knob comes out and she sits on the pig like that, right.
Guppie:	I bet ya mother's sat at 'ome now watchin' it right now, Jar. [Laughter]
Jar:	She gets this 'orse right, fuckin' 'ell and she starts blowin' it off and she takes it out of 'er mouth and its all over 'er face, like and she like sighs with pleasure. [Laughter]
George:	I feel sick after that fish cake and chips for dinner.
Jar:	Fuckin' 'ilarious it is! It's just a laff, isn't it?
Alice:	Well tha must 'ave 'ad sex, George?
George:	No I 'aven't! And I shan't ever want it again.
Jar:	Wing-nut still thinks it's for pissin' out off, don't ya? Goes out into the country in 'is rolled down wellies sheep shaggin'. [Laughter]
Guppie:	Sheep bummin', ya mean!
George:	How much do you pay for these films?
Jar:	Nowt! They're copies like, a couple of quid for the tape. Ya get them from people in pubs and ya swap.
Alice:	I'll post a couple to tha Mrs, George with a letter ''E left these at our house when 'e came!' See what she thinks. [Laughter]

Wolf returns from his Review.

Wolf:	Feast ya eyes on that! [Reading] . . . *Concrete work, tarmacing work, laying of flags; drain laying; measuring skills, numeracy ability, quantifying costs, paving. College report: Very good progress and developing skills and he has the potential to be employed. I shall pursue the possibility of employment status for Craig at Haythornthwaites especially as he finishes this September.* It's a reet report is that, i'n't it? They talked abart 'ow good I am.
Kamikaze:	I ain't interested me. I 'ate it. It's fuckin' borin! I ain't bothered! I do it f' money that's all.

George: If it's so boring how come you got on this particular scheme?

Wing-nut: I wanted t' do weldin' but they sent me on this.

Kamikaze: Because we're daft! I wanted t' be a bricklayer, CITB [Construction Industry Training Board]. I didn't get on that. I wa' just left with this one. I wanted t' do buildin'. I wanted t' be a bricklayer. A skill, a trade. I thought this were bricklayin' at first but when I came I found it were labourin' and there's no skill t' it.

Guppie: It's not worth lookin' f' a job though. Ya can make money! I got extra money from tha gaffers on top of YTS money! Ya can make a lot of money on ya placement! I made 75 quid once! Ya get some reet good gaffers. Mine signed me card, got paid even when I weren't there! Reet good boss!

Wolf: I'd rather do this than be bored. I don't give a fuck me! It's better than 'ard labour. Ya stick along with it f' tha brass. I want a proper job! The choice is sod all or 35 quid on this, i'n't it? And bein' on ya own without ya mates!

Alice: Ay, and gettin' into trouble! College is reet cushy, i'n't it? Seriously! Ya can piss abart at college, can't ya?

Kamikaze: I'm not bothered! It's alreet!

Alice: I don't mind doin' borin' things, so long as it pays reet! It's great, i'n't it? It's like that programme, that advertisement on tha tele with these YTS people. '*I was in the YTS and I got a job at the end of it.*' The lyin' bastards! I wandered 'ow much tha bastards get paid f' that! They're all fuckin' actors, gettin' paid! Real YTS would say, '*This is a load of bollocks and ya go on it for them t' rip ya off!*' It's reet i'n't it? It makes me laugh for people t' go and say things like that! It gets reet up ma nose! It's a load of fuckin' wank!

Wolf: It's fuckin' borin' this. I want t' go 'ome! Waitin' around! I'm fed up! Alice go see what Mason and Aggregate are doin'.

The lads change their clothes if they have not done so already. Mr Mason appears and checks the work.

Mr Mason: You've done really well. I'm very pleased with your performance today. Let's check everything, the tools and then you can go home. Get those cement bags there. Don't forget straight off the premises, don't hang around the college. We don't want any silly billies, any trouble. I'm doing you a favour letting you go, so no hanging about, drawing attention to yourselves. Don't go in the main building. It's a privilege, so don't abuse it! OK. Wait a minute, there's a tape missing. Where is it?

Wolf:	We've 'ad no tape today! We've done no measurin', 'ave we? We ain't seen it, 'ave we?
Mr Mason:	No-one goes home until we find it! Come on everyone get Looking. If you've not lost it, someone's lost it. Look in your bags and in your coats. Look throughout the workshop, starting that end and doing a thorough search! We haven't got the money to lose on tools!
All:	We've not 'ad one! We've not used any, 'ave we? The bricklayers 'ave 'ad 'em! Can we go?
Mr Mason:	I shan't be signing any cards until it is found. Get searching! Has anybody had an overall on and taken it off and left it there. Check 'em.
All:	We never used one! What would we need one for? Can we go?
Mr Mason:	Look in your bags! Look everywhere! Check everything!
All:	You can look in my bag and pockets. I ain't gorrit! Look!
Mr Mason:	I hope you are not going to let yourselves down. Are you sure you have not had it!
All:	Certain! Absolutely certain!
Mr Mason:	Have you had it or seen it Wolf? You Guppie? You Graffiti? You Alice? You Wing-nut? You Pods? You Jar? You Kamikaze?
All:	No! No! No! No! No! No! No! No! No!
Mr Mason:	Right, well I'll believe you. I don't think anyone would lie to me! But I'm looking in your bags and pockets before you go to be absolutely certain. Then we'll look for it tomorrow!
All:	'Ere check me! 'Ere feel ma pockets! I've turned ma pocket inside out f' ya! Look in ma bag! And me! And me! See ya! See ya! See ya tomorra!

Home time

'The Boys' race out to all parts of the compass. George, Alice and Guppie walk out together. 'Zzzound!', 'Zzzound!' echoes in the college corridors despite Mr Mason's injunction.

Alice:	What's tha doin' exactly, George? What' tha doin'? Can tha just do as tha wants? 'Aven't tha got no bosses then?
George:	I tell them all about you and they think I'm doin' a good job. I'll go in tomorrow to the university and say Alice told me about these stolen tellies. Do you want to buy one cheap? [Laughter]
Alice:	Do ya say things like that?
George:	No.
Guppie:	'E fuckin' does. 'E'll have an order f' tha tomorrow. They're all fuckin' crooks up there. [Laughter]

George: I write all about you and go around the country saying Alice says this and Wolf says that and Guppie says the other. By hanging around with you, I can say 'These young people think and do this and that.'

Guppie: But why does they want to know? Why?

George: I'm not too sure. I'd like to think it is so we can change things but I'm not sure. Maybe it's to police you better. [Laughter]

Alice: No-one cares abart us. It's every fucker out for theesens, aint it?

Guppie: Does tha get paid for doin' tha! Does tha get paid? Are there lots of people doin' what tha's doin'.

George: Yeh, I get paid! They say to me 'This is really very, very interesting, George. How do you manage to get those lads to talk to you like this?' And I say, 'It is very, very easy, just get on a bus up to the college and talk. They are just people.' I think they are scared of animals like you. [Laughter] . . . And I then say, 'You do not understand. They are not animals, they are normal human beings. They are geniuses. Professors of everyday life.'

Alice: But we are animals, be 'onest! [Laughter]

Guppie: I can do better than you, George. You're second-'and! Can tha get me a job doin' that? Can tha? They must be fuckin' mad! 'Ow much do ya get paid? Come on 'ow much?

George: I told Wolf earlier. £100 pounds an hour including danger money. But to be honest with you, it is a labour of love! I'd do it for nothing! [Laughter]

Guppie: Wha' can they learn from us?

Alice: 'Ow to be a yob?

Guppie: Why don't tha get a job as a lecturer 'ere instead?

George: They wouldn't employ me. I wouldn't get one with all the associated trouble I have with you lot. Besides what could I teach you? What could I teach? Life has already taught you too many lessons.

Alice: Takin' YTS lads out for a drink, like wha' tha learnt us! Tha learned us all I know about teenage drinkin', George. [Laughter]

George: Lies, all lies. You behave with such maturity I forget how young you are! [Laughter] . . . It is you who have taught me. It is you who has reminded me what you and I might have been and what you and I might yet become. You have changed me forever!

Alice: What's 'e fuckin' on about?

Guppie: I don't know. It's Uni-talk, vegetarianism and John Lennon gigs. Take no notice. 'Ere ask 'em at the Uni tomorrow, 'What's fifty foot long, got no pubic hair and is only good for fuckin'?' I bet they don't know that for all their learnin'! [Laughter]

George: Don't tell me.

Guppie: The front row at a Bros concert! I'll learn 'em if tha wants? Why do Pakis carry shit in their wallets? 'Cos they think that's what ya need for a dirty weekend! [Laughter]

Alice: Why d' niggers wear trilbies? T' stop birdshit landin' on their lips? Why do they wear long pointed shoes? To stop their knuckles scrapin' on the floor! [Laughter]

George: Come on, don't be like that, you racists!

Guppie: I'll tell ya a reet good joke – George! [Laughter]

George: Go on then. [Not picking up the nuance of his pronunciation]

Guppie: Ya university mong! Ya dosey cunt! That's it! [Laughter]

Note

1. This study was part of the ESRC 16–19 Initiative ethnography studies undertaken in the Division of Education, Sheffield University. I would like to thank the staff of 'Artisan College' for their support in this research. Last but not least, eternal thanks must go to 'the YTS Boys' for their cooperation and comradeship.

References

Edwards, R. (1979) *Contested Terrain*. London, Heinemann.

Gold, R. (1958) Roles in sociological field observations. *Social Forces*, 36, March, 217–23.

Riseborough, G.F. (forthcoming) 'The Wolf Pack!': An ethnography of YTS classroom politics in a further education college. *International Journal of Qualitative Studies in Education*.

Manpower Services Commission (1988) *YTS and You: Know Where You Stand*. Sheffield, MSC.

Chapter 9

Career Trajectories and the Mirage of Increased Social Mobility

Ken Roberts

Decade of Opportunity?

The 16–19 Initiative commenced in 1986 with the aim of identifying young people's main routes from education into the labour market, establishing which young people followed different career trajectories, and exploring the implications for their economic and political socialization, their self-concepts and subsequent prospects. In the event all mention of career routes and trajectories became controversial, especially the connotation of young people being somehow propelled along awaiting channels towards predetermined destinations. The researchers themselves became uncertain of whether these terms were helpful in analysing young people's movements towards, then into, the labour market. Indeed, the preceding chapters have contained much evidence of young people striving despite numerous obstacles to create paths for themselves towards their own goals. None of the groups studied in depth gave an appearance of moving passively towards destinations presented to them by the wider society. Beyond the research community, there was much talk in the 1980s about the social structure loosening and opportunities widening. Maybe earlier generations' paths into the labour market, and the jobs in which they would end up, had been clearly signposted. It was more debatable whether this still applied at the end of the 1980s. The virtual disappearance of youth employment in many parts of Britain had destroyed some former routes. It was possible to talk of school-leavers' prospects having deteriorated, though some young people, certainly the more enterprising among them, were supposed to be benefiting from new opportunities.

Enterprise became a buzz-word in the 1980s. Margaret Thatcher declared that there was no such thing as society, but we all knew that she did not intend to be taken literally. She meant that the shape of society was not the determinant so much as the outcome of the actions of individuals, families, businesses and other constituent groups. Her view was that people could and should be allowed to build their own lives and shape their society accordingly. Her successor, John Major, declared in favour of a classless Britain. Again, we all knew that he was not really advocating the abolition of socio-economic inequalities. He was arguing that his own biography, like his predecessor's, suggested that former barriers were being dismantled and would continue to be eroded. And this erosion was to be achieved by releasing capitalist market forces, not through socialist engineering. Margaret Thatcher was a grocer's daughter. John Major was a circus artist's son. Neither of these prime ministers' careers followed an established trajectory. Nevertheless, the results of the 16–19 Initiative show that, for most school-leavers in the late 1980s, Britain was still a land of very unequal opportunities.

To begin with, the samples' prospects at age 16 had depended heavily on their prior education. Margaret Thatcher and John Major were both eleven-plus successes. They attended grammar schools. One wonders if their careers could have been built from secondary modern backgrounds. Of course, by the 1980s, the eleven-plus had been consigned to history in most parts of Britain, including all the areas covered in the 16–19 enquiries, though private schools continued to co-exist alongside local education authority (LEA) comprehensives, and, possibly more crucial to the present point, pupils from LEA schools were not being given equal starts in life. Comprehensive pupils were streamed and setted, entered for different examinations, and by age 16 had very different levels of qualifications. Since 1988, all pupils have been entered for GCSE examinations, but some follow relatively easy syllabuses that cannot lead to the higher grade passes demanded by most universities and employers who can offer 'good jobs'. So everyone can still be graded at age 16 according to their number of ABCs, and so on. As types of secondary school have ceased to be divisive, qualifications earned in secondary education have become increasingly important. This was evident in the previous chapters. The sixth-formers on A-level courses (Chapters 6 and 7) had good O-level passes, the BTEC students preparing for careers in catering and fashion design (Chapters 3 and 4) were from the next rungs down the qualification ladder, while the young people training on the YTS for jobs in care and building (Chapters 2 and 9) were on their schemes largely because they lacked useful qualifications. The importance of qualifications was confirmed in the quantitative evidence from the questionnaire surveys in all four areas. Indeed, qualifications earned by age 16 proved the best single predictor of the directions that individuals' careers would then take, particularly whether they would remain in full-time education and, if so, on which courses. However qualifications also made a huge difference to the prospects of those who left full-time education at 16 (Roberts *et al.*,

1991). Among those who entered the YTS, the better-qualified usually obtained training on employer-led schemes where there were prospects of being kept on. When individuals sought employment immediately on leaving school at 16, the better qualified were the most likely to obtain jobs and avoid unemployment. Qualifications earned earlier on remained important even at later career stages. When individuals became unemployed, those with the better qualifications stood the best chances of escaping quickly. When jobs were obtained, the better-qualified tended to be given the higher pay, the most training and the best prospects.

The ethnographies in this book illustrate how some young people's options were further limited to the opportunities in their home areas. The majority of the teenagers had not enjoyed the freedom to roam throughout the national labour market. They had all been sent to local schools, then proceeded to local colleges, training schemes or jobs. The majority could not afford to relocate, or even pay for the expensive public transport journeys given the lack of educational grants for most 16- to 18-year-olds and the modest allowances paid to youth trainees. In Liverpool, a representative sample of young blacks was studied alongside the main 16–19 Initiative sample (Connolly *et al.*, 1991). The young blacks' opportunities were exceptionally restricted by a fear of venturing into most parts of their home city. The ethnographies in the preceding chapters have revealed how little scope for real choice many of the young people possessed, but they cannot portray how different their opportunities might have been had they lived in another part of Britain. The questionnaire findings from the area studies reveal the extent of these inequalities. Swindon, the one research area in southern England, was very different from all the others. A third of the Swindon sample made direct transitions from school into employment at age 16, whereas in Kirkcaldy, Liverpool and Sheffield only around one in ten made such 'traditional transitions'. Needless to say, unemployment was far lower in Swindon than in the other areas. Young people with just average or below-average educational attainments were the most affected by conditions in their local labour markets. The better-qualified could continue in education and eventually become part of the national labour market. Alternatively, if they sought jobs locally, their qualifications placed them at the head of the queues (Roberts *et al.*, 1991). The privately educated girls studied by Debra Roker (Chapter 7) and the sixth-formers studied by John Quicke (Chapter 6) were earning qualifications that would give them above-average chances were they to enter their local labour market. However, these young people did not need to remain in their home area; they had wider options in higher education. Less-qualified teenagers normally faced the additional disadvantage of having to remain home-based, which was a particularly severe handicap where the local labour market was depressed. One wonders whether the teenage John Major would have found it as easy to move into merchant banking after a succession of stop-gap jobs had he lived in the provinces instead of London.

Sociologists are renowned for stressing the governing role of social class and this chapter will eventually prove true to type; its main argument is that the career propects of the young people studied in the 16–19 Initiative had depended mainly on their social class origins. One hesitates to say 'determined by', but the young people's educational attainments, and whether they attended private or LEA schools, were very much class-related. At age sixteen, their immediate prospects varied greatly according to their social class backgrounds. A point to grasp is that focusing on individuals' success or failure at any particular career stage such as 16–19, then separating the different factors on which progress depends, inevitably obscures the influence of social class. This is because social origins do not directly determine adult positions but operate through a series of inter-mediaries – neighbourhoods, likelihood of attending a private school, qualifications earned whatever school attended, and so on. Also, the influence of social class is cumulative. Whether or not infants are well-prepared to make fast starts in infant school is class-related. Then, inde-pendently of prior preparation, so is progress within primary education. Then, whatever pupils' earlier attainments, so is progress in secondary education, and likewise from age 16 to 19, and then beyond. At each stage, social class may be well down the list of predictors of performance but its cumulative effects, gradually mounting over time, mean that its eventual hold on life chances proves considerable.

Even so, social class was certainly not the sole source of unequal opportunities among the young people studied in the 16–19 Initiative. Whatever their social class origins, the young people's subsequent oppor-tunities had varied according to their achievements in school and places of residence. Ethnic divisions were also of huge importance, especially to members of minority groups. In Liverpool in 1988–89, approximately 20 per cent of the city's 18- to 19-year-olds were unemployed, while roughly a half held full-time jobs. Among the city's black youth, these proportions were almost exactly reversed: only a fifth had full-time jobs while a half were unemployed (Connolly *et al.*, 1991). The greater part of this dif-ference could not be accounted for in terms of educational attainments or the blacks' residential concentration in inner-Liverpool. Of course, the blacks were disadvantaged by the depressed state of the Liverpool labour market. White youth in Liverpool were likely to see this as their main problem, but for the young blacks racism was the main barrier of which they were all too painfully aware.

Sex had proved to be another great and persistent divider. There were only minor differences between the proportions of males and females in the 16–19 Initiative who remained in full-time education beyond age 16, entered the YTS, and who were employed and unemployed at different stages. However, there were huge sex differences in the courses followed by those in education, the occupations for which others were trained, and in which they were subsequently employed. Inge Bates and George Riseborough were being entirely naturalistic in selecting pairs of vocational courses and training schemes that recruited mainly girls and boys, respectively. Their ethnographies also reveal how each sex had gendered expectations and aspirations. Males' and females' life chances were structured differently, not only by the different opportunities to which they had access but also by the young people having largely internalized their society's expectations. The same applied to some extent to the different opportunities associated with places of residence and qualifications. Males and females who completed their secondary education with different levels of attainments were already partly programmed so that they tended to avoid making choices which would have made it as plain to the individuals themselves as in our research evidence just how bounded their opportunities were, and how they were being propelled along awaiting career routes. It is true that some of the young people were attempting to break out. Some females were toying with aims untypical for their sex. Likewise, some of the less-qualified males and females were modestly ambitious and hoped to obtain apprenticeships or to become nurses, for example. Yet they only had to attempt to enact these aims to discover all too painfully, in most cases, the boundaries which fenced their opportunities. During the 1980s in Britain, school-leavers' opportunities were restructured rather than destructured in ways that would have widened their options and left their futures more open.

New Options

The 1980s' 16-year-olds were certainly offered a range of wholly new options. From 1983 onwards, the YTS guaranteed quality training to all who left education and were unable to obtain suitable employment. The YTS was introduced at a time of high unemployment, but it was intended to become a permanent bridge between school and work. The Manpower Services Commission (MSC), the scheme's parent, insisted that this measure was not just another alternative to joblessness. It proclaimed that, first and foremost, the YTS was a training measure. The scheme replaced the Youth Opportunities Programme which had begun in 1978 as a temporary measure, and which offered, at best, a mere six months of work experience. The YTS was to be different. It was to deliver quality training leading to real skills and recognized qualifications. This scheme quickly became the normal next step for 16-year-olds school-leavers in most parts of Britain. In three of the main 16–19 research areas – Kirkcaldy, Liverpool and Sheffield – approximately two-fifths of the samples entered the labour market through the scheme. Swindon was the sole area where more 16-year-olds made 'traditional transitions' straight into jobs at 16 (Roberts and Parsell, 1990). The YTS began as a one-year scheme, and was extended to two years in 1986, just before the younger respondents in the 16–19 enquiry left school.

The 1980s' 16-year-olds also had new options in full-time education. The days were gone when schools had no places for 16-year-olds without the qualifications deemed necessary to attempt the A-levels in England and Highers in Scotland required for higher education. By the 1980s, 'new sixth-formers' were welcome in virtually all comprehensives. Many schools and colleges operated 'open enrolment' – a place for everyone. There were opportunities to retake or add to existing successes in O-levels and CSEs. Then, in addition, there were new courses leading to BTECs, the Certificate of Pre-Vocational Education (CPVE) and other vocational qualifications. Vocational education was not newly invented in the 1980s. National Certificates and Diplomas had been available since the 1920s, and City and Guilds and Royal Society of Arts qualifications since the nineteenth century. What happened in the 1980s was that many more part-time and full-time courses were introduced linked to a wider range of occupations than formerly, and catering for young people ranging from those with excellent academic qualifications to none at all. By the end of the 1980s, the dense 'jungle' of vocational credentials and courses was being systematized into a matrix of National Vocational Qualifications (NVQs). The launch of the YTS in 1983 was accompanied by a decline in the proportion of 16-year-olds remaining in full-time education, but by 1985–86 Britain's schools and colleges were once again retaining a rising proportion of the age group. So across all four areas in the 16–19 Initiative, 45 per cent of the older respondents who reached age 16 in 1985, but 54 per cent of the younger cohort who became 16 in 1987, re-enrolled in full-time education (Roberts and Parsell, 1990). Many 16-year-olds must have been bewildered by their plethora of options in education and training. Even low-achievers discovered that their schools were keen to retain them. A crucial fact of this matter was that the schools needed the extra numbers to protect their rolls in a period when the size of the secondary school age group was declining. So sixth-forms and further education colleges began competing for young people at careers conventions. Meanwhile, television adverts told potential trainees that dozens of blue-chip companies, and even the England soccer team manager, were willing to train them.

A declared intention when these new opportunities were created was that they should be of greatest benefit to young people who were otherwise least advantaged. So the young unemployed were to be given the chance to learn skills that would equip them for the new technology jobs that were to come on stream. Young people who had not excelled on academic courses were to have the chance to acquire vocational knowledge and credentials. Those who did not thrive in classrooms were to be allowed to demonstrate their competence in real work situations. Unfortunately, there were serious hitches in these new opportunities. First, the chance of obtaining a real job at age sixteen was not among them, and in 1988 most 16- and 17-year-olds lost the right to be unemployed and claim social security. Throughout the 1980s, it remained normal throughout Britain for young people to test the labour market as they approached the statutory school-leaving age. Even those who intended to stay on for A-levels would often submit job applications, just in case they failed to earn the grades required for their first choices. Many other 16-year-olds returned to education or joined the YTS only because they were unable to obtain jobs. If it had remained on offer, the likelihood is that many, possibly the majority, of these 16 year-olds would have grasped the old infinitely preferable opportunity of immediate employment. Most of the ethnographies in this book report on young people who either remained in full-time education or entered the YTS at age sixteen. Until the 1980s, such a selection could have been criticized as unrepresentative, but by the time of the research in the late 1980s, only approximately one in ten of all 16-year-olds in Sheffield, Liverpool and Kirkcaldy were obtaining full-time employment. It was necessity rather than choice that had pushed many other young people onto the YTS and retained others in education.

A second hitch was that the new opportunities did not have equal status. In terms of the likelihood of obtaining a good job by age nineteen, the best proposition was to continue along the academic mainstream earning A-levels. The second best options were other types of full-time education and employer-led youth training. Employer-led schemes had the clear advantage over other forms of youth training of there being at least a chance of being kept on. Despite the stated intention that the new opportunities should be most helpful to less advantaged 16-year-olds, individuals' chances of entering the pathways with the best prospects were governed by their existing qualifications. So the girls who were training for care occupations in Chapter 2, and the boys on the college-based building YTS in Chapter 9, had not been offered the options of A-levels or even employer-led training.

A third hitch was that, when 16-year-olds were offered real choices, all the options often led to the same labour market destinations. Whether they sought employment immediately, stayed in full-time education or entered the YTS, poorly qualified 16-year-olds in Sheffield, Kirkcaldy and Liverpool were most likely to find themselves limited to non-skilled employment and competing for an inadequate number of jobs at age eighteen. In some cases, the different opportunities available at sixteen amounted to little more than a variety of ways of postponing the risk of unemployment. It may tax the credulity of the relevant further education and training staff to be told that they were not improving the young people's labour market prospects. They are likely to have seen the majority of the teenagers who they taught or trained proceeding into employment, often in directly related fields, and would have assumed that the young people's progress was due to the education and training received. Yet the statistical evidence from the 16–19 Initiative is unequivocal. Particular schemes and courses may have focused young people's opportunities upon particular firms and occupations, but without necessarily raising the levels at which they were most likely to find employment. Trainers and teachers can never be certain of what would have happened if the young people in their charge had taken different paths. What would have happened if they had persisted in seeking jobs and declined all the alternatives at age sixteen? The survey evidence from the 16–19 Initiative answers this question. In the late-1980, by age 18–20, young people overall would have had exactly the same likelihood of avoiding unemployment and holding jobs, and at precisely the same levels, as individuals who were equally qualified at age sixteen and then opted for youth training or further education. In terms purely of their relationships to the labour market, that is, excluding any implications for personal and social development, the principal role of a great deal of the new further education and training created in the 1980s was 'warehousing'.

With the passage of time, this role is likely to be obscured by a ratchet effect. As more 16-year-olds enter further education or training, employers tend to switch their recruitment to an older age group, and before long it becomes necessary to proceed through more education or formal training in order to stand any chance of obtaining jobs that were once available at age sixteen. The point is that the main propulsive force behind this development in the 1980s was not a technical need for the young people concerned to receive further education or training prior to taking up employment, but a straightforward shortage of jobs. At the time there was much talk of a skills revolution, impending shortages, and of the economy needing young people to reach higher standards in skills and qualifications than in the past. One plain fact, however, was that much of the additional education and training was in low-level skills and qualifications that were not in increasing demand. Another fact of the situation was that there was far more hard evidence, as opposed to talk, of an abundance of labour and talent in relation to demand in the labour markets in most parts of Britain. These were the structural determinants of the actual role of much further education and training in the 1980s.

The Main Routes

At the beginning of the 1970s, there were only two broad routes into Britain's labour markets. Academic high-fliers could remain in education at school or college until age eighteen or later, whereas most other young people entered employment at age sixteen. This is not to say that everyone fell into one or the other of these groups. For instance, some took full-time vocational courses in further education. However, the majority of full-time students after age sixteen were academic high-fliers, the remainder of the age group were most likely to start employment at age sixteen, and together these groups accounted for the vast majority of young people, whereas by the end of the 1980s the combined total of teenagers whose careers conformed to either of these types amounted to only a minority of the age group. There had been massive changes in 16- to 19-year-olds' opportunities. However, the new opportunities were stratified, and access was governed by the same predictors that had governed opportunities previously – sex, educational attainments – with social class origins lurking in the background – and places of residence. Beneath all the changes the old predictors remained in excellent working order. Perhaps even more remarkably, most of the new opportunities had been either absorbed within, or structured around, the longer-established routes – the academic mainstream, and employer-based experience and training from age sixteen.

One definite conclusion that can be drawn from the 16–19 Initiative's efforts to identify young people's main routes into the labour market is the impossibility of providing a definitive list. By the end of the 1980s, there were many possible ways of classifying young people's patterns of progression, or lack of progression, and which classifications worked best depended on the purposes. The ethnographies, rather than the statistical evidence from the questionnaires, describe 'real' trajectories and validate the concept. Every course and scheme selected for ethnographic study was drawing entrants from particular kinds of family and educational backgrounds, then pushing them irrespective of whether they went gently or were resistant, towards a specific set of labour market destinations. It is crystal clear from this evidence that there were definite links between young people's family and educational origins, their experiences from 16 to 19, and their subsequent employment prospects. The 'real trajectories' followed by the young people in the ethnographies were far narrower than categories such as 'vocational education' and 'YTS'; they were defined more precisely by the particular ranges of courses, schemes and subsequent jobs available to individuals of their sex, with their qualifications and in their localities. Throughout the UK, there would have been thousands of such trajectories defined by particular courses, schemes and local labour market conditions, though many of these unique routes shared a great deal in common. In analysing the Initiative's quantitative evidence, it was therefore possible to group the young people's transitional experiences to show how certain kinds of trajectory were occurring throughout the country and to highlight major differences.

An obvious grouping in the late 1980s was according to whether 16-year-olds remained in full-time education, entered the YTS, found jobs immediately, or obtained early experience of unemployment (Roberts and Parsell, 1989b). This particular classification proved particularly useful for demonstrating how the young people's sources and levels of income, and therefore their consumption opportunities, varied according to their routes into the labour market. There were obvious possibilities for subdividing all the routes in this typology. Post-compulsory education could be split into academic and vocational segments, training schemes into those led by employers and the rest, and jobs according to the pay, security, prospects and training that were offered. However, on introducing such subdivisions, it became evident that in terms of the types of young people recruited and their subsequent prospects, some varieties of youth training had more in common with certain types of jobs and educational programmes than other branches of the YTS. Hence the possibility of a further reclassification.

Different typologies served different purposes, and for revealing how 16-year-olds were being propelled along pre-set trajectories, with each step onwards increasing the probability of them reaching what had always been their most likely destinations, *the most useful classification identified just three main routes* – only two of which led towards the types of employment that virtually all the young people had hoped to enter prior to leaving school. These two routes had not been newly constructed during the 1980s. They were long-established and were absorbing or otherwise defining niches for, rather than being obliterated by, the new schemes and courses that had recently become available. One route was based on academic success, which secured entry to jobs with training and encouragement to earn further qualifications, leading eventually to professional, management and other high-level employment. It was possible to make the transition from education into this career stream at age sixteen, but it was more common for high achievers to remain full-time students at least up to A-levels and often through higher education. The second route was into 'good jobs' but not 'top jobs', whether manual or white-collar, which offered average or better security and pay. Access was by gaining experience in, and proving one's worth within, the firms that had such jobs to offer. The initial in-firm training could be in regular employment or under the YTS, but it had to be within a firm that could offer a 'good job' at the end. Vocational skills and qualifications from colleges and training schemes were doing little to strengthen their holders' chances in external labour markets (Roberts and Parsell 1989a).

Now these same routes were identified by Ashton and Field (1976) in the 1970s. They divided beginning workers at that time into those who embarked on extended and short careers. The main changes on the extended career route by the later 1980s were, first, that the path had broadened due to changes in the occupational structure with the proportion of high-level jobs having increased at the expense of low-level employment and, secondly, that well-qualified young people were more likely to remain in full-time education until age eighteen or later, so the transition into employment was normally at a later age than formerly. On the short career route, the main changes had been, first, that some of these transitions had been prolonged by the insertion of a YTS stage and, secondly, that qualifications had become more important in gaining entry. This was a result of the growth in the proportion of school-leavers, especially among those with average and below-average academic ability, who could offer paper qualifications, and the importance attached to this signal of potential in employers' selection procedures.

However, the main change since Ashton and Field's research had undoubtedly been in the prospects of young people who failed to gain entry even to short careers. From the Second World War until the 1970s, they were able to obtain non-skilled jobs and to move between a succession of such jobs if they so desired. The compensation for lack of long-term prospects was 'good money' at a young age. The lads in Paul Willis' *Learning to Labour* (1977) had seized such employment enthusiastically, but by the end of the 1980s most of these jobs had either been wiped out by economic and occupational restructuring or were filled by adults. So school-leavers and scheme-leavers who failed to progress to 'good jobs' were likely to move between unemployment, insecure low-paid jobs and temporary places on schemes such as the Community Programme up to 1988 and Employment Training subsequently. Needless to say, these individuals were at risk of longer-term unemployment. They were unable to save for deposits to purchase houses, or even to furnish rented accommodation and thereby cross other normal thresholds in the transition to adulthood.

The divisions between these three trajectories were clear in the survey evidence from the 16–19 Initiative, though not necessarily to the young people themselves. There were several reasons for this. First, individuals in all social locations tend to be most aware of, and sensitive to, the differences between their own and adjacent rather than more distant positions. So youth trainees were tending to judge their own experiences against those of friends on similar schemes. Those who failed to gain even non-skilled jobs typically compared their own lack of luck with individuals who managed to gain and hold on to such employment. Secondly, a norm of optimism prevailed among the young people, and possibly throughout adult society. Even those in the least advantaged positions seemed to believe that eventually they would overcome their difficulties; to have felt otherwise would have betrayed a lack of confidence in themselves. Thirdly, and related to the need to be optimistic and to feel in control, the young people seemed to have accepted that their futures were their own responsibility rather than dictated by society. To this extent, they had absorbed the enterprise culture. Fourthly, in the post-16 career stage, the young people were not only being channelled towards, but were typically experiencing further socialization which was adjusting their aspirations to, their actual prospects. So the girls being trained in care (Chapter 2), for example, were learning to hope for and to seek jobs with care organizations.

Class Origins and Trajectories

A further classification of the samples' career development was according to individuals' success or failure at three successive stages: before age sixteen, from age sixteen to eighteen, and thereafter. First, the samples were divided according to whether their examination performances at age sixteen were above or below average. In the second stage, the young people were rated as making successful transitions between sixteen and eighteen if they remained in full-time education throughout or if any youth training was employer-led, and if they avoided unemployment whatever their ages on entering the labour market proper. In the third stage, individuals were judged to have reached successful destinations at 18–20 if they either entered and remained in higher education, or if they obtained skilled manual or white-collar jobs and avoided unemployment completely.

It will be clear by now that this was just one of many ways in which the samples' career development could be and was analysed, but the scheme now being described was particularly useful for highlighting differences by social class origins. Young people from middle-class families were twice as likely as those from working-class homes to experience continuous success. Indeed, this was not just the most common but the majority pattern of career development for such young people. Seventy per cent were 'successful' as defined above at all three career stages. Transitions for young people from middle-class backgrounds had normally been relatively smooth. They had mostly been successful in their secondary schools. Subsequently, they either stayed on to take A-levels (Highers in Scotland), obtained good jobs immediately or proceeded to good jobs through employer-led youth training. A middle-class home background was not only a good predictor of educational success, but was also independently related to young people making the best possible use of their qualifications at later career stages. Pat Allatt's discussion of the relationships between middle-class parents and their teenage children in Chapter 7 provides insights into how this was occurring. The parents not only wanted but expected their children to succeed, and by age sixteen the young people had internalized these aspirations. Also, the parents could advise their children knowledgeably and confidently, and could use their own contacts if necessary, in order to ensure that the young people were give the opportunities that they wanted and were deemed to deserve. Debra Roker's chapter on girls at a private school describes how anyone contemplating dropping-out prior to *higher* education was considered a 'weirdo'. It is likely that anyone from this school whose examination performance was below-average for the entire age group, or who entered any branch of youth training, would have been a grave disappointment to the parents and teachers concerned. Even in LEA comprehensives, young people from middle-class homes were typically surrounded by social and cultural support systems which carried them across all the hurdles *en route* to good jobs. Succeeding did not appear to demand exceptional effort or enterprise from most of the young people themselves. Rather, dropping-out must have required the greater initiative and willingness to face censure from parents, teachers and friends.

The normal pattern of career development among young people from working-class homes was not continuous failure. Only 12 per cent of those from manual families in the questionnaire samples had below-average success at secondary school, followed by unemployment or low-status youth training between 16–18, then unemployment or poor quality jobs between 18–20. However, two-thirds of the respondents from working-class backgrounds had experienced failure at one or more stages. Major setbacks had been normal experiences for these young people, and it was this that set them apart from their middle-class contemporaries. The working-class child who rose smoothly to a good job or higher education by 18–20 was the exception rather than the norm within his or her peer group. In former years, the eleven-plus was a major hurdle, but none of the children in the 16–19 Initiative's areas had faced this particular obstacle. Nevertheless, in their comprehensive, the pupils from working-class homes had typically found themselves in the lower streams or sets, and had achieved only lower-grade passes in the sixteen-plus examinations. It is true that very few had left school without any qualifications at all, but some with graded passes considered that their qualifications were useless – indications of failure rather than success. The interviews with 16- to 18-year-olds on the lowest status trajectories – the care girls and the lads on the building course in Chapters 2 and 9, respectively – revealed several cases where individuals simply did not know what their school-leaving qualifications were; they had not bothered to find out and had assumed that any lower graded passes that they had achieved would be worthless.

Some recovered from poor performances at age sixteen by staying on to repeat exams or to earn vocational qualifications. Others managed to obtain good jobs or places on employer-led training schemes, despite their lack of impressive educational attainments. However, lack of such qualifications placed the individuals concerned at high risk of allocation to non-employer-led training, or unemployment if they sought jobs without passing through the YTS. Working-class teenagers with above-average educational attainments were more likely to fail during the 16–18 stage than similarly qualified young people from middle-class families. This seemed to be because, as indicated previously, the latter had internalized greater self-confidence and higher aspirations, and their families and friends were more likely to have useful contacts in education and industry. The case studies in Chapters 3 and 4 of young people pursuing BTEC qualifications in the hope of embarking on careers in hotels and catering, and fashion design, draw attention to the importance of the financial support that the students' families could or could not offer. Some, but not all, of the students, felt that they needed to do one or more part-time jobs alongside their full-time studies. So a working-class background increased the likelihood of individuals failing in secondary school, and also at 16–18. Of course, recovery was still possible, but for those with records of repeated failure up to age eighteen, further difficulties were probable. Even beyond age eighteen individuals from middle-class homes were continuing to benefit from the support, encouragement, aspirations and social networks that they had inherited. By this stage, some young people, mainly from working-class homes, were scarred by repeated experiences of failure.

A successful transition for young people from working-class backgrounds meant surviving though difficulties and failures. It would be wrong to create an impression that most respondents from working-class homes either regarded themselves as failures or were reconciled to whatever la-bour market fates awaited them. Many were not following their career trajectories enthusiastically or even passively. Some were non-compliant. Some were determined to break-out and get on, but ambitions alone were no guarantee of success. Moreover, working-class teenagers tended to measure their own success or failure against the norms for their own social groups. In general, the young people were optimistic about their prospects. In every wave of the questionnaire surveys, they collectively over-estimated their chances of being in jobs and under-estimated their risks of unem-ployment twelve months forward. Their self-confidence and belief in their ability to obtain suitable jobs eventually were normally surviving setbacks. However, the ethnographies illustrate how individuals were often adjusting their sights in line with their most likely opportunities. So 'the lads' studied by George Riseborough knew that they could expect nothing better than labouring jobs, and the 'care girls' in Inge Bates' chapter were eventually delighted if and when they were kept on by the employers with whom they were placed for training. Very few had felt this way about care jobs on starting their training scheme. Their experience on the YTS appeared to be teaching these groups of young people to be grateful for the chance to prove their worth to an employer, and to consider themselves successful if offered permanent employment. The girls at Debra Roker's independent school and the sixth-formers studied by John Quicke judged success using very different yardsticks.

The Mirage

The volume of social mobility revealed by the questionnaire surveys was far from trivial. Just over a third of the young people from working-class homes were experiencing continuous success as they moved through the sixteen-plus examinations, further education or training, then into higher education or good jobs. Only a minority of the privately educated girls in Debra Roker's study – generally those benefiting from assisted places – were from working-class families, but such origins were much in evidence among the LEA sixth-formers in John Quicke's chapter.

The 16–19 Initiative was insufficiently longitudinal to study trends over a generation or more, but there can be little doubt that in the 1980s the proportions of children from working-class homes who were succeeding in secondary school, proceeding to higher education, and entering skilled and other high-level jobs were higher than in the 1950s and 1960s. Other things had only to remain equal for this to result from the expansion of post compulsory education and the parallel increase in the proportion of professional and management jobs at the expense of manual employment. Increased upward mobility forced or facilitated by structural changes is a long-running trend in Britain. The 1944 Education Act increased the chances of working-class children receiving a grammar school education and, by the 1950s, across the country, approximately a half of all grammar school pupils were first-generation from working-class homes. Such figures and trends easily create an appearance of Britain becoming a more open and fluid society. The reason why this appearance is just a mirage is that the same developments that have drawn more working-class young people up the educational and occupational ladders have simultaneously reduced the chances of middle-class children descending. The net result, following the 1944 Education Act, was that relative inequalities in life chances, the greater likelihood of middle-class than working-class children reaching middle-class destinations, remained virtually unchanged (Goldthorpe *et al.*, 1980; Halsey *et al.*, 1980). This was probably happening during the 1980s when, according to the evidence from this research, just over a third of young people from working-class backgrounds, but over two-thirds from middle-class homes, were experiencing continuous success. This was a glaring flaw in the open society scenario.

Another was that only some of the young people in post-compulsory education and training had good prospects. From afar, from Westminster and London newspaper editorial suites, it may have been possible to believe that all young people who were being given new opportunities in further education and training were benefiting from enhanced life chances. Actually, the students with good prospects were generally those who had achieved good qualifications at age sixteen, especially those who then proceeded down the traditional academic route. The youth trainees with good prospects were mostly those with good enough qualifications to have won selection by employers offering high-quality training with prospects of retention and progressive careers to follow. The most likely sequels to other courses and training schemes were far less attractive. Upward mobility from the working class, when in process, was normally based on good performances at secondary school, as in the past, and the most common subsequent mobility channel was the traditional academic mainstream. A substantial proportion of those following this route were from working-class families and it is tempting to applaud both the young people's success and the educational route that they were following for enabling individuals from less advantaged backgrounds to prove their capability and get on. However, such approval simultaneously legitimizes the procedure and channels that were safeguarding middle-class youth from descent and excluding the majority with working-class origins.

The 1980s did create more opportunities for working-class young people to ascend. These opportunities were mostly constructed not from the enterprise initiatives that Robert MacDonald has described in Chapter 5, but by the expansion of high-level employment and the academic mainstream. However, from a working-class perspective, an equally significant change during the 1980s was the increased risks of descent. Young people who failed to enter short careers and reasonably secure jobs stood real risks of unemployment and survival on poverty incomes with no escapes in sight. For certain groups of young people, the risks of long-term unemployment, or joblessness broken only by low-paid, short-lived jobs and schemes, were considerable. At age 18–19, a half of all young blacks in Liverpool were unemployed, more than twice as many as held full-time jobs, and most of their jobs were from the bottom of the labour market. The YTS lads who spoke for themselves in Chapter 9 knew that unemployment following their training was a real possibility, as did the 'care girls' in Inge Bates' study, though their labour market problems were likely to be concealed by withdrawal into domesticity, as happened among earlier generations of young women. Young people who proceeded through the lower status branches of post-compulsory education and youth training were then at risk of unemployment, whereupon they became candidates for the Community Programme, subsequently Employment Training, and the other enterprise initiatives that Robert MacDonald described in Chapter 5. Most of the young adults in his study who were trying to embark into self-employment were doing so only because of their inability to obtain 'proper jobs'. Working-class striving was being sustained as much by a real fear of descent from the 'respectable' into the 'rough' as by the prospect of joining the middle classes.

Whenever social mobility is discussed, it tends to be the upward variety that commands attention. Education and training policies are presented as creating more opportunities for working-class youth to get ahead. How to promote more descents from the middle class is rarely considered, though this would be an inevitable aspect of a more open, fluid society. One has only to raise this problem to recognize why increased social fluidity proves so difficult to achieve. Downward mobility appears to be unacceptable in our society. Individuals will resort to all manner of social and psychological strategies to deny that it has happened or is happening to them (Roberts *et al.*, 1977). Downward mobility was not a fate to which the working-class respondents in this research could be easily reconciled. They all preferred to think of their futures in terms of overcoming immediate difficulties. Yet many knew that unemployment was a genuine risk. This was why the working-class teenagers and their parents could regard mere survival in the labour market as success. The working-class young people in Sheffield, Liverpool, Kirkcaldy, Durham and Teesside all had acquaintances if not close friends or family members with direct recent experience of unemployment. The increased risk of downward mobility from the working class was being obscured by the young people's own hopes and optimism, and by the training and education to which they had immediate access. For the middle classes long-range descent was a remote possibility. The contraction of manual employment was forcing more working-class young people upwards than in previous generations, but it was also threatening greater numbers with descent. For middle-class youth, the expansion of professional and management jobs meant that their positions were less vulnerable than before. Their typical problem was to choose between the widening range of occupations at, and routes towards, this level. For working-class youth, beneath the mirage of wider opportunities, descent into unemployment was the main new career trajectory created by trends in the 1980s.

References

Ashton, D.N. and Field, D. (1976) *Young Workers*. London, Hutchinson.

Connolly, M., Roberts, K., Ben-Tovim, G. and Torkington, P. (1991) *Black Youth in Liverpool*. Culemborg, Giordano Bruno.

Goldthorpe, J.H., Llewellyn, C. and Payne, C. (1980) *Social Mobility and Class Structure in Modern Britain*. Oxford, Clarendon Press.

Halsey, A.H., Heath, A.F. and Ridge, J.M. (1980) *Origins and Destinations*. Oxford, Clarendon Press.

Roberts, K. and Parsell, G. (1989a) The stratification of youth training. Occasional Paper 11, ESRC 16–19 Initiative. London, City University.

Roberts, K. and Parsell, G. (1989b) Recent changes in the pathways from school to work in Great Britain. In K. Hurrelman and U. Engel (eds) *The Social World of the Adolescent: International Perspectives*. New York, De Gruyter.

Roberts, K. and Parsell, G. (1990) Young people's routes into UK labour markets in the late-1980s. Paper presented to the *Conference on Understanding Unemployment*. Department of Employment/University of York.

Roberts, K., Clark, S., Cook, F. and Semeonoff, E. (1977) *The Fragmentary Class Structure*. London, Heinemann.

Roberts, K., Parsell, G. and Connolly, M. (1991) Young people's transitions into the labour market. In M. Cross and G. Payne (eds) *Work and the Enterprise Culture*. London, Falmer Press.

Willis, P. (1977) *Learning to Labour*. Farnborough, Saxon House.

Index

CAREERS AND IDENTITIES

Michael Banks, Inge Bates, Glynis Breakwell, John Bynner, Nicholas Emler, Lynn Jamieson and Kenneth Roberts

The generation that left school in the mid 1980s encountered a new world of work, politics and family life. How did they come to terms with the new routes into employment and the changing social and political terrain? *Careers and Identities* uses findings from the Economic and Social Research Council's 16–19 Initiative – an interdisciplinary programme of research on young people growing up in four areas of Britain – to chart their progress into adult life and to uncover the processes by which their adult occupational and political identities were established.

One theme that emerges strongly is the disparity in opportunities and resources between those embarking on different career paths in different parts of the country. Another is the critical role of education in mediating the effects of family background and gender on the rate of transition, occupational destinations, political participation and attitudes.

To prepare young people for the demands of adulthood in the next century, a new agenda for social and educational policy is needed with a major emphasis on transforming the content and quality of post-16 educational and occupational experience.

Contents
Contexts and issues – Studying young people in context – Career patterns – Home life, sociability and leisure – Labourer, carer, designer, chef . . . : the making and shaping of some careers and identities – Self and identity – Beliefs, attitudes and values – Politics – Careers and identities reconsidered – Appendices – References – Index.

240pp   0 335 09714 6 (Paperback)   0 335 09715 4 (Hardback)

YOUTH WORK AND WORKING CLASS YOUTH CULTURE
RULES AND RESISTANCE IN WEST BELFAST

Norman Gillespie, Tom Lovett and Wendy Garner

This book examines the youth service and the values, attitudes, culture and needs of working a class youth in Northern Ireland. It explores why some young people participate in youth clubs and others do not; how patterns of participation differ by gender, class and religion; how young people use their leisure time if they are not involved with youth clubs (and whether youth clubs *could* meet their needs). It concentrates on letting the young people speak for themselves, exploring working class youth culture, with all its tensions and contradictions, as they experience it.

Contents
Introduction – Youth and youth cultures in West Belfast – Two communities in West Belfast; the Shankhill and the Upper Springfield – The youth service in Northern Ireland – Youth work in West Belfast – Formal youth club participants – Youth and youth sub-culture in the Shankhill – Working class youth in Ballymurphy – Conclusions – Glossary and abbreviations – Bibliography – Index.

224pp   0 335 09480 5 (Paperback)   0 335 09481 3 (Hardback)

YOUTH, FAMILY AND CITIZENSHIP

Gill Jones and Claire Wallace

This important text examines how young people growing up come to be recognized as independent citizens and to what extent access to citizenship is determined by their economic circumstances and level of economic dependency. It explores how the transition from dependent child to independent adult is structured by relationships with family members, the market place and the institutions of the state. It considers how much freedom young people really have to make decisions about their lives, and identifies inequalities of opportunity and choice, stemming from their social class, gender, ethnicity, location and economic status. The text integrates often separated aspects of young people's lives – as family and peer group members, as trainees or workers, and as consumers.

This is essential reading for students and researchers across the social sciences, especially those concerned with social policy, youth and community work, sociology and education.

Contents

Youth, family and citizenship – structuring economic dependency – Social citizenship by proxy? – Dependence on their families? – Independence from their families? – Consumer citizens? – Rethinking youth and citizenship – Appendix – References – Indexes.

192pp   0 335 09294 2 (Paperback)   0 335 09299 3 (Hardback)